A Manual of Gardening: Instruction, Guideline and Techniques

A Manual of Gardening: Instruction, Guideline and Techniques

Surinder Bhanot

RANDOM

RANDOM PUBLICATIONS
NEW DELHI (INDIA)

A Manual of Gardening: Instruction, Guideline and Techniques

ISBN 978-93-5111-835-0

Published in 2016 in India by

RANDOM PUBLICATIONS

4376-A/4B, Gali Murari Lal, Ansari Road
New Delhi-110 002
Phone : +9111-43580356, 011-23289044, 011-43142548
e-mail: sales@randompublications.com,
info@randompublications.com, randomexports@gmail.com

Type Setting by : Friends Media, Delhi-110089
Printed at : Sanat Printers

Preface

Gardening is the practice of growing and cultivating plants as part of horticulture. In gardens, ornamental plants are often grown for their flowers, foliage, or overall appearance; useful plants, such as root vegetables, leaf vegetables, fruits, and herbs, are grown for consumption, for use as dyes, or for medicinal or cosmetic use. Gardening is considered to be a relaxing activity for many people.

Garden design is the art and process of designing and creating plans for layout and planting of gardens and landscapes. Garden design may be done by the garden owner themselves, or by professionals of varying levels of experience and expertise.

Most professional garden designers have some training in horticulture and the principles of design, and some are also landscape architects, a more formal level of training that usually requires an advanced degree and often a state license.

Amateur gardeners may also attain a high level of experience from extensive hours working in their own gardens, through casual study, serious study in Master Gardener Programs, or by joining gardening clubs.

The vegetated landscape that covered most of the Earth's continents before humans began to build still surrounds and penetrates even the largest metropolises. Efforts to design gardens and to preserve and develop green open space in and around cities are efforts to maintain contact with the original pastoral, rural landscape.

Gardens and designed landscapes, by filling the open areas in cities, create a continuity in space between structural urban landscapes and the open rural landscapes beyond. Moreover, gardens and designed landscapes have a special type of continuity in time. Buildings, paintings, and sculpture may survive longer than specific plants, but the constant cyclical growth and change in plants provide a continuous time dimension that static structures and sculpture can never achieve.

Gardening is the practice of growing and cultivating plants as part of horticulture. In gardens ornamental plants are often grown for their flowers foliage or overall appearances useful plants such as root vegetables, leaf vegetables fruits and herbs are grown for consumption for use as dyes, or for medicinal or cosmetic use. A gardener is someone who practices gardening.

– Author

Contents

1

Introduction

Wherever there is soil, plants grow and produce their kind, and all plants are interesting; when a person makes a choice as to what plants he shall grow in any given place, he becomes a gardener or a farmer; and if the conditions are such that he cannot make a choice, he may adopt the plants that grow there by nature, and by making the most of them may still be a gardener or a farmer in some degree.

Every family, therefore, may have a garden. If there is not a foot of land, there are porches or windows. Wherever there is sunlight, plants may be made to grow; and one plant in a tin-can may be a more helpful and inspiring garden to some mind than a whole acre of lawn and flowers may be to another.

The satisfaction of a garden does not depend on the area, nor, happily, on the cost or rarity of the plants. It depends on the temper of the person. One must first seek to love plants and nature, and then to cultivate the happy peace of mind that is satisfied with little.

In the vast majority of cases a person will be happier if he has no rigid and arbitrary notions, for gardens are moodish, particularly with the novice. If plants grow and thrive, he should be happy; and if the plants that thrive chance not to be the ones that he planted, they are plants nevertheless, and nature is satisfied with them.

We are wont to covet the things that we cannot have; but we are happier when we love the things that grow because they must. A patch of lusty pigweeds, growing and crowding in luxuriant abandon, may be a better and more worthy object of affection than a bed of coleuses in which every spark of life and spirit and individuality has been sheared out and suppressed. The man who worries morning and night about the dandelions in the lawn will find great relief in loving the dandelions. Each blossom is worth more than a gold coin, as it shines in the exuberant sunlight of the growing spring, and attracts the insects to its bosom. Little children like the dandelions: why may not we? Love the things nearest at hand; and love intensely. If I were to write a motto over the gate of a garden, I should choose the remark that Socrates is said to have made as he saw the luxuries in the market, "How much there is in the world that I do not want!"

I verily believe that this paragraph I have just written is worth more than all the advice with which I intend to cram the succeeding pages, notwithstanding the fact that I have most assiduously extracted this advice from various worthy but, happily, long-forgotten authors. Happiness is a quality of a person, not of a plant or a garden; and the anticipation of joy in the writing of a book may be the reason why so many books on garden-making have been written. Of course, all these books have been good and useful. It would be ungrateful, at the least, for the present writer to say otherwise; but books grow old, and the advice becomes too familiar. The sentences need to be transposed and the order of the chapters varied, now and then, or interest lags. Or, to speak plainly, a new book of advice on handicraft is needed in every decade, or perhaps oftener in these days of many publishers. There has been a long and worthy procession of these handbooks,—Gardiner & Hepburn, M'Mahon, Cobbett—original, pungent, versatile Cobbett!—Fessenden, Squibb, Bridgeman, Sayers, Buist, and a dozen more, each one a little richer because the others had been written. But even the fact that all books pass into oblivion does not deter another hand from making still another venture.

I expect, then, that every person who reads this book will make a garden, or will try to make one; but if only tares grow where roses are desired, I must remind the reader that at the outset I advised pigweeds. The book, therefore, will suit everybody,—the experienced gardener, because it will be a repetition of what he already knows; and the novice, because it will apply as well to a garden of burdocks as of onions.

WHAT IS GARDEN ?

A garden is the personal part of an estate, the area that is most intimately associated with the private life of the home. Originally, the garden was the area inside the inclosure or lines of fortification, in distinction from the unprotected area or fields that lay beyond; and this latter area was the particular domain of agriculture. This book understands the garden to be that part of the personal or home premises devoted to ornament, and to the growing of vegetables and fruits. The garden, therefore, is an ill-defined demesne; but the reader must not make the mistake of defining it by dimensions, for one may have a garden in a flower-pot or on a thousand acres. In other words, this book declares that every bit of land that is not used for buildings, walks, drives, and fences, should be planted. What we shall plant—whether sward, lilacs, thistles, cabbages, pears, chrysanthemums, or tomatoes—we shall talk about as we proceed.

The only way to keep land perfectly unproductive is to keep it moving. The moment the owner lets it alone, the planting has begun. In my own garden, this first planting is of pigweeds. These may be followed, the next year, by ragweeds, then by docks and thistles, with here and there a start of clover and grass; and it all ends in June-grass and dandelions.

GARDENING

Fig. Part of a parterre in an English garden

Gardening is the practice of growing and cultivating plants as part of horticulture. In gardens, ornamental plants are often grown for their flowers, foliage, or overall appearance; useful plants, such as root vegetables, leaf vegetables, fruits, and herbs, are grown for consumption, for use as dyes, or for medicinal or cosmetic use. Gardening is considered to be a relaxing activity for many people.

Gardening ranges in scale from fruit orchards, to long boulevard plantings with one or more different types of shrubs, trees, andherbaceous plants, to residential yards including lawns and foundation plantings, to plants in large or small containers grown inside or outside. Gardening may be very specialized, with only one type of plant grown, or involve a large number of different plants in mixed plantings. It involves an active participation in the growing of plants, and tends to be labor-intensive, which differentiates it from farming or forestry.

History

Fig. Robert Hart's forest garden in Shropshire, England

Ancient times

Forest gardening, a forest-based food production system, is the world's oldest form of gardening.

Forest gardens originated in prehistoric times along jungle-clad river banks and in the wet foothills of monsoon regions. In the gradual process of families improving their immediate environment, useful tree and vine species were identified, protected and improved while undesirable species were eliminated. Eventually foreign species were also selected and incorporated into the gardens.

After the emergence of the first civilizations, wealthy individuals began to create gardens for aesthetic purposes. Egyptian tomb paintings from around 1500 BC provide some of the earliest physical evidence of ornamental horticulture and landscape design; they depict lotusponds surrounded by symmetrical rows of acacias and palms. A notable example of ancient ornamental gardens were the Hanging Gardens of Babylon—one of the Seven Wonders of the Ancient World and now a World Heritage Site—while ancient Rome had dozens of gardens.

Wealthy ancient Egyptians used gardens for providing shade. Egyptians associated trees and gardens with gods as they believed that their deities were pleased by gardens. Gardens in ancient Egypt were often surrounded by walls with trees planted in rows. Among the most popular species planted were date palms, sycamores, fir trees, nut trees, and willows. These gardens were a sign of higher socioeconomic status. In addition, wealthy ancient Egyptians grew vineyards, as wine was a sign of the higher social classes. Roses, poppies, daisies andirises could all also be found in the gardens of the Egyptians.

The Assyrians were also renowned for their beautiful gardens. These tended to be wide and large, some of them used for hunting game—rather like a game reserve today—and others as leisure gardens. Cypresses and palms were some of the most frequently planted types of trees.

Ancient Roman gardens were laid out with hedges and vines and contained a wide variety of flowers—acanthus, cornflowers, crocus, cyclamen, hyacinth, iris, ivy, lavender, lilies, myrtle, narcissus, poppy, rosemary and violets—as well as statues and sculptures. Flower beds were popular in the courtyards of rich Romans.

THE MIDDLE AGES

The Middle Age represented a period of decline in gardens for aesthetic purposes, in what concerns gardening. After the fall of Rome, gardening was done for the purpose of growing medicinal herbs and/or decorating church altars. Monasteries carried on a tradition of garden design and intense horticultural techniques during the medieval period in Europe. Generally, monastic garden types consisted of kitchen gardens, infirmary gardens, cemetery orchards, cloister garths and vineyards. Individual monasteries might also have had a "green court", a plot of grass and trees where horses could graze, as well as a cellarer's garden or private gardens for obedientiaries, monks who held specific posts within the monastery.

Islamic gardens were built after the model of Persian gardens and they were usually enclosed by walls and divided in 4 by watercourses. Commonly, the center of the garden would have a pool or pavilion. Specific to the Islamic gardens are the mosaics and glazed tiles used to decorate the rills and fountains that were built in these gardens.

By the late 13th century, rich Europeans began to grow gardens for leisure and for medicinal herbs and vegetables. They surrounded the gardens by walls to protect them from animals and to provide seclusion. During the next two centuries, Europeans started planting lawns and raising flowerbeds and trellises of roses. Fruit trees were common in these gardens and also in some, there were turf seats. At the same time, the gardens in the monasteries were a place to grow flowers and medicinal herbs but they were also a space where the monks could enjoy nature and relax.

The gardens in the 16th and 17th century were symmetric, proportioned and balanced with a more classical appearance. Most of these gardens were built around a central axis and they were divided into different parts by hedges. Commonly, gardens had flowerbeds laid out in squares and separated by gravel paths.

Gardens in Renaissance were adorned with sculptures, topiary and fountains. In the 17th century, knot gardens became popular along with the hedge mazes. By this time, Europeans started planting new flowers such as tulips, marigolds and sunflowers.

Cottage gardens

Cottage gardens, which emerged in Elizabethan times, appear to have originated as a local source for herbs and fruits. One theory is that they arose out of the Black Death of the 1340s, when the death of so many laborers made land available for small cottages with personal gardens. According to the late 19th-century legend of origin, these gardens were originally created by the workers that lived in the cottages of the villages, to provide them with food and herbs, with flowers planted among them for decoration. Farm workers were provided with cottages that had architectural quality set in a small garden—about an acre—where they could grow food and keep pigs and chickens.

Authentic gardens of the yeoman cottager would have included a beehive and livestock, and frequently a pig and sty, along with a well. The peasant cottager of medieval times was more interested in meat than flowers, with herbs grown for medicinal use rather than for their beauty. By Elizabethan times there was more prosperity, and thus more room to grow flowers. Even the early cottage garden flowers typically had their practical use—violets were spread on the floor (for their pleasant scent and keeping out vermin);calendulas and primroses were both attractive and used in cooking. Others, such as sweet william and hollyhocks, were grown entirely for their beauty.

18th century

In the 18th century, gardens were laid out more naturally, without any walls. This style of smooth undulating grass, which would run straight to the house, clumps, belts and scattering of trees and his serpentine lakes formed by invisibly damming small rivers, were a new style within the English landscape, a "gardenless" form of landscape gardening, which swept away almost all the remnants of previous formally patterned styles. The English garden usually included a lake, lawns set against groves of trees, and often contained shrubberies, grottoes, pavilions, bridges and follies such as mock temples, Gothic ruins, bridges, and other picturesque architecture, designed to recreate an idyllic pastoral landscape.

This new style emerged in England in the early 18th century, and spread across Europe, replacing the more formal, symmetrical Garden à la françaiseof the 17th century as the principal gardening style of Europe. The English garden presented an idealized view of nature. They were often inspired by paintings of landscapes by Claude Lorraine and Nicolas Poussin, and some were Influenced by the classic Chinese gardens of the East, which had recently been described by European travelers.

The work of Lancelot 'Capability' Brown was particularly influential. Also, in 1804 the Horticultural Society was formed. Gardens of the 19th century contained plants such as the monkey puzzle or Chile pine. This is also the time when the so-called "gardenesque" style of gardens evolved. These gardens displayed a wide variety of flowers in a rather small space. Rock gardens increased in popularity in the 19th century.

Types

Fig. Conservatory of Flowers inGolden Gate Park, San Francisco

Hanging baskets inThornbury, South Gloucestershire.

Residential gardening takes place near the home, in a space referred to as the garden. Although a garden typically is located on the land near a residence, it may also be located on a roof, in an atrium, on a balcony, in a windowbox, or on a patio or vivarium.

Gardening also takes place in non-residential green areas, such as parks, public or semi-public gardens (botanical gardens or zoological gardens), amusement and amusement parks, along transportation corridors, and around tourist attractions and garden hotels. In these situations, a staff of gardeners or groundskeepers maintains the gardens.

- Indoor gardening is concerned with the growing of houseplants within a residence or building, in a conservatory, or in a greenhouse. Indoor gardens are sometimes incorporated as part of air conditioning or heating systems. Indoor gardening extends the growing season in the fall and spring and can be used for winter gardening.
- Native plant gardening is concerned with the use of native plants with or without the intent of creating wildlife habitat. The goal is to create a garden in harmony with, and adapted to a given area. This type of gardening typically reduces water usage, maintenance, and fertilization costs, while increasing native faunal interest.
- Water gardening is concerned with growing plants adapted to pools and ponds. Bog gardens are also considered a type of water garden. These all require special conditions and considerations. A simple water garden may consist solely of a tub containing the water and plant(s). In aquascaping, a garden is created within an aquarium tank.
- Container gardening is concerned with growing plants in any type of container either indoors or outdoors. Common containers are pots,hanging baskets, and planters. Container gardening is usually used in atriums and on balconies, patios, and roof tops.
- Hügelkultur is concerned with growing plants on piles of rotting wood, as a form of raised bed gardening and composting in situ. An English loanword from German, it means "mound garden." Toby Hemenway, noted Permaculture author and teacher, considers wood buried in trenches to also be a form of hugelkultur referred to as a dead wood swale. Hugelkultur is practiced by Sepp Holzer as a method of forest gardening and agroforestry, and by Geoff Lawton as a method of dryland farming and desert greening. When used as a method of disposing of large volumes of waste wood and woody debris, hugelkultur accomplishes carbon sequestration. It is also a form of xeriscaping.
- Community gardening is a social activity in which an area of land is gardened by a group of people, providing access to fresh produce and plants as well as access to satisfying labor, neighborhood

improvement, sense of community and connection to the environment. Community gardens are typically owned in trust by local governments or nonprofits.

- Garden sharing partners landowners with gardeners in need of land. These shared gardens, typically front or back yards, are usually used to produce food that is divided between the two parties.
- Organic gardening uses natural, sustainable methods, fertilizers and pesticides to grow non-genetically modified crops.

Garden features and accessories

There is a wide range of features and accessories available in the market for both the professional gardener and the amateur to exercise their creativity. These are used to add decoration or functionality, and may be made from a wide range of materials such as copper, stone, wood, bamboo, stainless steel, clay, stained glass, concrete, or iron. Examples include trellis, arbors, statues, benches, water fountains, urns, bird baths and feeders, and garden lighting such as candle lanterns and oil lamps. The use of these items can be part of the expression of a gardener's gardening personality.

Gardening departments and centers

Gardening departments and centers mainly sell plants, sundries, and garden accessories, but in recent times, many now stock outdoor leisure products as diverse as spas, furniture, and barbecues. Many garden centers now include food halls, and sections for clothing, gifts, pets, and power tools. There are also a number of online garden centers that now deliver directly to customers' doors.

Comparison with farming

Fig. Hand gardening tools

Gardening for beauty is likely nearly as old as farming for food, however for most of history for the majority of people there was no real distinction since the need for food and other useful product trumped other concerns. Small-scale, subsistence agriculture (called hoe-farming) is largely indistinguishable from gardening. A patch of potatoes grown by a Peruvian peasant or an Irish smallholder for personal use could be described as either a garden or a farm. Gardening for average people evolved as a separate discipline, more concerned with aesthetics and recreation, under the influence of the pleasure gardens of the wealthy. Meanwhile, farming has evolved (in developed countries) in the direction of commercialization, economics of scale, and monocropping.

In respect to its food producing purpose, gardening is distinguished from farming chiefly by scale and intent. Farming occurs on a larger scale, and with the production of salable goods as a major motivation. Gardening is done on a smaller scale, primarily for pleasure and to produce goods for the gardener's own family or community. There is some overlap between the terms, particularly in that some moderate-sized vegetable growing concerns, often called market gardening, can fit in either category.

Fig. Planting in a garden

The key distinction between gardening and farming is essentially one of scale; gardening can be a hobby or an income supplement, but farming is generally understood as a full-time or commercial activity, usually involving more land and quite different practices. One distinction is that gardening is labor-intensive and employs very little infrastructural capital, sometimes no more than a few tools, e.g. a spade, hoe, basket andwatering can. By contrast, larger-scale farming often involves irrigation systems, chemical fertilizers and harvesters or at least ladders, e.g. to reach up into fruit trees. However, this distinction is becoming blurred with the increasing use of power tools in even small gardens.

In part because of labor intensity and aesthetic motivations, gardening is very often much more productive per unit of land than farming. In the Soviet Union, half the food supply came from small peasants' garden plots on the huge government-run collective farms, although they were tiny patches of land. Some argue this as evidence of the superiority of capitalism, since the peasants were generally able to sell their produce. Others consider it to be evidence of a tragedy of the commons, since the large collective plots were often neglected, or fertilizers or water redirected to the private gardens.

The term precision agriculture is sometimes used to describe gardening using intermediate technology (more than tools, less than harvesters), especially of organic varieties. Gardening is effectively scaled up to feed entire villages of over 100 people from specialized plots.

Gardens as art

Fig. Garden at the Schultenhof inMettingen, North Rhine-Westphalia, Germany

Garden design is considered to be an art in most cultures, distinguished from gardening, which generally means *garden maintenance*. Garden design can include different themes such as perennial, butterfly, wildlife, Japanese, water, tropical, or shade gardens. In Japan, Samurai and Zen monks were often required to build decorative gardens or practice related skills like flower arrangement known as *ikebana*. In 18th-century Europe, country estates were refashioned by landscape gardeners into formal gardens or landscaped park lands, such as at Versailles, France, or Stowe, England. Today, landscape architects and garden designers continue to produce artistically creative designs for private garden spaces. In the USA, professional landscape designers are certified by the Association of Professional Landscape Designers.

Social aspects

People can express their political or social views in gardens, intentionally or not. The lawn vs. garden issue is played out in urban planning as the debate over the "land ethic" that is to determine urban land use and whether hyper hygienist bylaws (e.g. weed control) should apply, or whether land should generally be allowed to exist in its natural wild state. In a famous Canadian Charter of Rights case, "Sandra Bell vs. City of Toronto", 1997, the right to cultivate all native species, even most varieties deemed noxious or allergenic, was upheld as part of the right of free expression.

Community gardening comprises a wide variety of approaches to sharing land and gardens.

People often surround their house and garden with a hedge. Common hedge plants are privet, hawthorn, beech, yew, leyland cypress, hemlock, arborvitae, barberry, box, holly,oleander, forsythia and lavender. The idea of open gardens without hedges may be distasteful to those who enjoy privacy. The Slow Food movement has sought in some countries to add an edible school yard and garden classrooms to schools, e.g. in Fergus, Ontario, where these were added to a public school to augment the kitchen classroom.Garden sharing, where urban landowners allow gardeners to grow on their property in exchange for a share of the harvest, is associated with the desire to control the quality of one's food, and reconnect with soil and community.

In US and British usage, the production of ornamental plantings around buildings is called *landscaping*, *landscape maintenance* or *grounds keeping*, while international usage uses the term *gardening* for these same activities.

Also gaining popularity is the concept of "Green Gardening" which involves growing plants using organic fertilizers and pesticides so that the gardening process - or the flowers and fruits produced thereby - doesn't adversely affect the environment or people's health in any manner.

Garden pests

Garden pests are generally plants, fungi, or animals (frequently insects) that engages in activity that the gardener considers undesirable. It may crowd out desirable plants, disturb soil, stunt the growth of young seedlings, steal or damage fruit, or otherwise kill plants, hamper their growth, damage their appearance, or reduce the quality of the edible or ornamental portions of the plant. Aphids, spider mites, slugs, snails, ants, birds, and even cats are commonly considered to be garden pests.

Because gardeners may have different goals, organisms considered "garden pests" vary from gardener to gardener. *Tropaeolum speciosum*, for example, may be considered a desirable and ornamental garden plant, or it may be considered a pest if it seeds and starts to grow where it is not wanted. As another example, in lawns, moss can become dominant and be impossible to eradicate. In some lawns, lichens, especially very damp lawn lichens such as *Peltigera lactucfolia* and *P. membranacea*, can become difficult to control and be considered pests.

GARDEN PEST CONTROL

There are many ways by which unwanted pests are removed from a garden. The techniques vary depending on the pest, the gardener's goals, and the gardener's philosophy. For example, snails may be dealt with through the use of a chemical pesticide, an organic pesticide, hand-picking, barriers, or simply growing snail-resistant plants.

Pest control is often done through the use of pesticides, which may be either organic or artificially synthesized. Pesticides may affect the ecology of a garden due to their effects on the populations of both target and non-target species. For example, unintended exposure to some neonicotinoid pesticides has been proposed as a factor in the recent decline in honey bee populations. A mole vibrator can deter mole activity in a garden.

Other means of control include the removal of infected plants, using fertilizers and biostimulants to improve the health and vigour of plants so they better resist attack, practisingcrop rotation to prevent pest build-up, using companion planting, and practising good garden hygiene, such as disinfecting tools and clearing debris and weeds which may harbour pests.

History of gardening

Fig. the renaissance style gardens at Chateau Villandry

The history of ornamental gardening may be considered as aesthetic expressions of beauty through art and nature, a display of taste or style in civilized life, an expression of an individual's or culture's philosophy, and sometimes as a display of private status or national pride—in private and public landscapes.

Fig. Robert Hart's forest garden in Shropshire, England.

Forest gardening, a plant-based food pro-system, is the world's oldest form of gardening. Forest gardens originated in prehistoric timesalong jungle-clad river banks and in the wet foothills of monsoon regions. In the gradual process of families improving their immediate environment, useful tree and vine species were identified, protected and improved whilst undesirable species were eliminated. Eventually foreign species were also selected and incorporated into the gardens.

The enclosure of outdoor space began in 10,000 BC. Though no one knows the specific details of the first garden, historians imagine the first enclosure was a type of barrier for the purpose of keeping out animals and marauders. Garden-making and design was a key precursor to landscape architecture, and it began in West Asia, eventually spreading westward into Greece, Spain, Germany, France, Britain, etc. Modern words of "garden" and "yard" are descendants of the Old English term "geard," which means fence or enclosure.

Vitruvius, a Roman author and engineer, wrote the oldest surviving design manual in 27 BC. De architecture libri decem (The Ten Books on Architecture) addressed design theory, landscape architecture, engineering, water supply and public projects, such as parks and squares. Vitruvius asserted that firmitas (firmness, durability, strength), utilitas (commodity, convenience, utility) and venustas (delight, loveliness, beauty) were the main design objectives, and some consider these elements centrally important to quality landscape design.

After the emergence of the first civilizations, wealthy individuals began to create gardens for purely aesthetic purposes. Egyptian tomb paintings of the 16th century BC are some of the earliest physical evidence of ornamental horticulture and landscape design; they depictlotus ponds surrounded by symmetrical rows of acacias and palms. Another ancient gardening tradition is of Persia: Darius the Great was said to have had a "paradise garden" and the Hanging Gardens of Babylon were renowned as a Wonder of the World. Persian gardens were also organized symmetrically, along a center line known as an axis.

Persian influences extended to post-Alexander's Greece: around 350 BC there were gardens at the Academy of Athens, and Theophrastus, who wrote on botany, was supposed to have inherited a garden from Aristotle. Epicurus also had a garden where he walked and taught, and bequeathed it to Hermarchus of Mytilene. Alciphron also mentions private gardens.

The most influential ancient gardens in the western world were the Ptolemy's gardens at Alexandria and the gardening tradition brought to Rome by Lucullus. Wall paintings inPompeii attest to elaborate development later. The wealthiest Romans built extensive villa gardens with water features, topiary and cultivated roses and shaded arcades. Archeological evidence survives at sites such as Hadrian's Villa.

Byzantium and Moorish Spain kept garden traditions alive after the 4th century and the fall of Rome. By this time, a separate gardening tradition had arisen in China, which was transmitted to Japan, where it developed into aristocratic miniature landscapes centered on ponds and separately into the severe Zen gardens of temples.

In Europe, gardening revived in Languedoc and the Île-de-France in the 13th century. The rediscovery of descriptions of antique Roman villas and gardens led to the creation of a new form of garden, the Italian Renaissance garden in the late 15th and early 16th century. The first public parks were built by the Spanish Crown in the 16th century, in Europe and the Americas. The formal Garden à la française, exemplified by the Gardens of Versailles, became the dominant style of garden in Europe until the middle of the 18th century when it was replaced by the English landscape garden and the French landscape garden. The 19th century saw a welter of historical revivals and Romantic cottage-inspired gardening. In England, William Robinson and Gertrude Jekyll were strong proponents of the wild garden and the perennial garden respectively. Andrew Jackson Downing and Frederick Law Olmsted adapted European styles for North America, especially influencing public parks, campuses and suburban landscapes. Olmsted's influence extended well into the 20th century.

The 20th century saw the influence of modernism in the garden: from the articulate clarity of Thomas Church to the bold colors and forms of Brazilian Roberto Burle Marx.

A strong environmental consciousness and Sustainable design practices, such as green roofs and rainwater harvesting, are driving new considerations in gardening today.

THE HISTORICAL DEVELOPMENT OF GARDEN STYLES

MESOPOTAMIAN GARDENS

Mesopotamia - the "land between the Rivers" Tigris and Euphrates - comprises a hilly and mountainous northern area and a flat, alluvial south. Its peoples (Sumerians, Akkadians, Assyrians, and Babylonians) were urban and literate from about 3,000BC. Evidence for their gardens comes from written texts, pictorial sculpture and archaeology. In western tradition Mesopotamia was the location of the Garden of Eden and the Hanging Gardens of Babylon. Temple gardens developed from the representation of a sacred grove; several distinct styles of royal garden are also known.

The courtyard garden was enclosed by the walls of a palace, or on a larger scale was a cultivated place inside the city walls. At Mari on the Middle Euphrates (c 1,800BC) one of the huge palace courtyards was called the Court of the Palms in contemporary written records. It is crossed by raised walkways of baked brick; the king and his entourage would dine there. At Ugarit (c1,400BC) there was a stone water basin, not located centrally as in later Persian gardens, for the central feature was probably a tree (date palm or tamarisk).

The 7th century BC Assyrian king Assurbanipal is shown on a sculpture feasting with his queen, reclining on a couch beneath an arbour of vines, attended by musicians. Trophies of conquest are on display, including the dismembered head of the king of Elam hanging from a fragrant pine branch! A Babylonian text from the same period is divided into sections as if showing beds of soil with the names of medicinal, vegetable and herbal plants written into each square, perhaps representing a *parterre* design.

On a larger scale royal hunting parks were established to hold the exotic animals and plants which the king had acquired on his foreign campaigns. King Tiglath-Pileser I (c 1,000BC) lists horses, oxen, asses, deer of two types, gazelle and ibex, boasting "I numbered them like flocks of sheep."

From around 1,000 BC the Assyrian kings developed a style of city garden incorporating a naturalistic layout, running water supplied from river headwaters, and exotic plants from their foreign campaigns. Assurnasirpal II (883-859BC) lists pines of different kinds, cypresses and junipers of different kinds, almonds, dates, ebony, rosewood, olive, oak, tamarisk, walnut, terebinth and ash, fir pomegranate, pear, quince, fig and grapevines: "The canal water gushes from above into the gardens; fragrance pervades the walkways; streams of water as numerous as the stars of heaven flow in the pleasure garden.... Like a squirrel I pick fruit in the garden of delights." The city garden reached its zenith with the palace design of Sennacherib (704-681BC) whose water system stretched for 50 km into the hills, whose garden was higher and more ornate than any others, and who boasted of the complex technologies he deployed, calling his palace and garden "a Wonder for all Peoples".

The biblical Book of Genesis mentions the Tigris and Euphrates as two of the four rivers bounding the Garden of Eden. No specific place has been identified although there are many theories.

The Hanging Gardens of Babylon are listed by classical Greek writers as one of the Seven Wonders of the World - places to see before you die. The excavated ruins of Babylon do not reveal any suitable evidence, which has led some scholars to suggest that they may have been purely legendary. Alternatively the story may have originated from Sennacherib's garden in Nineveh.

Persian gardens

All Persian gardens, from the ancient to the high classical were developed in opposition to the harsh and arid landscape of the Iranian Plateau. Unlike historical European gardens, which seemed carved or re-ordered from within their existinglandscape, Persian gardens appeared as impossibilities. Their ethereal and delicate qualities emphasized their intrinsic contrast to the hostile environment. Trees and trellises largely feature as biotic shade; pavilions and walls are also structurally prominent in blocking the sun.

The heat also makes water important, both in the design and maintenance of the garden. Irrigation may be required, and may be provided via a form of underground tunnel called a qanat, that transports water from a local aquifer. Well-like structures then connect to the qanat, enabling the drawing of water. Alternatively, an animal-driven Persian well would draw water to the surface.

Such wheel systems also moved water around surface water systems, such as those in the chahar bâgh style. Trees were often planted in a ditch called a juy, which prevented water evaporation and allowed the water quick access to the tree roots.

The Persian style often attempts to integrate indoors with outdoors through the connection of a surrounding garden with an inner courtyard. Designers often place architectural elements such as vaulted arches between the outer and interior areas to open up the divide between them.

Egyptian gardens

Gardens were much cherished in the Egyptian times and were kept both for secular purposes and attached to temple compounds. Gardens in private homes and villas before the New Kingdom were mostly used for growing vegetables and located close to a canal or the river. However, in the New Kingdom they were often surrounded by walls and their purpose incorporated pleasure and beauty besides utility. Garden produce made out an important part of foodstuff but flowers were also cultivated for use in garlands to wear at festive occasions and for medicinal purposes.

Fig. A funerary model of a garden, dating to the Eleventh dynasty of Egypt, c. 2009–1998 BC. Made of painted and gessoed wood, originally fromThebes.

While the poor kept a patch for growing vegetables, the rich people could afford gardens lined with sheltering trees and decorative pools with fish and waterfowl. There could be wooden structures forming pergolas to support vines of grapes from which raisins and wine were produced. There could even be elaborate stone kiosks for ornamental reasons, with decorative statues.

Temple gardens had plots for cultivating special vegetables, plants or herbs considered sacred to a certain deity and which were required in rituals and offerings like lettuce to Min. Sacred groves and ornamental trees were planted in front of or near both cult temples and mortuary temples. As temples were representations of heaven and built as the actual home of the god, gardens were laid out according to the same principle. Avenues leading up to the entrance could be lined with trees, courtyards could hold small gardens and between temple buildings gardens with trees, vineyards, flowers and ponds were maintained.

The ancient Egyptian garden would have looked different from a modern garden. It would have seemed more like a collection of herbs or a patch of wild flowers, lacking the specially bred flowers of today. Flowers like the iris, chrysanthemum, lily and delphinium (blue), were certainly known to the ancients but do not feature much in garden scenes. Formal boquets seem to have been composed of mandrake, poppy, cornflower and or lotus and papyrus.

Due to the arid climate of Egypt, tending gardens meant constant attention and depended on irrigation. Skilled gardeners were employed by temples and households of the wealthy. Duties included planting, weeding, watering by means of a shaduf, pruning of fruit trees, digging the ground, harvesting the fruit etc.

Hellenistic and Roman gardens

Hellenistic gardens

It is curious that although the Egyptians and Romans both gardened with vigor, the Greeks did not own private gardens. They did put gardens around temples and they adorned walkways and roads with statues, but the ornate and pleasure gardens that demonstrated wealth in the other communities is seemingly absent.

Roman gardens

Roman gardens were a place of peace and solitude, a refuge from urban life. Ornamental horticulture became highly developed during the development of Roman civilization. The administrators of the Roman Empire (c.100 BC - 500 AD) actively exchanged information on agriculture, horticulture, animal husbandry, hydraulics, and botany. Seeds and plants were widely shared. The Gardens of Lucullus (Horti Lucullani) on the Pincian Hill on the edge of Rome introduced the Persian garden to Europe, about 60 BC.

Chinese and Japanese gardens

Both Chinese and Japanese garden design traditionally is intended to evoke the natural landscape of mountains and rivers. However, the intended viewpoint of the gardens differs: Chinese gardens were intended to be viewed from within the garden and are intended as a setting for everyday life. Japanese gardens, with a few exceptions, were intended to be viewed from within the house, somewhat like adiorama. Additionally, Chinese gardens more often included a water feature, while Japanese gardens, set in a wetter climate, would often get by with the suggestion of water. (Such as sand or pebbles raked into a wave pattern.) Traditional Chinese gardens are also more likely to treat the plants in a naturalistic way, while traditional Japanese gardens might feature plants sheared into mountain shapes. This contrasts with the handling of stone elements: in a Japanese garden, stones are placed in groupings as part of the landscape, but in a Chinese garden, a particularly choice stone might even be placed on a pedestal in a prominent location so that it might be more easily appreciated.

Chinese scholar gardens

The style of Chinese garden varies among economic groups and differs by dynasties. Rocks, water, bridges and pavilions are among the most common features of scholar gardens for the wealthy classes, while courtyards, wells, and terra cotta fish tanks are common among general population. Other features such as moon gates and leaky windows (openwork screens that pierce surrounding walls) are seen in both groups.

The development of landscape design in China was historically driven by philosophies of both Confucianism and Taoism. Geometric symmetry and reinforcement of class boundaries were typical characteristics of landscape design in Asian cities, and both characteristics reflect Confucian ideals. While the British used nature outside the home to provide privacy, Chinese homes were compounds made of a number of buildings which all faced one or more courtyards or common areas. Rather than around the home, the Chinese valued natural spaces inside the compound, which is where the family socialized. Furthermore, Courtyards in the Chinese home reflected Taoist philosophies, where families would try to create abstractions of nature rather than recreations of it. For example, a Taoist garden would avoid straight lines and use stone and water instead of trees, whereas Asian cities followed Confucian, geometric designs and North American parks typically feature trees and lawns.

There are two ways of looking at the signature design characteristics of the Chinese garden: first, the concept of Yin and Yang and second, the myths of longevity that arose during the Qin Dynasty.

The philosophy of Yin and Yang portrays the idea of balance and harmony. The Chinese garden expresses the relationship to nature and the idea of balance through the art of mimicking natural setting, thus the existence of mountains, rocks, water, and wind elements. Yin and Yang juxtapose complementary opposites: as hard as rock can be, the softness of water can dissolve it. Tai Hu rocks, limestone eroded by the water of Lake Tai, are the quintessential example. Water, air and light run through the rock as it sit still on display. The leaky windows of the Chinese garden wall portray both steadiness and movement. The windows create a solid painting on walls, however that steadiness changes once the wind blows or the eyes move.

Chinese garden's structure is based upon the culture's creation myth, rooted in rocks and water. To have longevity is to live among mountains and water; it is to live with nature, to live like an immortal being (Xian). The garden evokes a healthy lifestyle that makes one immortal, free from the problems of civilization. Thus, Chinese landscape is known as Shan (mountain) and Shui (water). (Add Roger's citation).

Symbolism is a key element of Chinese garden design. To the earthy tones of the Chinese garden, a touch of red or gold is often added to bring forth the Yin/Yang contrast. The colors red and gold also represent luck and wealth. Bats, dragons and other mystic creatures carved on wooden doors are also commonly found in Chinese gardens; these are signs of luck and protection.

Circles portray togetherness, especially for family members, and are depicted in moon gates and round tables placed within square backgrounds. The moon gate and other whimsical doorways also act to frame views and to force the viewer to pause for a transition into a new space.

Paths in Chinese gardens are often uneven and sometimes consciously zigzag. These paths are like the passages of a human life. There is always something new or different when seen from a different angle, while the future is unknown and unpredictable.

EUROPEAN GARDENS

Gardens of Byzantium

The Byzantine empire span a period of more than 1000 years (330-1453 AD) and a geographic area from modern day Spain and Britain to the Middle East and north Africa. Probably due to this temporal and geographic spread and its turbulent history, there is no single dominant garden style that can be labeled "Byzantine style". Archaeological evidence of public, imperial, and private gardens is scant at best and researchers over the years have relied on literary sources to derive clues about the main features of Byzantine gardens.

Romance novels such as Hysmine and Hysminias (12th century) included detailed descriptions of gardens and their popularity attests to the Byzantines' enthusiasm for pleasure gardens (locus amoenus). More formal gardening texts such as the Geoponika (10th century) were in fact encyclopedias of accumulated agricultural practices (grafting, watering) and pagan lore (astrology, plant sympathy/antipathy relationships) going back to Hesiod's time. Their repeated publications and translations to other languages well into the 16th century is evidence to the value attributed to the horticultural knowledge of antiquity. These literary sources worked as handbooks promoting the concepts of walled gardens with plants arranged by type. Such ideals found expression in the suburban parks (Philopation, Aretai) and palatial gardens (Mesokepion,Mangana) of Constantinople.

The Byzantine garden tradition was influenced by the strong undercurrents of history that the empire itself was exposed to. The first and foremost influence was the adoption of Christianity as the empire's official religion by its founder Constantine I. The new religion signaled a departure from the ornamental pagan sculptures of the Greco-Roman garden style. The second influence was the increasing contact with the Islamic nations of the Middle East especially after the 9th century. Lavish furnishings in the emperor's palace and the adoption of automata in the palatial gardens are evidence of this influence. The third factor was a fundamental shift in the design of the Byzantine cities after the 7th century when they became smaller in size and population as well as more ruralized. The class of wealthy aristocrats who could finance and maintain elaborate gardens probably shrank as well. The final factor was a shifting view toward a more "enclosed" garden space (hortus conclusus); a trend dominant in Europe at that time. The open views and vistas so much favored by the garden builders of the Roman villas were replaced by garden walls and scenic views painted on the inside of these walls. The concept of the heavenly paradise was an enclosed garden gained popularity during that time and especially after the iconoclastic period (7th century) with the emphasis it placed on divine punishment and repentance.

An area of horticulture that flourished throughout the long history of Byzantium was that practiced by monasteries. Although archaeological evidence has provided limited evidence of monastic horticulture, a great deal can be learned by studying the foundation documents (ôõðéêüí, typikon) of the numerous Christian monasteries as well as the biographies of saints describing their gardening activities. From these sources we learn that monasteries maintained gardens outside their walls and watered them with complex irrigation systems fed by springs or rainwater. These gardens contained vineyards, broadleaf vegetables, and fruit trees for the sustenance of monks and pilgrims alike. The role of the gardener was frequently assumed by monks as an act of humility. Monastic horticultural practices established at that time are still in use in Christian monasteries throughout Greece and the Middle East.

Medieval

Monasteries carried on a tradition of garden design and intense horticultural techniques during the medieval period in Europe. Rather than any one particular horticultural technique employed, it is the variety of different purposes the monasteries had for their gardens that serves as testament to their sophistication. As for gardening practices, records are limited, and there are no extant monastic gardens that are entirely true to original form. There are, however, records and plans that indicate the types of garden a monastery might have had, such as those for St. Gall in Switzerland.

Generally, monastic garden types consisted of kitchen gardens, infirmary gardens, cemetery orchards, cloister garths and vineyards. Individual monasteries might also have had a "green court", a plot of grass and trees where horses could graze, as well as a cellarer's garden or private gardens for obedientiaries, monks who held specific posts within the monastery.

From a utilitarian standpoint, vegetable and herb gardens helped provide both alimentary and medicinal crops, which could be used to feed or treat the monks and, in some cases, the outside community. As detailed in the plans for St. Gall, these gardens were laid out in rectangular plots, with narrow paths between them to facilitate collection of yields. Often these beds were surrounded with wattle fencing to prevent animals from entry. In the kitchen gardens, fennel, cabbage, onion, garlic, leeks, radishes, and parsnips might be grown, as well as peas, lentils and beans if space allowed for them. The infirmary gardens could contain *Rosa gallica* ("The Apothecary Rose"), savory, costmary, fenugreek, rosemary, peppermint, rue, iris, sage, bergamot, mint, lovage, fennel and cumin, amongst other herbs. From a utilitarian standpoint, vegetable and herb gardens helped provide both alimentary and medicinal crops, which could be used to feed or treat the monks and, in some cases, the outside community.

The herb and vegetable gardens served a purpose beyond that of production, and that was that their installation and maintenance allowed the monks to fulfill the manual labor component of the religious way of life prescribed by Rule of St. Benedict.

Orchards also served as sites for food production and as arenas for manual labor, and cemetery orchards, such as that detailed in the plan for St. Gall, showed yet more versatility. The cemetery orchard not only produced fruit, but manifested as a natural symbol of the garden of Paradise. This bi-fold concept of the garden as a space that met both physical and spiritual needs was carried over to the cloister garth.

The cloister garth, a claustrum consisting of the viridarium, a rectangular plot of grass surrounded by peristyle arcades, was barred to the laity, and served primarily as a place of retreat, a locus of the 'vita contempliva'. The viridarium was often bisected or quartered by paths, and often featured a roofed fountain at the center or side of the garth that served as a primary source for wash water and for irrigation, meeting yet more physical needs. Some cloister gardens contained small fish ponds as well, another source of food for the community. The arcades were used for teaching, sitting and meditating, or for exercise in inclement weather.

There is much conjecture as to ways in which the garth served as a spiritual aid. Umberto Eco describes the green swath as a sort of balm on which a monk might rest weary eyes, so as to return to reading with renewed vigor. Some scholars suggest that, though sparsely planted, plant materials found in the cloister garth might have inspired various religious visions. This tendency to imbue the garden with symbolic values was not inherent to the religious orders alone, but was a feature of medieval culture in general. The square closter garth was meant to represent the four points of the compass, and so the universe as a whole. As Turner puts it,

Augustine inspired medieval garden makers to abjure earthliness and look upward for divine inspiration. A perfect square with a round pool and a pentagonal fountain became a microcosm, illuminating the mathematical order and divine grace of the macrocosm (the universe).

Walking around the cloister while meditating was a way of devoting oneself to the "path of life"; indeed, each of the monastic gardens was imbued with symbolic as well as palpable value, testifying to the ingenuity of its creators.

In the later Middle Ages, texts, art and literary works provide a picture of developments in garden design. During the late 12th through 15th centuries, European cities were walled for internal defense and to control trade. Though space within these walls was limited, surviving documents show that there were animals, fruit trees and kitchen gardens inside the city limits.

Pietro Crescenzi, a Bolognese lawyer, wrote twelve volumes on the practical aspects of farming in the 13th century and they offer a description of medieval gardening practices. From his text we know that gardens were surrounded with stonewalls, thick hedging or fencing and incorporated trellises and arbors. They borrowed their form from the square or rectangular shape of the cloister and included square planting beds.

Grass was also first noted in the medieval garden. In the *De Vegetabilibus* of Albertus Magnus written around 1260, instructions are given for planting grass plots. Raised banks covered in turf called "Turf Seats" were constructed to provide seating in the garden. Fruit trees were prevalent and often grafted to produce new varieties of fruit. Gardens included a raised mound or mount to serve as a stage for viewing and planting beds were customarily elevated on raised platforms.

Two works from the late Middle Ages discuss plant cultivation. In the English poem "The Feate of Gardinage" by Jon Gardener and the general household advice given in Le Ménagier de Paris of 1393, a variety of herbs, flowers, fruit trees and bushes were listed with instructions on their cultivation. The Menagier provides advice by season on sowing, planting and grafting. The most sophisticated gardening during the Middle Ages was done at the monasteries. Monks developed horticultural techniques, and cultivated herbs, fruits and vegetables. Using the medicinal herbs they grew, monks treated those suffering inside the monastery and in surrounding communities.

During the Middle Ages, gardens were thought to unite the earthly with the divine. The enclosed garden as an allegory for paradise or a "lost Eden" was termed the *Hortus Conclusus*. Freighted with religious and spiritual significance, enclosed gardens were often depicted in the visual arts, picturing the Virgin Mary, a fountain, a unicorn and roses inside an enclosed area.

Though Medieval gardens lacked many of the features of the Renaissance gardens that followed them, some of the characteristics of these gardens continue to be incorporated today.

The Renaissance

- The Italian Renaissance inspired a revolution in private gardening. Renaissance private gardens were full of scenes from ancient mythology and other learned allusions. Water during this time was especially symbolic: it was associated with fertility and the abundance of nature.
- The first public gardens were built by the Spanish Crown in the 16th century, in Europe and the Americas.
- Terraced Italian Renaissance gardens

French Baroque

- The Garden à la française, or Baroque French gardens, in the tradition of André Le Nôtre.

The French Classical garden style, or Garden à la française, climaxed during the reign of Louis XIVof France (1638–1715) and his head gardener of Gardens of Versailles, André Le Nôtre (1613–1700). The inspiration for these gardens initially came from the Italian Renaissance garden of the 14th and 15th centuries and ideas of French philosopher René Descartes (1576–1650). At this time the

French opened the garden up to enormous proportions compared to their Italian predecessor. Their gardens epitomize monarch and 'man' dominating and manipulating nature to show his authority, wealth, and power.

Renée Descartes, the founder of analytical geometry, believed that the natural world was objectively measurable and that space is infinitely divisible. His belief that "all movement is a straight line therefore space is a universal grid of mathematical coordinates and everything can be located on its infinitely extendable planes" gave us Cartesian mathematics. Through the classical French gardens this coordinate system and philosophy is now given a physical and visual representation.

This French formal and axial garden style placed the house centrally on an enormous and mainly flat property of land. A large central axis that gets narrower further from the main house, forces the viewer's perspective to the horizon line, making the property look even larger. The viewer is to see the property as a cohesive whole but at the same time is unable to see all the components of the garden. One is to be led through a logical progression or story and be surprised by elements that aren't visible until approached. There is an allegorical story referring to the owner through statues and water features which have mythological references. There are small, almost imperceptible grade changes that help conceal the gardens surprises as well as elongate the gardens views.

These grand gardens have organized spaces meant to be elaborate stages for entertaining the court and guests with plays, concerts and fireworks displays. The following list of garden features were used:

- Allée
- Axis
- Bosquet
- Canal
- Cul de sac
- Fountains
- Grottos with rocaille
- Orangerie
- Parterre de broderie
- Patte d'oie (Goose foot)
- Tapis Vert
- Topiary

Mediterranean Gardens

Due to being an early hub for Western society and being used for centuries, Mediterranean soil was fragile, and one could think of the region's landscape culture to be a conflict between fruitfulness and frugality. The area consisted largely of small-scale agricultural plots. Later, following World War II, Mediterranean immigrants brought this agricultural style to Canada, where fruit trees and vegetables in the backyard became common.

Anglo-Dutch gardens

- Anglo-Dutch formal gardens

Picturesque and English Landscape gardens

Forested areas played a number of roles for the British in the Middle Ages, and one of those roles was to produce game for the gentry. Lords of valuable land were expected to provide a bounty of animals for hunting during royal visits. Despite being in natural locations, forested manor homes could symbolize status, wealth and power if they appeared to have all amenities. After the Industrial Revolution, Britain's forest industry shrank until it no longer existed. In response, the Garden City Movement brought urban planning into industrialized areas in the early 20th century to offset negative industrial effects such as pollution.

There were several traditions that influenced English gardening in the 18th century, the first of which was to plant woods around homes. By the mid-17th century, coppiceplanting became consistent and was considered visually and aesthetically pleasing. Whereas forested areas were more useful for hunting purposes in Britain during the Middle Ages, 18th century patterns demonstrate a further deviation in gardening approach from practicality toward design meant to please the senses.

Likewise, English pleasure grounds were influenced by medieval groves, some of which were still in existence in 18th century Britain. This influence manifest in the form of shrubbery, sometimes organized in mazes or maze-like formations. And though also ancient, shredding became a common characteristic of these early gardens, as the method enabled light to enter the understory. Shredding was used to make garden groves, which ideally included an orchard with fruit trees, fragrant herbs and flowers, and moss-covered pathways.

The picturesque garden style emerged in England in the 18th century, one of the growing currents of the larger Romantic movement. Garden designers like William Kent andCapability Brown emulated the allegorical landscape paintings of European artists, especially Claude Lorraine, Poussin and Salvator Rosa. The manicured hills, lakes and trees dotted with allegorical temples were sculpted into the land.

By the 1790s there was a reaction against these stereotypical compositions; a number of thinkers began to promote the idea of picturesque gardens. The leader of the movement was landscape theorist William Gilpin, an accomplished artist known for his realistic depictions of Nature. He preferred the natural landscape over the manicured and urged designers to respond to the topography of a given site. He also noted that while classical beauty was associated with the smooth and neat, picturesque beauty had a wilder, untamed quality. The picturesque style also incorporated architectural follies—castles, Gothic ruins, rustic cottages—built to add interest and depth to the landscape

Controversy between the picturesque school and proponents of the more manicured garden raged well into the 19th century. Landscape designer Humphrey

Repton supported Gilpin's ideas, particularly that of the garden harmonizing with surrounding landforms. He was attacked in the press by two rival theorists, Richard Payne Knight and Uvedale Price. Repton countered by highlighting the differences between painting and landscape gardening. Unlike a painting, the viewer moves through a garden, constantly shifting viewpoints.

The French landscape garden, also called the *jardin anglais* or *jardin pittoresque*, was influenced by contemporary English gardens. Rococo features like Turkish tents and Chinese bridges are prevalent in French gardens in the 18th century. The French Picturesque garden style falls into two categories: those that were staged, almost like theatrical scenery, usually rustic and exotic, called *jardin anglo-chinois*, and those filled with pastoral romance and bucolic sentiment, influenced by Jean-Jacques Rousseau. The former style is represented by the Désert de Retz and Parc Monceau, the latter by the Moulin Jolie.

The rusticity found in French Picturesque gardens is also derived from an admiration of Dutch 17th century landscape painting and works of French 18th century artists Claude-Henri Watelet, François Boucher and Hubert Robert.

English gardens: the common name in the English speaking world, of interpretations, derivations, and revivals in the style of the original Landscape Garden examples.

'Gardenesque' gardens

The 'Gardenesque' style of English garden design evolved during the 1820s from Humphry Repton's Picturesque or 'Mixed' style, largely under the impetus of J. C. Loudon, who invented the term.

In a Gardenesque plan, all the trees, shrubs and other plants are positioned and managed in such a way that the character of each plant can be displayed to its full potential. With the spread of botany as a suitable avocation for the enlightened, the Gardenesque tended to emphasize botanical curiosities and a collector's approach. New plant material that would have seemed bizarre and alien in earlier gardening found settings: Pampas grass from Argentina and

Monkey-puzzle trees. Winding paths linked scattered plantings. The Gardenesque approach involved the creation of small-scale landscapes, dotted with features and vignettes, to promote beauty of detail, variety and mystery, sometimes to the detriment of coherence. Artificial mounds helped to stage groupings of shrubs, and island beds became prominent features.

"Wild" gardens and herbaceous borders

The books of William Robinson describing his own "wild" gardening at Gravetye Manor in Sussex, and the sentimental picture of a rosy, idealized "cottage garden" of the kind pictured by Kate Greenaway, which had scarcely existed historically, both influenced the development of the mixed herbaceous borders that were advocated by Gertrude Jekyllat Munstead Wood in Surrey from the 1890s. Her plantings, which mixed shrubs with perennial and annual plants and bulbs in deep beds within more formal structures of terraces and stairs designed by Edwin Lutyens, set the model for high-style, high-maintenance gardening until the Second World War. Vita Sackville-West's garden atSissinghurst Castle, Kent is the most famous and influential garden of this last blossoming of romantic style, publicized by the gardener's own gardening column in *The Observer*. The trend continued in the gardening of Margery Fish at East Lambrook Manor. In the last quarter of the 20th century, less structured Wildlife gardening emphasized the ecological framework of similar gardens using native plants. A leading proponent in the United States was the landscape architect Jens Jensen. He designed city andregional parks, and private estates, with a honed aesthetic of art and nature.

Pattern gardens: revived parterres

Contemporary gardens

- Romantic English cottage garden revival.
- Modernist gardens.
- Naturalistic habitat gardens

In the 20th century, modern design for gardens became important as architects began to design buildings and residences with an eye toward innovation and streamlining the formal Beaux-Arts and derivative early revival styles, removing unnecessary references and embellishment. Garden design, inspired by modern architecture, naturally followed in the same philosophy of "form following function".

Thus concerning the many philosophies of plant maturity. In post-war United States people's residences and domestic lives became more outdoor oriented, especially in the western states as promoted by 'Sunset Magazine', with the backyard often becoming an outdoor room.

Frank Lloyd Wright demonstrated his interpretation for the modern garden by designing homes in complete harmony with natural surroundings. Taliesin and Fallingwater are both examples of careful placement of architecture in nature so the relationship between the residence and surroundings become seamless.

His son Lloyd Wright trained in architecture and landscape architecture in the Olmsted Brothers office, with his father, and with architect Irving Gill. He practiced an innovative organic integration of structure and landscape in his works.

Subsequently Garrett Eckbo, James Rose, and Dan Kiley - known as the "bad boys of Harvard", met while studying traditional landscape architecture became notable pioneers in the design of modern gardens. As Harvard embraced modern design in their school of architecture, these designers wanted to interpret and incorporate those new ideas in landscape design. They became interested in developing functional space for outdoor living with designs echoing natural surroundings.

Modern gardens feature a fresh mix of curved and architectonic designs and many include abstract art in geometrics and sculpture. Spaces are defined with the thoughtful placement of trees and plantings. Thomas Church work in California was influential through his books and other publications. In Sonoma County, California his 1948 Donnell garden's swimming Pool, kidney-shaped with an abstract sculpture within it, became an icon of modern outdoor living.

In Mexico Luis Barragán explored a synthesis of International style modernism with native Mexican tradition. in private estates and residential development projects such asJardines del Pedregal *(English: Rocky Gardens)* and the San Cristobal 'Los Clubes' Estates in Mexico City. In civic design the Torres de Satélite are urban sculptures of substantial dimensions in Naucalpan, Mexico. His house, studio, and gardens, built in 1948 in Mexico City, was listed as a UNESCO World Heritage site in 2004.

Roberto Burle Marx is accredited with having introduced modernist landscape architecture to Brazil. He was known as a modern nature artist and a public urban space designer.

He was landscape architect (as well as a botanist, painter, print maker, ecologist, naturalist, artist, and musician) who designed of parks and gardens in Brazil,Argentina, Venezuela, Kuala Lumpur, Malaysia, and in the United States in Florida.

He worked with the architects Lúcio Costa and Oscar Niemeyer on the landscape design for some of the prominent modernist government buildings in Brazil's capitol Brasília.

Container garden

Container gardening or pot gardening is the practice of growing plants, including edible plants, exclusively in containers instead of planting them in the ground.

Fig. Container garden on front porch

A container is the general term used in gardening for a small, enclosed and usually portable object used for displaying live flowers or plants. It may take the form of a pot, box, tub, pot, basket, tin, barrel or hanging basket.

Pots, traditionally made of terracotta but now more commonly plastic, and window boxes have been the most commonly seen. Small pots are commonly called flowerpots. In some cases, this method of growing is used for ornamental purposes. This method is also useful in areas where the soil or climate is unsuitable for the plant or crop in question. Using a container is also generally necessary forhouseplants. Limited growing space, or growing space that is paved over, can also make this option appealing to the gardener.

Planting

Containers range from simple plastic pots, teacups to complex automatic-watering irrigation systems. This flexibility in design is another reason container gardening is popular with growers. They can be found on porches, front steps, and in urban locations, on rooftops. Sub-irrigated planters (SIP) are a type of container that may be used in container gardens. Potting material must be loose and allow drainage to offer proper aeration for roots to breathe, preventing root rot.

Re-potting

Re-potting is the action of placing an already potted plant into a larger or smaller pot. A pot that fits a plant's root system better is normally used. Plants are usually re-potted according to the size of their root system. Most plants need to be re-potted every few years, because they become "pot-bound" or "root-bound." Plants' roots can sense its surroundings, including the size of the pot it is in, and increasing the pot size allows plant size to increase proportionally.

Advantages

Many types of plants are suitable for the container, including decorative flowers, herbs, cacti, vegetables, and small trees. There are many advantages to growing plants in containers, namely:

- Less risk of soil-borne disease
- Virtually eliminate weed problems
- Mobile plants gives more control over moisture, sunlight & temperature

Pot farming

Tomato plants growing in a pot farming alongside a small house in New Jersey in fifteen garbage cans filled with soil, grew over 700 tomatoes during the summer of 2013.

Crops can be grown in flowerpots and it is called pot farming or pot agriculture.

Compost

Compost is organic matter that has been decomposed and recycled as a fertilizer and soil amendment. Compost is a key ingredient in organic farming. At the simplest level, the process of composting simply requires making a heap of wetted organic matter known as green waste (leaves, food waste) and waiting for the materials to break down into humus after a period of weeks or months.

Modern, methodical composting is a multi-step, closely monitored process with measured inputs of water, air, and carbon- and nitrogen-rich materials. The decomposition process is aided by shredding the plant matter, adding water and ensuring proper aeration by regularly turning the mixture. Worms and fungi further break up the material. Bacteria requiring oxygen to function (aerobic bacteria) and fungi manage the chemical process by converting the inputs into heat, carbon dioxide and ammonium. The ammonium (NH_4) is the form of nitrogen used by plants. When available ammonium is not used by plants it is further converted by bacteria into nitrates (NO_3) through the process of nitrification. Compost is rich in nutrients. It is used in gardens, landscaping, horticulture, and agriculture. The compost itself is beneficial for the land in many ways, including as a soil conditioner, a fertilizer, addition of vital humus or humic acids, and as a natural pesticide for soil. In ecosystems, compost is useful for erosion control, land and stream reclamation, wetland construction, and as landfill cover. Organic ingredients intended for composting can alternatively be used to generate biogas through anaerobic digestion.

Terminology

The term "composting" is used worldwide with differing meanings. Some composting textbooks narrowly define composting as being an aerobic form of decompostion, primarily by microbes. For many people, however, composting is used to refer to several different types of biological process. In North America, "anaerobic composting" is still a common term, but in much of the rest of the world and in technical publications the more accurate term anaerobic digestion is used as the microbes used and the processes involved are quite different.

Ingredients

Fig. Home compost barrel in the Escuela Barreales, Santa Cruz, Chile.

Carbon, nitrogen, oxygen, water

Composting organisms require four equally important ingredients to work effectively:

- Carbon — for energy; the microbial oxidation of carbon produces the heat, if included at suggested levels.
- High carbon materials tend to be brown and dry.
- Nitrogen — to grow and reproduce more organisms to oxidize the carbon.
- High nitrogen materials tend to be green (or colorful, such as fruits and vegetables) and wet.
- Oxygen — for oxidizing the carbon, the decomposition process.
- Water — in the right amounts to maintain activity without causing anaerobic conditions.

Certain ratios of these materials will provide beneficial bacteria with the nutrients to work at a rate that will heat up the pile. In that process much water will be released as vapor ("steam"), and the oxygen will be quickly depleted, explaining the need to actively manage the pile. The hotter the pile gets, the more often added air and water is necessary; the air/water balance is critical to maintaining high temperatures (135°-160° Fahrenheit / 50° - 70° Celsius) until the materials are broken down. At the same time, too much air or water also slows the process, as does too much carbon (or too little nitrogen).

The most efficient composting occurs with an optimal carbon:nitrogen ratio of about 10:1 to 20:1. Nearly all plant and animal materials have both carbon and nitrogen, but amounts vary widely, with characteristics noted above (dry/wet, brown/green). Fresh grass clippings have an average ratio of about 15:1 and dry autumn leaves about 50:1 depending on species. Mixing equal parts by volume approximates the ideal C:N range. Few individual situations will provide the ideal mix of materials at any point. Observation of amounts, and consideration of different materials as a pile is built over time, can quickly achieve a workable technique for the individual situation.

Animal manure and bedding

On many farms, the basic composting ingredients are animal manure generated on the farm and bedding. Straw and sawdust are common bedding materials. Non-traditional bedding materials are also used, including newspaper and chopped cardboard. The amount of manure composted on a livestock farm is often determined by cleaning schedules, land availability, and weather conditions. Each type of manure has its own physical, chemical, and biological characteristics. Cattle and horse manures, when mixed with bedding, possess good qualities for composting. Swine manure, which is very wet and usually not mixed with bedding material, must be mixed with straw or similar raw materials. Poultry manure also must be blended with carbonaceous materials - those low in nitrogen preferred, such as sawdust or straw.

Microorganisms

With the proper mixture of water, oxygen, carbon, and nitrogen, micro-organisms are allowed to break down organic matter to produce compost. The composting process is dependent on micro-organisms to break down organic matter into compost. There are many types of microorganisms found in active compost of which the most common are:

- Bacteria- The most numerous of all the microorganisms found in compost. Depending on the phase of composting, mesophilic or thermophilic bacteria may predominate.
- Actinobacteria- Necessary for breaking down paper products such as newspaper, bark, etc.
- Fungi- Molds and yeast help break down materials that bacteria cannot, especially lignin in woody material.
- Protozoa- Help consume bacteria, fungi and micro organic particulates.
- Rotifers- Rotifers help control populations of bacteria and small protozoans.

In addition, earthworms not only ingest partly composted material, but also continually re-create aeration and drainage tunnels as they move through the compost. A lack of a healthy micro-organism community is the main reason why composting processes are slow in landfills with environmental factors such as lack of oxygen, nutrients or water being the cause of the depleted biological community.

Phases of composting

Under ideal conditions, composting proceeds through three major phases:

- An initial, mesophilic phase, in which the decomposition is carried out under moderate temperatures by mesophilic microorganisms.
- As the temperature rises, a second, thermophilic phase starts, in which in decomposition is carried out by various thermophilic bacteria under high temperatures.
- As the supply of high-energy compounds dwindles, the temperature starts to decrease, and the mesophiles once again predominate in the maturation phase.

Human waste

Human waste (excreta) can also be added as an input to the composting process, like it is done in composting toilets, as human waste is a nitrogen-rich organic material.

People excrete far more water-soluble plant nutrients (nitrogen, phosphorus, potassium) in urine than in feces. Human urine can be used directly as fertilizer or it can be put onto compost. Adding a healthy person's urine to compost usually will increase temperatures and therefore increase its ability to destroy pathogens and unwanted seeds.

Urine from a person with no obvious symptoms of infection is much more sanitary than fresh feces. Unlike feces, urine does not attract disease-spreading flies (such as house flies orblow flies), and it does not contain the most hardy of pathogens, such as parasitic worm eggs. Urine usually does not stink for long, particularly when it is fresh, diluted, or put onsorbents.

Urine is primarily composed of water and urea. Although metabolites of urea are nitrogen fertilizers, it is easy to over-fertilize with urine, or to utilize urine containing pharmaceutical (or other) content, creating too much ammonia for plants to absorb, acidic conditions, or other phytotoxicity.

Humanure

"Humanure" is a combination of the words *human* and *manure*, designating human excrement (feces and urine) that is recycled via composting for agricultural or other purposes.

The term was first used in a 1994 book by Joseph Jenkins that advocates the use of this organic soil amendment. The term humanure is used by compost enthusiasts in the US but not generally elsewhere. Because the term "humanure" has no authoritative definition it is subject to various uses; news reporters occasionally fail to correctly distinguish between humanure and sewage sludge or "biosolids".

Uses

Compost is generally recommended as an additive to soil, or other matrices such as coir and peat, as a tilth improver, supplying humus and nutrients. It provides a rich *growing medium*, or a porous, absorbent material that holds moisture and soluble minerals, providing the support and nutrients in which plants can flourish, although it is rarely used alone, being primarily mixed with soil, sand, grit, bark chips, vermiculite, perlite, or clay granules to produce loam. Compost can be tilled directly into the soil or growing medium to boost the level of organic matter and the overall fertility of the soil. Compost that is ready to be used as an additive is dark brown or even black with an earthy smell.

Generally, direct seeding into a compost is not recommended due to the speed with which it may dry and the possible presence of phytotoxins that may inhibit germination, and the possible tie up of nitrogen by incompletely decomposed lignin.

It is very common to see blends of 20–30% compost used for transplantingseedlings at cotyledon stage or later.

Composting can destroy pathogens or unwanted seeds. Unwanted living plants (or weeds) can be discouraged by covering with mulch/compost. The "microbial pesticides" in compost may include thermophiles and mesophiles, however certain composting detritivores such as black soldier fly larvae and redworms, also reduce many pathogens.

Thermophilic (high-temperature) composting is well known to destroy many seeds and nearly all types of pathogens (exceptions may include prions). The sanitizing qualities of (thermophilic) composting are desirable where there is a high likelihood of pathogens, such as with manure.

Composting technologies

Fig. A modern compost bin constructed from plastics

Overview

In addition to the traditional compost pile, various approaches have been developed to handle different composting processes, ingredients, locations, and applications for the composted product.

There is a large number of different composting systems on the market, for example:

- At the household level: Composting toilet, container composting, vermicomposting
- At the industrial composting (large scale): Aerated Static Pile Composting, vermicomposting, windrow composting etc.

Examples

Vermicomposting

Fig. Food waste - after three years

Vermicompost is the product or process of composting through the utilization of various species of worms, usually red wigglers, white worms, and earthworms, to create a heterogeneous mixture of decomposing vegetable or food waste (excluding meat, dairy, fats, or oils), bedding materials, and vermicast. Vermicast, also known as worm castings, worm humus or worm manure, is the end-product of the breakdown of organic matter by species of earthworm. Vermicomposting is widely used in North America for on-site institutional processing of food waste, such as in hospitals and shopping malls. This type of composting is sometimes suggested as a feasible indoor home composting method. Vermicomposting has gained popularity in both these industrial and domestic settings because, as compared with conventional composting, it provides a way to compost organic materials more quickly (as defined by a higher rate ofcarbon-to-nitrogen ratio increase) and to attain products that have lower salinity levels that are therefore more beneficial to plant mediums.

The earthworm species (or composting worms) most often used are red wigglers (*Eisenia fetida*or *Eisenia andrei*), though European nightcrawlers (*Eisenia hortensis* or *Dendrobaena veneta*) could also be used. Red wigglers are recommended by most vermiculture experts, as they have some of the best appetites and breed very quickly.

Containing water-soluble nutrients, vermicompost is a nutrient-rich organic fertilizer and soil conditioner in a form that is relatively easy for plants to absorb. Worm castings are sometimes used as an organic fertilizer. Because the earthworms grind and uniformly mix minerals in simple forms, plants need only minimal effort to obtain them. The worms' digestive systems also add beneficial microbes to help create a "living" soil environment for plants.

Vermicompost tea in conjunction with 10% castings has been shown to cause up to a 1.7 times growth in plant mass over plants grown without.

Researchers from the Pondicherry University discovered that worm composts can also be used to clean up heavy metals. The researchers found substantial reductions in heavy metals when the worms were released into the garbage and they are effective at removing lead, zinc, cadmium, copper and manganese.

Hügelkultur (raised garden beds or mounds)

Fig. An almost completed Hügelkultur bed (does not have dirt on it yet).

The practice of making raised garden beds or mounds filled with rotting wood is also called "Hügelkultur" in German. It is in effect creating a Nurse log, however, covered with dirt.

Benefits of hügelkultur garden beds include water retention and warming of soil. Buried wood becomes like a sponge as it decomposes, able to capture water and store it for later use by crops planted on top of the hügelkultur bed.

The buried decomposing wood will also give off heat, as all compost does, for several years. These effects have been used by Sepp Holzer for one to allow fruit trees to survive at otherwise inhospitable temperatures and altitudes.

Black soldier fly larvae composting

Black Soldier Fly (*Hermetia illucens*) larvae have been shown to be able to rapidly consume large amounts of organic waste when kept at 31.8°C, the optimum temperature for reproduction. Enthusiasts have experimented with a large number of different waste productsand some even sell starter kits to the public.

Cockroach composting

Cockroach composting is another insect-mediated composting method. In this case the adults of any number of cockroach species (such as the Turkestan cockroach or *Blaptica dubia*) are used to quickly convert manure or kitchen waste to nutrient dense compost. Depending on species used and environmental conditions, excess composting insects can be used as an excellent animal feed for farm animals and pets.

Bokashi

Bokashi is a method that uses a mix of microorganisms to cover food waste to decrease smell. It derives from the practice of Japanesefarmers centuries ago of covering food waste with rich, local soil that contained the microorganisms that would ferment the waste. After a few weeks, they would bury the waste.

Most practitioners obtain the microorganisms from the product Effective Microorganisms (EM1), first sold in the 1980s. EM1 is mixed with a carbon base (e.g. sawdust or bran) that it sticks to and a sugar for food (e.g. molasses). The mixture is layered with waste in a sealed container and after a few weeks, removed and buried.

Newspaper fermented in a lactobacillus culture can be substituted for bokashi bran for a successful bokashi bucket.

Compost tea

Compost teas are defined as water extracts brewed from composted materials and can be derived from aerobic or anaerobic processes. Compost teas are generally produced from adding one volume of compost to 4-10 volumes of water, but there has also been debate about the benefits of aerating the mixture. Field studies have shown the benefits of adding compost teas to crops due to the adding of organic matter, increased nutrient availability and increased microbial activity. They have also been shown to have an effect on plant pathogens.

Composting toilets

A composting toilet does not require water or electricity, and when properly managed does not smell. A composting toilet collects human excreta which is then added to a compost heap together with sawdust and straw or other carbon rich materials, where pathogens are destroyed to some extent. The amount of pathogen destruction depends on the temperature (mesophilic or thermophilic conditions) and composting time. A composting toilet tries to process the excreta in situ although this is often coupled with a secondary external composting step. The resulting compost product has been given various names, such as humanure and EcoHumus.

A composting toilet can aid in the conservation of fresh water by avoiding the usage of potable water required by the typical flush toilet. It further prevents the pollution of ground water by controlling the fecal matter decomposition before entering the system. When properly managed, there should be no ground contamination from leachate.

Compost and land-filling

As concern about landfill space increases, worldwide interest in recycling by means of composting is growing, since composting is a process for converting decomposable organic materials into useful stable products. Composting is one of the only ways to revitalize soil vitality due to phosphorus depletion in soil. Industrial scale composting in the form of in-vessel composting, aerated static pile composting, and anaerobic digestion takes place in most Western countries now, and in many areas is mandated by law. There are process and product guidelines in Europe that date to the early 1980s (Germany, the Netherlands, Switzerland) and only more recently in the UK and the US. In both these countries, private trade associations within the industry have established loose standards, some say as a stop-gap measure to discourage independent government agencies from establishing tougher consumer-friendly standards. The USA is the only Western country that does not distinguish sludge-source compost from green-composts, and by default in the USA 50% of states expect composts to comply in some manner with the federal EPA 503 rule promulgated in 1984 for sludge products.Compost is regulated in Canada and Australia as well.

Industrial systems

Industrial composting systems are increasingly being installed as a waste management alternative to landfills, along with other advanced waste processing systems. Mechanical sorting of mixed waste streams combined with anaerobic digestion or in-vessel composting is called mechanical biological treatment, and are increasingly being used in developed countries due to regulations controlling the amount of organic matter allowed in landfills. Treating biodegradable waste before it enters a landfill reduces global warming from fugitivemethane; untreated waste breaks down anaerobically in a landfill, producing landfill gas that contains methane, a potent greenhouse gas.

Vermicomposting, also known as vermiculture, is used for medium-scale on-site institutional composting, such as for food waste from universities and shopping malls: selected either as a more environmental choice, or to reduce the cost of commercial waste removal.

Large-scale composting systems are used by many urban areas around the world. Co-composting is a technique that combines solid waste with de-watered biosolids, although difficulties controlling inert and plastics contamination from municipal solid waste makes this approach less attractive. The World's largest MSW co-composter is the Edmonton Composting Facility in Edmonton, Alberta, Canada, which turns 220,000 tonnes of residential solid waste and 22,500 dry tonnes of biosolids per year into 80,000 tonnes of compost.

The facility is 38,690 meters^2 (416,500 ft^2), equivalent to 4½ Canadian football fields, and the operating structure is the largest stainless steel building in North America, the size of 14 NHL rinks. In 2006, the State of Qatar awarded Keppel Seghers Singapore, a subsidiary of Keppel Corporation to begin construction on a 275,000 tonne/year Anaerobic Digestion and Composting Plant licensed by Kompogas (de) Switzerland. This plant, with 15 independent anaerobic digestors will be the world's largest composting facility once fully operational in early 2011 and forms part of the Qatar Domestic Solid Waste Management Center, the largest integrated waste management complex in the Middle East.

Another large MSW composter is the Lahore Composting Facility in Lahore, Pakistan, which has a capacity to convert 1,000 tonnes of municipal solid waste per day into compost. It also has a capacity to convert substantial portion of the intake into Refuse-derived fuel (RDF) materials for further combustion use in several energy consuming industries across Pakistan e.g., in cement manufacturing companies where it is used to heat up the Cement Kiln systems. This project has also been approved by the Executive Board of the United Nations Framework Convention on Climate Change (UNFCCC) for reduction of emission of methane gas into the climate and has been registered with a capacity of reducing 108,686 metric tonnes CO2 equivalent per annum.

Related technologies

Anaerobic digestion is another possible process for converting organic waste into a useful produce (biogas). In central Europe, anaerobic digestion is now more common than composting as a process for treating organic waste. The two processes can also be used in combination: sewage sludge is often anaerobically digested first, followed by a composting process before selling or giving away the compost to farmers.

History

Composting as a recognized practice dates to at least the early Roman Empire since Pliny the Elder (AD 23-79). Traditionally, composting involved piling organic materials until the next planting season, at which time the materials would have decayed enough to be ready for use in the soil. The advantage of this method is that little working time or effort is required from the composter and it fits in naturally with agricultural practices in temperate climates. Disadvantages (from the modern perspective) are that space is used for a whole year, some nutrients might be leached due to exposure to rainfall, and disease-producing organisms and insects may not be adequately controlled.

Composting was somewhat modernized beginning in the 1920s in Europe as a tool for organic farming. The first industrial station for the transformation of urban organic materials into compost was set up in Wels, Austria in the year 1921. Early frequent citations for propounding composting within farming are for the German-speaking world Rudolf Steiner, founder of a farming method called biodynamics, and Annie Francé-Harrar, who was appointed on behalf of the government in Mexico and supported the country 1950–1958 to set up a large humus organization in the fight against erosion and soil degradation. In the English-speaking world it was Sir Albert Howardwho worked extensively in India on sustainable practices and Lady Eve Balfour who was a huge proponent of composting. Composting was imported to America by various followers of these early European movements by the likes of J.I. Rodale (founder of Rodale Organic Gardening), E.E. Pfeiffer (who developed scientific practices in biodynamic farming), Paul Keene (founder of Walnut Acres in Pennsylvania), and Scott and Helen Nearing (who inspired the back-to-the-land movement of the 1960s). Coincidentally, some of the above met briefly in India - all were quite influential in the U.S. from the 1960s into the 1980s.

There are many modern proponents of rapid composting that attempt to correct some of the perceived problems associated with traditional, slow composting. Many advocate that compost can be made in 2 to 3 weeks. Many such short processes involve a few changes to traditional methods, including smaller, more homogenized pieces in the compost, controlling carbon-to-nitrogen ratio (C:N) at 30 to 1 or less, and monitoring the moisture level more carefully. However, none of these parameters differ significantly from the early writings of Howard and Balfour, suggesting that in fact modern composting has not made significant advances over the traditional methods that take a few months to work. For this reason and others, many modern scientists who deal with carbon transformations are sceptical that there is a "super-charged" way to get nature to make compost rapidly.

In fact, both sides are right to some extent. The bacterial activity in rapid high heat methods breaks down the material to the extent that pathogens and seeds are destroyed, and the original feedstock is unrecognizable. At this stage, the compost can be used to prepare fields or other planting areas. However, most professionals recommend that the compost be given time to cure before using in a nursery for starting seeds or growing young plants. The curing time allows fungi to continue the decomposition process and eliminating phytotoxic substances.

Many countries such as Wales and some individual cities such as Seattle and San Francisco require food and yard waste to be sorted for composting.

Kew Gardens in London has one of the biggest non-commercial compost heaps in Europe.

2

Origin and Development of Gardening

A recently opened Visitor's Center in the oldest garden in South Africa explains to visitors the history and significance of 'The Company's Garden'.

The origins of The Dutch East India Company's Garden in Cape Town are set against the dramatic background of 'The Voyages of Discovery' in the late 15th century. The sole purpose of these voyages of exploration was the search for a sea-route around Africa to access the fabulous wealth to be gained from the Spice Trade. Thus it was plants such as pepper, cloves, cinnamon and nutmeg that played a fundamental role in the connection of Western Europe, Asia and Africa, with all the subsequent far-reaching consequences for these continents.

With the discovery of the 'trade-winds' that allowed ships to sail from 'The Cape of Good Hope' directly across the Indian Ocean to Asia came also the associated problem of provisioning ships for this arduous voyage. It was the 'Company's Garden' at the half-way point on the sea route from Europe to the Spice Islands which sustained the spice trade with fresh water from Table Mountain and, through it's production of fruit and vegetables, prevented the ravages of scurvy, thereby enabling sailing ships to embark on this voyage across the Indian Ocean.

Cape Town became known as 'The Tavern of the Seas' and European settlement of 'The Cape of Good Hope' and of South Africa began with this garden. 'The Company's Garden' as it is known today, nestles below the slopes of Table Mountain and is framed by Devil's peak to the east and Lion's Head to the west. Rain falling on Table Mountain, which rises to more than a thousand meters above sea level, filters through the upper ramparts of Table Mountain and emerges as perennial streams in Table Valley below, these springs were an important factor drawing people to this area from stone-age times.

This fresh water also drew sailors to this landmark, early Portuguese explorers stopped to provision their ships here while trying to find a sea-route to the east and the lucrative spice trade. One of these explorers, Bartolomew

Dias, was the first to discover the Cape in 1488 and named it 'The Cape of Storms'. Fatefully, he and half his fleet were lost in a storm off the Cape in 1500.

There were many superstitions about the Cape including the legend of the 'Flying Dutchman' and the captain of this ghost ship that was doomed to perpetually battle the stormy seas around the Cape. There was also the legend of the terrifying monster 'Adamastor' who, infuriated about his discovery, sent storms down upon passing ships.

It was these superstitions and myths as well as conflict with indigenous people known as the Khoekhoen and the political vagaries of Europe at the time, which together, militated against the settlement of the Cape during the late 16th and early 17th centuries.

All this was to change forever when the crew of a Dutch ship, the 'Haarlem' were shipwrecked in 1647 on the shores of Table Bay and in order to survive, sowed vegetable seeds near a stream of fresh water beneath Table Mountain. They were rescued some six months later by a fleet of Dutch ships returning to Holland and which carried aboard a young VOC (Verenigde Oost-Indische Compagnie) merchant returning home in disgrace after being accused of private trading – his name was Jan Van Riebeeck.

Back in Holland, the ship-wrecked sailor's reports of the fertility of the land and abundant water convinced the VOC to establish a permanent supply station at the Cape of Good Hope. This decision was also influenced by the fear that at any time the British might annex the Cape. In order to rehabilitate his good name, Jan van Riebeeck volunteered to lead this expedition and so it was that in April 1652 he and 5 ships arrived in Table Bay at Cape Town.

From Jan van Riebeeck's diary we learn that master gardener Hendrik Boom prepared the first ground in the garden for sowing seed on the 29th April 1652. This makes the garden 358 years old and a Pyrus communis tree (Saffraan Pear) planted around this time still exists in the garden to this day and is thus the oldest cultivated tree in South Africa.

The size of the garden slowly increased until, some ten years later, it had grown to 18 ha. Apart from a vegetable and fruit garden, Boom also laid out a herb and medicinal garden. Once these were established, various ornamental plants were also introduced, amongst which were Oak trees and Roses, the first of these Roses were reported to have bloomed on 1st November 1659.

" The story of the Garden does not end with vegetables and fruits. Man does not live by food alone, and the utilitarian motive leads on to the aesthetic and civilized, so that as time passed The Company's Garden became a place of beauty and pleasantness....and of special enchantment for the ocean-weary travellers setting foot in an otherwise strange and perhaps alarming land. And then came the further stage in development, when the Garden became botanical and appealed to the mind as well as the senses.." *

From 1679, Simon van der Stel, Governor of the Cape, and his master gardeners, Hendrik Bernard Oldenland and Jan Hartog, transformed the original fruit and vegetable garden into a world famous botanical garden with indigenous and exotic plants, shrubs and trees. They built an elaborate system of canals fed by mountain water, and many ornamental species were introduced.

Johan Andries Auge, who became Superintendent of the Garden in 1751, planted many indigenous species gathered on expeditions throughout the Cape. A Streletzia nicolai (Wild banana) which is thought to have been planted by Auge still grows in the Company's Garden today.

By the mid eighteenth century, the Garden had become famous, firstly for its beauty and delight; and secondly for the propagation and export of African plants. This had proceeded under the direction of master gardener J. A. Auge, under whose auspices bulbs and plants were exported to an increasingly lucrative European market. The arrival of Pelargoniums or Geraniums (and their hybrids) and other Cape plants in Europe, date from about this period.

The British occupied the Cape in 1795 to forestall any French interest in the strategic sea route to India and elsewhere. It was during this period that Governor Yonge tried to turn the Garden into his private domain, but there was such on outcry that the traditions of public access to the Garden remain to this day.

In 1848 the Company's Garden became 'The Botanical Garden' which had general public access and at that time began to take on many of the landscape features which remain until the present, chiefly the sinuous curving pathways indicative of the English naturalistic landscape style which overlaid the Dutch formal grid-layout. In 1892 it became the responsibility of the Municipal Authority of Cape Town and by 1913 the National Botanic Gardens at Kirstenbosch were founded on an estate bequeathed by Cecil Rhodes and the Company's Garden became a public recreation garden.

This layered landscape has become one of the unique features of The Company's Garden today. It is a garden in which the formal 'Dutch Baroque' landscape style of the early 18th century was overlaid by the informal, 'Victorian Romantic' or 'Picturesque' landscape style influenced by the late 18th century English landscape designers, namely, Capability Brown, William Kent and Humphrey Repton.

Typical of the Dutch landscape style were formal walkways lined with avenues of Oak trees and clipped hedges which were crossed at right angles by smaller paths. Two such examples still exist : Government Avenue, which is the traditional public promenade through the garden precinct, as well as the main axial walkway through the 'old garden' itself. These long straight walkways lead the eye to distant vistas – which may be prominent buildings or natural views. Government

Avenue, for example leads the eye to views of Table Mountain and makes it part of a 'borrowed landscape'. The Dutch Baroque landscape style also included rectangular plant-beds grouped into fours with corners cut away at central focal points. Parterre gardens were prominent and today these still exist at the old Governor's residence, Tuynhuis, which has become the modern President's Cape Town residence.

This is situated about halfway along Government Avenue, and itself forms a vista from the garden. These elements were typical of the Baroque-era garden style and the Company's Garden reflected this influence with the combination of the ordered style of the Dutch Kitchen Garden and the " flamboyant expression of grandeur and power of the officials of the Dutch East India Company " * who were largely inspired by contemporary landscape influences in Europe at the time, the epitome of which was the Palace Garden at Versailles.

This era of landscape design that emphasised man's control over wild nature and it's transformation to his will gave way to the English Picturesque style, which sought to emulate nature in it's natural beauty and was influenced by the landscape painters of the time who portrayed idyllic landscapes. Victorian landscape design was characterised by this new romanticism that featured curved lines, flowing contours and idealised natural plantings.

The transition between these two landscape styles is captured by The Company's Garden in which the two landscape design periods are interwoven and layered on top of one another. Axis pathways are linked by a curving 'sinuous' pathway that encircles the garden and links the many outdoor rooms within this matrix. The Company's Garden is unique in this blend of styles and has been conserved as an unbroken link with the past history of The Cape of Good Hope and is a tangible reminder of Cape Town's heritage which residents and tourists enjoy to this day.

A BRIEF HISTORY OF GARDENING

Gardening In The Ancient World

The earliest gardens were grown for practical reasons. People grew herbs or vegetables. However when man became civilized an upper class emerged with the leisure to enjoy purely decorative gardens. They also had servants (or slaves) to do the gardening for them.

Gardening in Ancient Egypt

In the hot and arid climate of ancient Egypt rich people liked to rest in the shade of trees. They created gardens enclosed by walls with trees planted with trees in rows. Sometimes the Egyptians planted alternating species. They grew trees like sycamores, date palms, fig trees, nut trees and pomegranate trees. They also grew willows. The Egyptians also grew vineyards. (Although beer was the drink of the common people the rich liked drinking wine).

The Egyptians also grew a wide variety of flowers including roses, poppies, irises, daisies and cornflowers. Egyptians also liked their gardens to have rectangular ponds. Sometimes they were stocked with fish. The Egyptians also liked to grow fragrant trees and shrubs.

The Egyptians believed that the gods liked gardens and so temples usually had gardens by them. In ancient Egypt gardens also had religious significance as different trees were associated with different gods.

However in Egypt there was no strict division between gardens for pleasure and gardens for produce. As well as being beautiful gardens were used to grow fruit and vegetables and to produce wine and olive oil.

Gardening in Ancient Iraq

In the ancient world beautiful gardens were created in what is now Iraq. The Assyrians came from Iraq and in the period 900 BC - 612 BC they ruled a great empire in the Middle East. Like the Egyptians upper class Assyrians enjoyed gardens.

They created large hunting parks but they also made pleasure gardens irrigated by water canals. The Assyrians planted trees such as palms and cypresses. Like the Egyptians they planted the trees in rows, sometimes alternating species. They also created ponds and they cultivated vines and some flowers.

When the Assyrian Empire was destroyed in 612 the city-state of Babylon created another huge empire. King Nebuchadnezzar is supposed to have built the hanging gardens of Babylon, one of the seven wonders of the ancient world. According to tradition his wife Amyitis missed the mountainous terrain of her homeland so the king built a stepped terrace garden for her. Man-powered pumps watered it. (Probably a chain pump).

At any rate the Babylonians liked formal gardens. They enjoyed the shade of trees planted in straight lines.In 539 the Babylonian Empire was destroyed by the Persians who created yet another great empire. The Persians were superb gardeners. They built underground aqueducts to bring water to their gardens without it evaporating on the way. These were called qanats.

Like the earlier civilizations the Persians grew fruit trees and fragrant shrubs and flowers. Their gardens also contained pools, fountains and watercourses or rills.

Greek Gardening

The Greeks were not great gardeners. They sometimes planted trees to provide shade around temples and other public places but pleasure gardens were rare. The Greeks did grow flowers but usually in containers.

Although Greek travelers admired the gardens of the east in Greece gardens were usually grown for practical reasons. The Greeks grew orchards, vineyards and vegetable gardens.

Roman Gardening

When they conquered Egypt in 30 BC the Romans introduced eastern ideas about gardening. Rich Romans created gardens next to their palaces and villas. The Romans were masters of the art of topiary. Roman gardens were adorned with statues and sculptures.

Roman gardens were laid out with hedges and vines. They also contained a wide variety of flowers including acanthus, cornflowers and crocus, cyclamen, hyacinth, iris and ivy, lavender, lilies, myrtle, narcissus, poppy, rosemary and violet.

In the towns wealthy Romans built houses around a courtyard. The courtyard usually contained a colonnaded porch, a pool and a fountain as well as beds of flowers.

After the Romans conquered Britain they introduced a number of new plants including roses, leeks, turnips and plums. They may also have introduced cabbages.

Gardening In The Middle Ages

After the fall of Rome gardening declined in Western Europe. However the church still made some gardens for growing herbs (e.g. for medicines) and some flowers were grown to decorate church altars.

Islamic Gardening

Meanwhile in the 7th century the Arabs created a huge empire. When they conquered Persia they took over many Persian ideas about gardens.

Islamic gardens were surrounded by walls and very often they were divided into 4 by watercourses. In the center was a pool or pavilion. Islamic gardens also contained rills and fountains and they were decorated with mosaics and glazed tiles. Rows of plane or cypress were planted for shade. The Arabs also grew fruit trees.

In the early 8th century the Arabs conquered Spain. The Moors as they were called, grew ash, laurel, hazel, walnut, poplar, willow and elm. They also grew orange and lemon trees as well as dates, figs, almonds, apricots, apples, pears, quinces, plums and peaches. They also grew a wide variety of flowers including roses, hollyhocks, narcissus, violets, wallflowers and lilies.

Gardening in Medieval Europe

Gradually order was restored in Europe and by the late 13th century the rich began to grow gardens for pleasure as well as those for medicinal herbs and vegetables.

In the Middle Ages gardens were walled both to protect them from wild animals and to provide seclusion. In the 14th and 15th centuries gardens were planted with lawns sprinkled with fragrant herbs. They had raised flowerbeds and trellises of roses or vines. Gardens also contained fruit trees and sometimes they had turf seats.

In the Middle Ages monasteries grew gardens of medicinal herbs. They also grew orchards and vineyards as well as vegetables. They also grew flowers for their altars. However monastery gardens were not purely functional. They were a place for the monks to relax and enjoy nature.

16TH AND 17TH CENTURY GARDENING

In the 16th century there was a revival of the ideas of ancient Greece and Rome. Ideas about gardening changed, influenced by classical ideas. In the 16th and 17th century symmetry, proportion and balance became important. Very often gardens were laid out with a central axis leading down from the house with a number of cross axes forming a grid pattern. The garden was divided into parts by hedges. In the 16th and 17th centuries flowerbeds were often laid out in squares, separated by gravel paths. 16th century gardens were adorned with sculptures, fountains and topiary. Often they also contained water jokes (unsuspecting visitors were sprayed with jets of water). Water organs played music or imitated bird song. Gardens also often contained grottoes (cave like buildings).

Fig. Petersfield Physic Garden, a recreated 17th century herb garden

Furthermore knot gardens were popular. Intricate patterns like knots were made by planting lines of box and herbs like lavender. Furthermore in the 16th and 17th centuries hedge mazes were very popular in Europe.

Also in the 16th and 17th centuries many new plants were introduced into Europe including tulips, marigolds and sunflowers. The horse chestnut was also introduced into Europe in the 16th century. Potatoes and tomatoes were also introduced into Europe at that time.

18th Century Gardening

In the early 18th century many people rebelled against formal gardens and preferred a more 'natural' style.

However in the 18th century gardens often contained shrubberies, grottoes, pavilions, bridges and follies such as mock temples.

Two of the most famous gardeners of the 18th century were William Kent (1685-1748) and Charles Bridgeman (1690-1738). In 1731 William Kent was employed to redesign a garden at Chiswick. He also created a garden at

Rousham, which still exists much as he designed it. The most famous gardener of the 18th century was Lancelot 'Capability' Brown. Kent and Bridgeman mixed formal and informal elements in their gardens but Capability Brown adopted a completely informal style. He wanted to 'improve' nature not rework it. Brown sought to remove the 'roughness' of a landscape and perfect it but afterwards it should be almost indistinguishable from a landscape created entirely by nature.

After Brown came the famous gardener Humphry Repton (1752-1818). He first became a gardener in 1788 and even within his lifetime a reaction began against the informal landscaping style towards more formal gardens.

Meanwhile in 1725 the Society of Gardeners was founded in England. In London public gardens were created - although you had to pay to view them. However in the 18th century pleasure gardens were still only for the upper class and the middle classes. If poor people had a garden they had to use it for growing herbs or vegetables. They had neither the time nor the money to grow plants for pleasure.

Meanwhile in the North American colonies life was, at first, rough but by the end of the 17th century the wealthy began to create pleasure gardens. However the Americans preferred more formal gardens.

LIFE IN THE 18TH CENTURY

19th Century Gardening

In 1804 the Horticultural Society was formed. (It became a royal society in 1861).

In 1829 Dr Nathaniel Bagshaw Ward accidentally discovered that if plants were kept sealed under glass they formed their own micro-climate. During the day the plants transpired water. At night it condensed on the glass and fell onto the soil where it was reabsorbed by the plants. Creating sealed micro-climates made it much easier to transport plants around the world.

Many new plants were introduced into Europe in the 19th century including the monkey puzzle or Chile pine. Then, in 1830 Edwin Beard Budding (1796-1846) invented the lawn mower.

In the 19th century gardeners began to build large greenhouses or conservatories to provide plants with both heat and light. The largest was Crystal Palace, built in 1851 by Joseph Paxton (1806-1865). (Paxton was one of the great gardeners of the 19th century although he was also an engineer and architect).

In the 19th century as well as well-trimmed lawns massed or carpet bedding of flowers became popular. There were other changes. In the 19th century the middle class grew in numbers and in wealth. As well as great estates gardens attached to suburban villas became important. A new style of garden evolved called gardenesque, which displayed a wide variety of plants in a limited space.

Many 19th century gardens also had rock gardens. They were only invented at the end of the 18th century but they became popular in the 19th century.

In the early 19th century the most famous gardener was John Claudius Loudon (1783-1843). Loudon led a return to geometric gardens when he published his book Remarks on Laying out Public Gardens and Promenades in 1835. Loudon also wrote a book for middle class gardeners, The Suburban Gardener and Villa Companion in 1838. His wife Jane Loudon (1807-1858) also wrote books including The Ladies Companion to the Flower Garden and Instructions in Gardening for Ladies.

Slightly later the famous gardener Sir Charles Barry (1795-1860) introduced the Italian style into England. It was a return to geometric gardens and it proved to be popular.

In the 19th century Chinese style gardens were also popular. In the late 19th century some gardeners tried to imitate Japanese gardens. Meanwhile in the late 19th century a more natural style of gardening became fashionable led by the famous gardener William Robinson (1838-1935). He published his ideas in The Wild Garden in 1870. Robinson advocated planting a mixture of trees and shrubs, perennials and bulbs.

Furthermore in the 19th century towns and cities boomed in size. Workers were herded together in cramped and unsanitary houses but in the later half of the 19th century local authorities began creating public parks for them.

20th Century Gardening

At the end of the 19th century and the beginning of the 20th century some gardeners were influenced by the arts and crafts movement. Its followers fled that the industrial revolution and mass production had led to a decline in taste. They yearned for a past age of individual craftsmen. Influenced by the movement some gardeners had an idealized view of old fashioned cottage gardens. They designed gardens with trellises of flowers, neat hedges and old fashioned English flowers.

In the early 20th century Gertrude Jekyll (1843-1932) became a famous gardener and she designed many gardens. Sir Edward Lutyens (1869-1944) sometimes worked with Jekyll. Other famous gardeners of the 20th century were Frederick Gibberd (1908-1984), Sylvia Crowe (1901-1997) and Russell Page (1906-1985) who wrote an influential book The Education of a Gardener. Other famous gardeners were Harold Peto (1854-1933) and Lawrence Johnston (1871-1958).

In the 20th century there was a new movement in architecture and gardening called modernism. The modernists rejected copying old styles of gardening and advocated starting afresh using modern materials. Modernists liked gardens to be 'uncluttered'.

In 1926 a German engineer called Andreas Stihl developed the chain saw and in 1963 the first hover mower went on sale.

In the 20th century as incomes rose gardening became a popular hobby. Meanwhile the Garden History Society was founded in 1965 and the Museum of Garden History opened in London in 1977.

he nature of gardening

Gardening in its ornamental sense needs a certain level of civilization before it can flourish. Wherever that level has been attained, in all parts of the world and at all periods, people have made efforts to shape their environment into an attractive display. The instinct and even enthusiasm for gardening thus appear to arise from some primitive response to nature, engendering a wish to produce growth and harmony in a creative partnership with it.

It is possible to be merely an admiring spectator of gardens. However, most people who cultivate a domestic plot also derive satisfaction from involvement in the processes of tending plants. They find that the necessary attention to the seasonal changes, and to the myriad small "events" in any shrubbery or herbaceous border, improves their understanding and appreciation of gardens in general.

A phenomenal upsurge of interest in gardening began in Western countries after World War II. A lawn with flower beds and perhaps a vegetable patch has become a sought-after advantage to home ownership. The increased interest produced an unprecedented expansion of business among horticultural suppliers, nurseries, garden centres, and seedsmen. Books, journals, and newspaper columns on garden practice have found an eager readership, while television and radio programs on the subject have achieved a dedicated following.

Several reasons for this expansion suggest themselves. Increased leisure in the industrial nations gives more people the opportunity to enjoy this relaxing pursuit. The increased public appetite for self-sufficiency in basic skills also encourages people to take up the spade. In the kitchen, the homegrown potato or ear of sweet corn rewards the gardener with a sense of achievement, as well as with flavour superior to that of store-bought produce. An increased awareness of threats to the natural environment and the drabness of many inner cities stir some people to cultivate the greenery and colour around their own doorsteps. The bustle of 20th-century life leads more individuals to rediscover the age-old tranquillity of gardens.

The varied appeal of gardening

The attractions of gardening are many and various and, to a degree perhaps unique among the arts and crafts, may be experienced by any age group and at all levels of ambition. At its most elemental, but not least valuable, the gardening experience begins with the child's wonder that a packet of seeds will produce a charming festival of colour. At the adult level, it can be as simple as helping to raise a good and edible carrot, and it can give rise to almost parental pride. At higher levels of appreciation, it involves an understanding of the complexity of the gardening process, equivalent to a chess game with nature, because the variables are so many.

The gardening experience may involve visiting some of the world's great gardens at different seasons to see the relation of individual groups of plants, trees, and shrubs to the whole design; to study the positioning of plants in terms of their colour, texture, and weight of leaf or blossom; and to appreciate the use of special features such as ponds or watercourses, pavilions, or rockeries. Garden visiting on an international scale provides an opportunity to understand the broad cultural influences, as well as the variations in climate and soil, that have resulted in so many different approaches to garden making.

The appeal of gardening is thus multifaceted and wide in range. The garden is often the only place where someone without special training can exercise creative impulses as designer, artist, technician, and scientific observer. In addition, many find it a relaxing and therapeutic pursuit. It is not surprising that the garden, accorded respect as a part of nature and a place of contemplation, holds a special place in the spiritual life of many.

Practical and spiritual aspects of gardening are shown in an impressive body of literature. In Western countries manuals of instruction date to classical Greece and Rome. Images of plants and gardens are profuse in the works of the major poets, from Virgil to Shakespeare, and on to some of the moderns.

Another of gardening's attractions is that up to a certain level it is a simple craft to learn. The beginner can produce pleasing results without the exacting studies and practice required by, for example, painting or music. Gardens are also forgiving to the inexperienced to a certain degree. Nature's exuberance will cover up minor errors or short periods of neglect, so gardening is an art practiced in a relatively nonjudgmental atmosphere. While tolerant in many respects, nature does, however, present firm reminders that all gardening takes place within a framework of natural law; and one important aspect of the study of the craft is to learn which of these primal rules are imperatives and which may be stretched.

Control and cooperation

Large areas of gardening development and mastery have concentrated on persuading plants to achieve what they would not have done if left in the wild and therefore "natural" state. Gardens at all times have been created through a good deal of control and what might be called interference. The gardener attends to a number of basic processes: combating weeds and pests; using space to allay the competition between plants; attending to feeding, watering, and pruning; and conditioning the soil. Above this fundamental level, the gardener assesses and accommodates the unique complex of temperature, wind, rainfall, sunlight, and shade found within his own garden boundaries. A major part of the fascination of gardening is that in problems and potential no one garden is quite like another; and it is in finding the most imaginative solutions to challenges that the gardener demonstrates artistry and finds the subtler levels of satisfaction.

Different aesthetics require different balances between controlling nature and cooperating with its requirements. The degree of control depends on the gardener's objective, the theme and identity he is aiming to create. For example, the English wild woodland style of gardening in the mid-19th century dispensed with controls after planting, and any interference, such as pruning, would have been misplaced. At the other extreme is the Japanese dry-landscape garden, beautifully composed of rock and raked pebbles. The artistic control in this type of garden is so firm and refined that the intrusion of a single "natural" weed would spoil the effect.

Choice of plants

The need for cooperation with nature is probably most felt by the amateur gardener in choosing the plants he wants to grow. The range of plants available to the modern gardener is remarkably rich, and new varieties are constantly being offered by nurseries. Most of the shrubs and flowers used in the Western world are descendants of plants imported from other countries. Because they are nonnative, they present the gardener with some of his most interesting problems but also with the possibility of an enhanced display. Plants that originated in subtropical regions, for example, are naturally more sensitive to frost. Some, like rhododendrons or azaleas, originated in an acid soil, mainly composed of leaf mold. Consequently, they will not thrive in a chalky or an alkaline soil. Plant breeding continues to improve the adaptability of such exotic plants, but the more closely the new habitat resembles the original, the better the plant will flourish. Manuals offer solutions to most such problems, and the true gardener will always enjoy finding his own. In such experiments, he may best experience his work as part of the historical tradition of gardening.

HISTORICAL BACKGROUND

Early history

Western gardening had its origins in Egypt some 4,000 years ago. As the style spread, it was changed and adapted to different localities and climates, but its essentials remained those of disciplined lines and groupings of plants, usually in walled enclosures. Gardening was introduced into Europe through the expansion of Roman rule and, second, by way of the spread of Islam into Spain. Though clear evidence is lacking, it is presumed that Roman villas outside the confines of Italy contained native and imported plants, hedges, fruit trees, and vines, in addition to herbs for medicinal and culinary purposes.

In medieval times the monasteries were the main repositories of gardening knowledge and the important herbal lore. Though little is certainly known about the design and content of the monastic garden, it probably consisted of a walled courtyard built around a well or an arbour, with colour provided by flowers (some of which, including roses and lilies, served as ecclesiastical symbols), all of which maintained the ancient idea of the garden as a place of contemplation.

The earliest account of gardening in English, *The Feate of Gardening*, dating from about 1400, mentions the use of more than 100 plants, with instructions on sowing, planting, and grafting of trees and advice on cultivation of herbs such as parsley, sage, fennel, thyme, camomile, and saffron. The vegetables mentioned include turnip, spinach, leek, lettuce, and garlic.

Early gardening was largely for utility. The emergence of the garden as a form of creative display properly began in the 16th century. The Renaissance, with its increased prosperity, brought an upsurge of curiosity about the natural world and, incidentally, stirred interest in composing harmonious forms in the garden. This awakening took especially firm root in Elizabethan England, which notably developed the idea that gardens were for enjoyment and delight. Echoing the Renaissance outlook, the mood of the period was one of exuberance in gardening, seen in the somewhat playful arrangements of Tudor times, with mazes, painted statuary, and knot gardens (consisting of beds in which various types of plants were separated by dwarf hedges). Flowers began to appear profusely in paintings and, as mentioned above, were used by poets in their verbal images.

This enthusiasm was accompanied by an earnest search for knowledge, and the period saw the birth of botanical science. A leading figure in this work wasCarolus Clusius (Charles de l'Écluse), whose botanical skills and introduction of the tulip and other bulbous plants to the botanical gardens at Leiden, Netherlands, laid the foundation for Dutch prominence in international horticulture.

The earliest botanical garden was that of Pisa (1543), followed by that of Padua (1545). The first in England was founded at Oxford in 1621, followed by Scotland's first, at Edinburgh, in 1667.

The gardens at Kew, near London, were founded almost a century later, in 1759. These centres of experiment and learning have contributed greatly to the art and science of horticulture.

The advances from the simple medieval style were marked and rapid at this time. The English statesman and scholar Francis Bacon could already, by 1625, advance a sophisticated and almost modern conception of the garden in his essay "On Gardens." He saw it as a place that should be planted for year-round enjoyment, offering a wide range of experiences through colour, form and scent, exercise and repose. The flower garden, already well established by the early 17th century, was set against a background of tall, clipped hedges and neatly scythed lawns. The taste of the time, as contemporary lists show, was for perfumed varieties such as carnations, lavender, sweet marjoram, musk roses, and poppies.

The plant trade

As interest in gardening developed in Europe, the new trade of nurseryman was established, and the trade became highly important to the spread of knowledge and materials. By the end of the 17th century, nurserymen were relatively numerous in England, France, and the Low Countries, with keen customers among the nobility and gentry for all the exotica they could provide. The catalog of the Tradescant family's private botanical garden in London listed 1,600 plants in 1656. A number of them had been brought back by the family from visits to Virginia. These early exotica from the New World included now familiar plants such as the Michaelmas daisy, the Virginia creeper, hamamelis, goldenrod, the first perennial lupine, and such fine autumn-colouring trees as liquidambar and the staghorn sumac. The work of the nurserymen thus spread new plants more widely and, as breeding skills developed, contributed to the acclimatizing of foreign imports.

Vegetables and fruits

The history of vegetables is imprecise. Though familiar types, including the radish, turnip, and onion, are known to have been in cultivation from early times, it is fairly supposed that they were meagre and would bear little clear resemblance to modern equivalents. The early range available to European gardens and, later, to those in America, included such native plants as kale, parsnips, and the Brussels sprout family, with peas and broad beans grown as field crops.

The Romans introduced the globe artichoke, leek, cucumber, cabbage, asparagus, and the Mediterranean strain of garlic to their imperial territory wherever these plants would flourish. Among plants imported to Europe from the Americas were the scarlet runner bean and tomato (both originally grown for ornament), corn (maize), and the vastly important potato. The numerous herbs in use were mostly native to European locations. One curiosity to the modern mind is that certain flowers, such as marigolds, violets, and primroses, were used as flavourings in the kitchen.

The cultivation of fruit trees was one of the most advanced skills and interests from the 16th century onward. Pride was taken in variety, and, judging by the opulent still-life paintings of the period, the quality was remarkably high. Among the challenges bravely taken up in the 17th century in northern Europe was the growing of orange and lemon trees, though this was done more for the pleasure of their evergreen qualities than for their fruit. The catalog of the British royal gardens in 1708 shows 14 varieties of cherry, 14 apricots, 58 kinds of peach and nectarine, 33 plums, eight figs, 23 vines, 29 pears, and numerous varieties of apple.

The French style

The most favoured style for great house gardens in Europe during much of this period derived from the influence of the French designer André Le Nôtre, creator of the gardens at Versailles. The French style represented an extreme of formality, with box-edged parterres (elaborate and geometrical beds) typically placed near the residence to provide an arranged view. Trees were grouped in neat plantations or in bold lines along avenues, with terraces and statuary carefully placed to emphasize the architectural symmetry of the grand manner. The widespread adoption of this style among the European nobility and gentry reflected the potency of French cultural influence at the time. It was also related, on a practical basis, to the limited availability of planting materials, especially those offering autumn and winter display.

The change to a more natural style of gardening came about when, in the latter part of the 18th century, the opinion arose among leading gardeners, particularly those of the English gentry, that the formal manner brought with it a certain monotony. The increasing importation of foreign plants also brought with it opportunities for a large-scale transformation.

The plant hunters

The early importation of plants to Europe was managed through informal channels, following the increase in exploration and the spread of empires. Seeds and tubers were sent home by diplomats and missionaries, sea captains and travelers. An example of this type of collecting is afforded by Henry Compton, bishop of London, whose diocese included the American colonies. He was an avid collector, and he corresponded with like-minded experts in Europe and America and thus brought numerous fine plants to his exceptional garden in Fulham, west London. He also encouraged his missionaries to send home seeds. From one such source in Virginia came the *Magnolia virginiana*, the first magnolia to be cultivated. This was the beginning of what became known as the American garden, based upon magnolias, azaleas, and other woodland species.

As the appetite for exotica developed, plant collecting around the world became more systematized. Expeditions to foreign parts were organized and financed by nurserymen, botanical gardens, or syndicates of private gardeners. The botanist plant hunters thus sent out were exceptional and patient. They were required to endure long voyages and residence for up to several years in an often hostile environment. Their goal was to find the plant in flower, return in due season to collect seed, then see their delicate specimens back to Europe through varying climatic zones.

North America's potential to yield countless new specimens was recognized early: the first book on American plants, published in London in 1577, was entitled *Joyfull Newes out of the New Founde Worlde*and was in itself a hint of the excited spirit of contemporary gardening. The jacaranda, flowering catalpa, and wisteria were among the finds made by Compton's missionaries in the Carolinas. An early resident collector in North America was John Bartram, regarded as the founder of American botany. He settled on a farm near Philadelphia in 1728 and, in 30 years of collecting in the Alleghenies, Carolinas, and other areas of North America, sent some 200 important plants to British gardens in sufficient quantity that they became widespread there.

The extremely rich west coast of North America was not exploited by plant collectors until the early 19th century. The contemporary importance of such discoveries is suggested by the fact that, in their celebrated crossing of the American continent in 1804–06, Lewis and Clark found time to collect the seeds of *Mahonia aquifolium* and *Symphoricarpos racemosus*. Perhaps the most distinguished collector among an exceptional fraternity was David Douglas, one of the numerous Scotsmen who contributed to international botany. His expeditions to the North American Far West brought to Europe such important timber trees as the Douglas fir, the Sitka spruce, the Monterey pine, and a number of now familiar shrubs such as *Garrya elliptica* and *Ribes sanguineum*. The California annuals he discovered made a lasting impact on the colour of Western gardens. In the 19th century, plant collectors began to explore South America, where two Cornish brothers, William and Thomas Lobb, gained prominence. They are credited with carrying back to Europe the monkey puzzle tree (*Araucaria araucana*), native to the Andes mountains; the *Berberis darwinii*; and the *Escallonia macrantha*.

Collectors went to a number of countries in the 19th century, but the most important area was China. Its flora was more intact than that in the West, because the erosions of the Ice Age had been less severe for climatic reasons, and it had a long history of skilled gardening. Plant collection was difficult, however, because for many years the only foreigners allowed to travel within its borders were Jesuit priests.

They aided botanists by sending many specimens to Paris and London. The first professional collector to live in China was William Kerr, who sent out 238 new plants. Real exploration of the interior did not begin until the 1840s. China, Japan, and the Himalayas produced unparalleled riches in rhododendrons, azaleas, flowering cherries, ornamental maples, roses, lilies, primulas, poppies, kerrias, and quinces.

The conditions for transporting plants from such distances had been much improved by Nathaniel B. Ward's invention of the wardian case, an airtight glass box that protected the plants from sea air and harsh climate. Gradually almost all regions and countries were visited, and new plants and their progeny were dispersed around the Western world. And still the search for new specimens continues.

From the 19th century

By the early 19th century, with the expansion of the horticultural trade, gardening had become international in scope. Numerous handbooks spread knowledge. The founding of new garden and botanical societies, such as the London (later Royal) Horticultural Society, helped to increase interest, encourage science, and raise standards. Such moves signaled the rise of the small leisure gardener; a floral retreat was no longer the sole property of the rich. It now extended from the manor to the small suburban garden.

Gardens in North America had generally been smaller and trimmer than their European counterparts, with box edgings and pleached trees (that is, lines of trees allowed to grow with branches interlaced to form a screen), as seen in the reconstructed gardens of Williamsburg, Virginia. The "natural" gardening style (known on the European continent as the English style), which had overtaken earlier formality, allowed wider use of plant varieties. This approach became the pervasive trend in the west, notably through the views of John Claudius Loudon, whose*Encyclopaedia of Gardening* (1822) set the pattern of domestic cultivation over a long period with a style known as Gardenesque. His style encouraged the individual qualities of garden elements while ensuring that together they made a harmonious blend.

The natural style was further enhanced by an English artist and landscape architect, Gertrude Jekyll. In her opinion, the first purpose of a garden is to give happiness and repose of mind. With experience derived from the richly floral cottage gardens of Surrey, she developed the idea of supporting plants with an architectural base and allowing them to grow in a free form, encouraging natural shape and creating harmonious relationships of colour.

The period saw much progress in garden equipment and supplies. Heated greenhouses had been in use since the late 17th century, and mass production led to great strides in nursery gardening. The modern, bladed lawn mower was first seen in a design of 1832; in more recent times the application of the jet-engine principle led to the hover mower. Fertilizer development was also important, from the discovery of superphosphate to the devising of modern kinds of foliar feeding.

In the second half of the 20th century, interest in gardening brought in new adherents in unprecedented numbers; they were advised and encouraged by numerous publications and by television and radio programs. Though the process was very gradual, domestic gardening became somewhat more adventurous. Among the more ambitious, designs took a multiplicity of forms, from the Japanese garden, producing an austere magic out of rock and pebble, to the other extreme of the wild country garden, virtually left to seed itself.

Increasing numbers of professional designers at their best set high standards to emulate. But the art of gardening still depends on a simple empathy with the needs and nature of living things. Symbolic of this essential, the spade has remained much the same implement that it had been in medieval times.

Types of gardens

The domestic garden can assume almost any identity the owner wishes within the limits of climate, materials, and means. The size of the plot is one of the main factors, deciding not only the scope but also the kind of display and usage.

Limits on space near urban centres, as well as the wish to spend less time on upkeep, have tended to make modern gardens ever smaller. Paradoxically, this happens at a time when the variety of plants and hybrids has never been wider. The wise small gardener avoids the temptations of this banquet. Some of the most attractive miniature schemes, such as those seen in Japan or in some Western patio gardens, are effectively based on an austere simplicity of design and content, with a handful of plants given room to find their proper identities.

In the medium- to large-sized garden, the tradition generally continues of dividing the area to serve various purposes: a main ornamental section to enhance the residence and provide vistas; walkways and seating areas for recreation; a vegetable plot; a children's play area; and features to catch the eye here and there. Because most gardens are mixed, the resulting style is a matter of emphasis rather than exclusive concentration on one aspect. It may be useful to review briefly the main garden types.

Flower gardens

Though flower gardens in different countries may vary in the types of plants that are grown, the basic planning and principles are nearly the same, whether the gardens are formal or informal. Trees and shrubs are the mainstay of a well-designed flower garden. These permanent features are usually planned first, and the spaces for herbaceous plants, annuals, and bulbs are arranged around them. The range of flowering trees and shrubs is enormous. It is important, however, that such plants be appropriate to the areas they will occupy when mature. Thus it is of little use to plant a forest tree that will grow 100 feet (30 metres) high and 50 feet across in a small suburban front garden 30 feet square, but a narrow flowering cherry or redbud tree would be quite suitable.

Blending and contrast of colour as well as of forms are important aspects to consider in planning a garden. The older type of herbaceous border was designed to give a maximum display of colour in summer, but many gardeners now prefer to have flowers during the early spring as well, at the expense of some bare patches later. This is often done by planting early-flowering bulbs in groups toward the front. Mixed borders of flowering shrubs combined with herbaceous plants are also popular and do not require quite so much maintenance as the completely herbaceous border.

Groups of half-hardy annuals, which can withstand low night temperatures, may be planted at the end of spring to fill gaps left by the spring-flowering bulbs. The perpetual-flowering roses and some of the larger shrub roses look good toward the back of such a border, but the hybrid tea roses and the floribunda and polyantha roses are usually grown in separate rose beds or in a rose garden by themselves.

Woodland gardens

The informal woodland garden is the natural descendant of the shrubby "wilderness" of earlier times. The essence of the woodland garden is informality and naturalness. Paths curve rather than run straight and are of mulch or grass rather than pavement. Trees are thinned to allow enough light, particularly in the glades, but irregular groups may be left, and any mature tree of character can be a focal point. Plants are chosen largely from those that are woodlanders in their native countries: rhododendron, magnolia, pieris, and maple among the trees and shrubs; lily, daffodil, and snowdrop among the bulbs; primrose, hellebore, St.-John's-wort, epimedium, and many others among the herbs.

Rock gardens

Rock gardens are designed to look as if they are a natural part of a rocky hillside or slope. If rocks are added, they are generally laid on their larger edges, as in natural strata. A few large boulders usually look better than a number of small rocks. In a well-designed rock garden, rocks are arranged so that there are various exposures for sun-tolerant plants such as rockroses and for shade-tolerant plants such as primulas, which often do better in a cool, north-facing aspect. Many smaller perennial plants are available for filling spaces in vertical cracks among the rock faces.

The main rocks from which rock gardens are constructed are sandstone and limestone. Sandstone, less irregular and pitted generally, looks more restful and natural, but certain plants, notably most of the dianthuses, do best in limestone. Granite is generally regarded as too hard and unsuitable for the rock garden because it weathers very slowly.

Water gardens

The water garden represents one of the oldest forms of gardening. Egyptian records and pictures of cultivated water lilies date as far back as 2000 BCE.

The Japanese have also made water gardens to their own particular and beautiful patterns for many centuries. Many have an ornamental lantern of stone in the centre or perhaps a flat trellis roof of wisteria extending over the water. In Europe and North America, water gardens range from formal pools with rectangular or circular outline, sometimes with fountains in the centre and often without plants or with just one or two water lilies (*Nymphaea*), to informal pools of irregular outline planted with water lilies and other water plants and surrounded by boggy or damp soil where moisture-tolerant plants can be grown. The pool must contain suitable oxygenating plants to keep the water clear and support any introduced fish. Most water plants, including even the large water lilies, do well in still water two to five feet deep. Temperate water lilies flower all day, but many of the tropical and subtropical ones open their flowers only in the evening. In temperate countries water gardens also can be made under glass, and the pools can be kept heated. In such cases, more tropical plants, such as the great*Victoria amazonica* (*V. regia*) or the lotus (*Nelumbo nucifera*), can be grown together with papyrus reeds at the edge. The range of moisture-loving plants for damp places at the edge of the pool is great and includes many beautiful plants such as the candelabra primulas, calthas, irises, and osmunda ferns.

Herb and vegetable gardens

Most of the medieval gardens and the first botanical gardens were largely herb gardens containing plants used for medicinal purposes or herbs such as thyme, parsley, rosemary, fennel, marjoram, and dill for savouring foods. The term *herb garden* is usually used now to denote a garden of herbs used for cooking, and the medicinal aspect is rarely considered. Herb gardens need a sunny position, because the majority of the plants grown are native to warm, dry regions.

The vegetable garden also requires an open and sunny location. Good cultivation and preparation of the ground are important for successful vegetable growing, and it is also desirable to practice a rotation of crops as in farming. The usual period of rotation for vegetables is three years; this also helps to prevent the carryover from season to season of certain pests and diseases.

The old French *potager*, the prized vegetable garden, was grown to be decorative as well as useful; the short rows with little hedges around and the high standard of cultivation represent a model of the art of vegetable growing. The elaborate parterre vegetable garden at the Château de Villandry is perhaps the finest example in Europe of a decorative vegetable garden.

ROOF GARDENS

The modern tendency in architecture for flat roofs has made possible the development of attractive roof gardens in urban areas above private houses and commercial buildings. These gardens follow the same principles as others except that the depth of soil is less, to keep the weight on the rooftop low, and therefore the size of plants is limited. The plants are generally set in tubs or other containers, but elaborate roof gardens have been made with small pools and beds. Beds of flowering plants are suitable, among which may be stood tubs of specimen plants to produce a desired effect.

SCENTED GARDENS

Scent is one of the qualities that many people appreciate highly in gardens. Scented gardens, in which scent from leaves or flowers is the main criterion for inclusion of a plant, have been established, especially for the benefit of blind people. Some plants release a strong scent in full sunlight, and many must be bruised or rubbed to yield their fragrance. These are usually grown in raised beds within easy reach of visitors.

CONTENTS OF GARDENS

Permanent elements

The more or less permanent plants available for any garden plan are various grasses for lawns, other ground-cover plants, shrubs, climbers, and trees. More transitory and therefore in need of continued attention are the herbaceous plants, such as the short-lived annuals and biennials, and the perennials and bulbous plants, which resume growth each year.

LAWNS AND GROUND COVERS

Areas of lawn, or turf, provide the green expanse that links all other garden plantings together. The main grasses used in cool areas for fine-textured lawns are fescues (*Festuca* species), bluegrasses (*Poa* species), and bent grasses (*Agrostis* species), often in mixtures. A rougher lawn mixture may contain ryegrass (*Lolium* species). In drier and subtropical regions, Bermuda grass (*Cynodon dactylon*) is frequently used, but it does not make nearly as fine a lawn as those seen in temperate regions of higher rainfall.

Ground covers are perennial plants used as grass substitutes in regions where grasses do poorly, or they are sometimes combined with grassy areas to produce a desired design. The deep greens, bronzes, and other colours that ground-cover plants can provide offer pleasing contrasts to the green of a turf. Ground covers, however, are not so durable as lawns and do not sustain themselves as well under foot traffic and other activities. Among the better known plants used as ground covers are Japanese spurge (*Pachysandra terminalis*), common periwinkle (*Vinca minor*), lily of the valley (*Convallaria majalis*), ajuga, or bugleweed (*Ajuga reptans*), many stonecrops (*Sedum* species), dichondra (*Dichondra repens*), and many ivies (*Hedera* species).

SHRUBS AND VINES (CLIMBERS)

Smaller woody plants, such as shrubs and bushes, have several stems arising from the base. These plants attain heights up to about 20 feet (6 metres). They often form the largest part of modern gardens, because their cultivation requires less labour than that of herbaceous plants, and some flowering shrubs have extended blooming periods. Among the popular garden shrubs are lilac (*Syringa vulgaris*), privet(*Ligustrum* species), spirea (*Spiraea* species), honeysuckle (*Lonicera* species),forsythia (*Forsythia* species), mock orange (*Philadelphus* species), and hydrangea (*Hydrangea* species).

Bushlike azaleas and rhododendrons (both of which are species of *Rhododendron*) provide colourful blossoms in spots where there is semishade.

Climbers are often useful in softening the sharp lines of buildings, fences, and other structures. They can provide shade as an awning or cover on an arbour or garden house. Some species are also useful as ground covers on steep slopes and terraces. Among the many woody perennial climbers for the garden are the ivies, trumpet creeper (*Bignonia*, or *Campsis, radicans*), clematis (*Clematis* species), wisteria (*Wisteria sinensis*), climbing roses, annual herbaceous vines such as morning glory (*Ipomoea* species), and ornamental gourds, the last of which can provide rapid but temporary coverage of unsightly objects.

TREES

Trees are the most permanent features of a garden plan. The range of tree sizes, shapes, and colours is vast enough to suit almost any gardening scheme, from shrubby dwarf trees to giant shade trees, from slow to rapid growers, from all tones of green to bronzes, reds, yellows, and purples. A balance between evergreen trees, such as pines and spruces, and deciduous trees, such as oaks, maples, and beeches, can provide protection and visual interest throughout the year.

Transitory elements

HERBACEOUS PLANTS

Herbaceous plants, which die down annually and have no woody stem aboveground, are readily divided into three categories, as mentioned earlier: (1) Annuals, plants that complete their life cycle in one year, are usually grown from seed sown in the spring either in the place they are to flower or in separate containers, from which they are subsequently moved into their final position. Annuals flower in summer and die down in winter after setting seed. Many brilliantly coloured ornamental plants as well as many weeds belong in this category.

Examples of annuals are petunia and lobelia. (2) Biennials are plants sown from seed one year, generally during the summer. They flower the second season and then die. Examples are wallflower and sweet william. (3) Herbaceous perennialsare those that die down to the ground each year but whose roots remain alive and send up new top growth each year. They are an important group in horticulture, whether grown as individual plants or in the assembly of the herbaceous border. Because they flower each year, they help to create the structure of the garden's appearance, so their placement must be considered carefully. Examples are delphinium and lupine.

BULBOUS PLANTS

For horticultural purposes, bulbous plants are defined to include those plants that have true bulbs (such as the daffodil), those with corms (such as the crocus), and a few that have tubers or rhizomes (such as the dahlia or iris). A bulb is defined as a modified shoot with a disklike basal plate and above it a number of fleshy scales that take the place of leaves and contain foods such as starch, sugar, and some proteins.

Each year a new stem arises from the centre. A corm consists of the swollen base of a stem, generally rounded or flattened at the top and covered with a membranous tunic in which reserve food materials are stored. A tuber or rhizome is not the base of the stem but rather a swollen part of an underground stem; it is often knobbly. All such plants have evolved in places where they can survive in a semidormant state over long unfavourable seasons, either cold mountain winters or long droughty summers.

The principles of gardening

Soil: its nature and needs

Soil is the basic element in the cultivation of all plants, although soilless growth in water, with or without gravel or sand, enriched with suitable chemicals (hydroponics) can be very successful.

Soil consists of particles, mainly mineral, derived from the breakdown of rocks and other substances together with organic matter. In the pore spaces between the particles, both water (containing dissolved salts) and air circulate. The air contains more carbon dioxide and less oxygen than does the atmosphere. Minute living organisms are also present in soil in immense quantities and are what make it "alive." Plants must penetrate this pore space to reach much of their nourishment.

The soil must be managed for fertility (the ability to supply plant nutrients) and physical condition. Nutrients must be supplied and released in forms available to the plant. Sixteen elements are necessary for plant growth. Three of these, carbon, oxygen, and hydrogen, are provided through water and air; the other 13 are provided through the soil. The elements required in relatively large amounts are called major elements: nitrogen, phosphorus, potassium, calcium, magnesium, and sulfur. The minerals required in small quantities are called trace elements: iron, boron, manganese, zinc, molybdenum, copper, and chlorine.

Soils can be roughly divided into three main types on the basis of their usefulness horticulturally, but many areas contain a mixture.

CLAYS

Clays, in which the particles are very fine, are called in horticulture heavy soils, because it is difficult to turn them over with a spade. They can be very fertile but tend to be lacking in good drainage, holding their water closely adhered to the soil particles; therefore, they cannot be worked when wet, and under pressure they tend to compact tightly, driving out the air. During drought they tend to become hard and even to develop large cracks so that they cannot be worked satisfactorily. Clay soils can be lightened with as much humus as can be dug into them. Humus may be any decayed organic matter, such as farmyard manure, leaf mold, or compost made from kitchen scraps and grass clippings.

SANDS AND GRAVELS

Sands and gravels are opposite in properties to clay. The soil particles are large, and the soils are called light because they are easy to work and turn in nearly all weather. Since their water-holding capacity is very low, however, they tend to dry out quickly. They are "hungry" soils requiring great quantities of manures, humus, and fertilizers to keep them prolific.

PEATS AND HEATHS

Peats and heaths are usually very acid and ill-drained. They result where conditions have prevented the complete breakdown of old vegetable matter into humus, generally because of poor aeration and surplus acid bog water. Much peat is derived from the decaying roots of sphagnum moss, useful for mulching in the garden. A heath soil is generally less fertile, consisting of a large mixture of sand with the peat and tending to be very low in mineral content and in water-retaining capacity.

The ideal garden soil is a medium loam consisting of a mixture of clay and sand, fairly rich in humus and easily worked, and not forming large clods when dry. The consistency of the soil is important, for a porous, properly tilled soil provides a medium through which roots can penetrate readily and rapidly. Another factor of importance in soils is the degree of acidity or alkalinity. Soil alkalinity is usually derived from free calcium carbonate or a similar alkaline salt. Soil reaction can be modified. It may be made more alkaline by adding one of the organic salts, of which calcium is best, in the form of lime. Acidity may be increased by adding hydrogen, in the form of sulfur compounds such as ammonia sulfate or superphosphate.

Feeding: fertilizing and watering

Maximum return can be obtained only from soil with an ample supply of elements necessary for plant growth, combined with sufficient moisture to enable them to be dissolved and absorbed through the plant hairs.

Treatment with farmyard manure or garden compost can supply the majority of these requirements. Because manure and compost are scarce in urban areas it is often necessary to use mineral fertilizers as well as organics. The soil is such a complex substance that all fertilizers must be applied in moderation and in balance with each other according to the deficiencies of the soil and the requirements of the particular crop. Different crops have different fertilizer needs. Manures are generally best dug into the ground in autumn in a temperate climate but also may be used asmulches in spring to control weeds. A mulch is a surface layer of organic matter that helps the several needs of feeding, conserving moisture, and controlling weeds. Black polyethylene sheeting is now widely used for all the mulching functions except feeding.

Watering of newly placed plants and of all plants during periods of drought is an essential gardening chore. Deep and thorough watering—not simply sprinkling the soil surface—can result in greatly improved growth. Water is essential in itself, but it also makes minerals available to plants in solution, the only form usable by plants. About one inch of water applied each week to the soil surface will percolate down about six inches; this is a minimal subsistence amount for many herbaceous garden plants, and small trees and shrubs require more. Proper watering once a week encourages deep penetration of roots, which in turn enables plants to survive dry surface conditions.

Drainage

Drainage is the other important side of water management. All plants need water but the amount needed varies, and if plants are forced to absorb more than they need, a form of drowning occurs. The symptoms are most easily seen in overwatered pot plants but are also visible to an experienced eye in badly drained corners of a garden. Roots require air as well as water and depend on subsurface water to bring the necessary oxygen. In large private gardens and in commercial gardens, buried earthenware piping is commonly used. In smaller gardens drainage can be readily achieved by the use of sumps, that is, holes dug to a depth of about four feet in affected places. The bottom half of the sump is filled with stones, through which excess water drains. Such measures may greatly improve the potential of a garden and the workability of its soil.

Protecting plants

Most plants have a precise level of tolerance to cold, below which they are killed. Many plants from tropical or subtropical regions cannot survive frost and are killed by temperatures below 32 °F (0 °C). These are called frost-tender. Others, called half-hardy, can withstand a few degrees of frost. Fortunately, many of the best garden plants are completely hardy, a quality often encouraged by careful breeding, and will withstand any low temperatures likely to be reached in temperate regions.

Various measures can be taken to give frost protection, from the simple ones appropriate for smaller gardens to the elaborate coverings used to protect valuable horticultural crops. Removing weeds that shade the soil increases the amount of heat stored during the day. Well-drained soil is less susceptible. Any shield against wind in frosty weather enhances survival capability. The simplest form of protection is a wrapping to keep warmer air around the plant. This can be a mulch (leaves, soil, ashes) placed over the crown of a slightly tender plant in winter or a shield of sacking for leaf-shedding plants (not as desirable for evergreens, which utilize their leaves all the year).

Glass structures such as greenhouses or outdoor frames can provide additional protection for tender plants. Such structures can be heated and the temperature regulated by a thermostat to any required degree. Thus, in temperate regions, orchids and other tropical plants can be grown so that they flower throughout the winter, many being forced to flower earlier than their normal season by the higher temperature. Greenhouses are divided by gardeners into four rough categories: (1) The cold house, in which there is no supplementary heating and which is suitable only for plants that will not be killed by a few degrees of frost (such as alpines or potted bulbous plants). The combination of heat from the sun and protection from wind will keep such a house appreciably warmer than the temperature outside. (2) The coolhouse, in which the minimum temperature is kept to 45 °F (7 °C). Most amateurs' greenhouses fall into this class, and a very large range of plants can be grown in them. (3) The intermediate house, in which the minimum temperature is kept at 55 or 60 °F (13 or 16 °C) and which is suitable for a wide range of orchids. (4) The hothouse, or stove house, in which the minimum temperature is kept above 60 °F (16 °C) and in which tropical plants such as anthuriums and cattleyas (a genus of the orchid family) can be grown.

Training and pruning

Training, the orienting of the plant in space, is achieved by techniques that direct the shape, size, and direction of plant growth. It may be accomplished by use of supports to which plants can be bent, twisted, or fastened. Pruning, the judicious cutting away of plant parts, is performed for other purposes: to contain size, to encourage fruiting in orchard trees, or to improve the appearance of ornamental trees and shrubs. It is one of the most important horticultural arts.

Where trees and shrubs are left to grow naturally, they often become much too large for their space in the garden. Also they may grow lanky and misshapen and have much dead growth. Where a branch or shoot is cut, it will often be induced to make a number of young shoots from below the cut, and these are likely to flower more freely than the older branches. Fruit trees in particular when pruned annually often give fruit of finer quality, larger in size, freer of disease, and of better colour. The two basic pruning cuts are known as heading back and thinning out. Heading back consists of cutting back the terminal portion of a branch to a bud; thinning out is the complete removal of a branch to a lateral or main trunk. Heading back, usually followed by the stimulation of lateral budbreak below the cut, produces a bushy, compact plant, suitable for a hedgerow, and it is often used to rejuvenate shrubs that have become too large or that flower poorly. Thinning out, which encourages longer growth of the remaining terminals by reducing lateral branches, tends to open up the plant, producing a longer plant. In general, pruning, started when the plant is young, obviates the need for drastic and risky remedial pruning later of a large, old, or misshapen bush or tree.

f******Particular spatial arrangements may increase light utilization, facilitate harvesting or disease control, or improve productivity and quality. Thus, training and pruning form an essential part of fruit growing throughout the life of the plant. Special attention is given in the formative years to obtain desired shape and structure. The key to training is the point on the main stem from which branches form. In the central-leader system of training, the trunk forms a central axis with branches distributed laterally up and down and around the stem. In the open-centre or vase system, the main stem is terminated and growth forced through a number of branches originating close to the upper end of the trunk. An intermediate system is called the modified-leader system. In espaliersystems plants are trained to grow flat along a wire or trellis. Properly executed espaliers are extremely attractive as ornamentals. Espaliers in combination with dwarfing rootstocks allow high-density orchards that are very productive on a per-unit-area basis, with the fruit close to the ground for easy harvest. Extensive pruning is required annually to maintain the system.

There are a number of physiological responses to training and pruning. Orientation of the plant may have a marked effect on growth and fruiting. Thus fruit trees planted on an inclined angle become dwarfed and flower earlier; training branches in a horizontal position produces the same effect. This effect is achieved naturally when a heavy fruit load bends a limb down. The main effects of pruning are achieved by altering the root–shoot balance. Thus an explosion of vegetative growth normally occurs after extensive shoot pruning. Severely pruned plants, especially if they are in the juvenile stage of growth, tend to remain vegetative. Similarly the slowdown of vegetative growth by root pruning encourages flowering.

The training of plants to grow in unnatural shapes for ornamental purposes is called topiary.

In Roman and Renaissance times, when ingenious topiary was in high fashion, plants were trained to unusual and fantastic shapes such as beasts, ships, and building facades. Though more modestly, hedges and shrubs are still trained to geometric shapes in formal gardens.

Another extreme form of training is the Japanese art ofbonsai, the creation of dwarfed potted trees by a combination of pruning (both roots and tops) and restricted nutrition. Living trees more than 100 years old and only a few feet high are grown in special containers arranged to resemble the natural landscape.

Propagation

New plants are produced either from seed or by the techniques of division, taking cuttings, grafting, budding, or layering. For the ordinary gardener,propagation is a relatively simple but interesting process normally used for economic provision of more versions of favourite plants, as part of exchanges with other gardeners, or as a wise precaution against winter losses.

Propagation by cuttings is the most common practice. Young shoots of the current season are usually the most successful at rooting. Roses are usually propagated by budding, in which a bud from the rose desired is inserted in rootstock (that part of the plant tissue from which a root can form) just above ground level.

Fruit trees are usually propagated by layering, in which a young shoot is pegged down in the ground with the end twisted upward almost at right angles; the lower side of the wood just before the twist is wounded so as to induce rooting. When this has taken place, the layer is severed from the parent.

Control of weeds

Controlling weeds is a basic, and probably the most arduous, factor of cultivation and has been carried on from the time the earliest nomads settled down to an agricultural life. It has always been necessary to free the chosen crops of competition from other plants. For smaller weeds hoeing is practicable. The weeds are cut off by the action of the hoe and left to wither on the surface. Hand weeding, by pulling out individual weeds, is often necessary in gardens, particularly the rock garden, in seed boxes, and in the herbaceous border or among annuals. Chemical and biological control of weeds developed greatly after World War II and has made much mechanical cultivation unnecessary.

Control of pests and diseases

Damage to plants is most often caused by pests such as insects, mites, eelworms, and other small creatures but may also be caused by mammals such as deer, rabbits, and mice. Damage by disease is that caused by fungi, bacteria, and viruses.

Prevention is generally better than cure, and constant vigilance is necessary to prevent a pest infestation or a disease outbreak. Control can be obtained by the use of chemical sprays, dusts, and fumigants, but some of these are so potent that they should be used only by the experienced operator. Considerable evidence is available regarding the possible harmful long-term effects on the biological chain of excessive use of some of these noxious chemicals, particularly the hydrocarbons. Some control can be obtained through good garden practices: clearing up all dead and diseased material and burning it; pruning and thinning so that a reasonable circulation of air is obtained through the plants; and crop rotation. Some control may also be obtained through natural biological predators. The breeding of plants immune to certain pests and diseases is also a valuable means of control.

Mechanical aids

Mechanical devices to aid the gardener include tillers, lawn mowers, hedge cutters, sprinklers, and a variety of more esoteric equipment that has made gardening an easier pursuit. Such machines are not a substitute for good judgment and technique in the garden, however, nor will they give anyone a completely labour-free garden. They do enable a considerably larger area to be cultivated and maintained than if all labour is performed by hand.

Roots, a Potted History of Cottage Gardening

The roots of cottage gardening go back to the English Tudor period (1485 - 1603) and the potted history below is intended to explain the main developments over time since then.

The Dark Ages had ended and in this comparatively peaceful time, country folk were able to tend their gardens, outside the protection of the local castle walls, in the relative safety of the countryside.

Cottage (humble home, small dwelling) dwellers were usually poor peasants and had what we today politely call *"an extremely limited budget"*- they were dirt-poor and lived in abject poverty. It was the time of the European Renaissance and new plants were arriving regularly from the Americas, China and Japan. But they were only of interest to rich people, and were beyond the reach of mere peasants.

Gardens for pleasure and appearance were only within the means of the wealthy - the landed gentry. The major gardens of the period were large and often laid out in the *Renaissance style - e.g. Hampton Court* - or the romantic (landscape) style - e.g. *Chiswick House* and *Blenheim Palace.*

The English Cottage Garden

A cottage gardener had a very small plot of land and every inch of ground available had to produce fruit, vegetables and herbs to help ensure family survival. As he had to watch the pennies, he kept his choice of plants limited to tried and trusted varieties of local, English origin.

These plants, hardy and simple all, always gave good results and are today known as *"cottage garden plants"*.

Why were flowers, which aren't generally a source of food, so important in the cottage garden?

Simply because flowers attract bees, butterflies and other insects and they in turn pollinate fruit tree blossom, vegetables and flowering shrubs, e.g. apples and raspberries. Pollination is crucial for plant survival as it leads to the successful development of seed - fruit is, in effect, a pot of seeds.

Growing edible crops was the objective of cottage gardening and the flowers, with their colours, pollen and fragrance, were used as a lure - their beauty was of secondary importance.

Peak Flowering Season

Cottage gardening reached it's peak flowering season during the Victorian era (1837 - 1904).

The emergence of the worker or artisan and middle classes meant that for the first time in human history, many people had the time, and a little spare cash, to indulge themselves in gardening and garden food production for their pleasure, instead of as a basic necessity of existence.

One factor hadn't changed though - the new middle classes, like the original cottage gardeners, all had small gardens.

Relevance in the Modern Age - a Personal Learning Curve

We live in a time of accelerating climate change, the greenhouse effect, the *"red lists of endangered species"* of plants, animals, birds and insects and a polluted environment. We've also witnessed a rapid increase of many types of childhood and adult diseases, many of which were more or less unheard of when I was schoolboy.

As a teenager in the '60s, I read *"Silent Spring"* by *Rachel Carson* (1907 - 1964, the earth mother of the environmental movement in my opinion), and my eyes were opened forever to the realization that we humans were - and are - destroying our planet. Her book led to the banning of the pesticide DDT: Rachel Carson had defeated big business and changed the policies of the WHO and national governments all over the world.

I've been a keen amateur gardener and designer all my life and in the '70s, while still working as a marketing manager, the ideas of *E. F. Schumacher* (1911 - 1977, in his book *"Small is Beautiful"*, proved to me that *"big"* just doesn't work in organizations. The modern farming industry (usually based on one type of crop, be it animal or plant - mono-cultivation, awful word isn't it?) has had continuous problems with all kinds of diseases and pests for many years, and only exists by the profitable grace of the pesticide and fertilizer companies.

But cottage gardens are living proof that small is definitely beautiful: They rarely suffer from diseases and pests due to the wide variety of plants used in small numbers - I believe this is known as *"bio-diversity"* in modern-day *"techno-speak."*

The last stage in my discovery of cottage gardening was my first visit in 1985 to a nursery that advertised in my gardening magazine that:

If you want the usual assortment of pansies, petunias and marigolds, don't visit us as we cannot help you so and a visit will be a waste of your time.

If, however, you're looking for plants that will turn your garden into a romantic place filled with flowers, birds and insects, then we can help you.

That got to me - it takes guts to make such a statement in advertising. I had to go and visit the Stam family in Ochten (sorry, no link, today they live in a cottage in Ireland). At that time they were the only nursery in the Netherlands specialized in cottage garden plants, and I was converted from the first visit.

Points to Ponder

- None of our leaders and governments have managed to do anything about climate change and pollution in my lifetime - hell no, instead of taking action they wasted decades of valuable time telling us the problems didn't exist!
- Yet I've noticed the steady advance in flowering time of our botanic crocuses from early March to mid February during the last 30 years and I'm sure you too will have noticed similar changes in your area.
- *"The End of Nature"* by *Bill McKibben*, the first book for a general audience about global warming, proved - for me in any event - back in 1990 that the process of global warming was a work in progress

which had started more than 150 years earlier with the advent of the Industrial Revolution.

- Our wee friends - the animals, birds and insects - desperately need all the help they can get. All it takes is a glance at the list of the number of species we've already lost, let alone the endangered species lists.
- Plants are becoming more and more unnatural - we lost the fragrance in roses after WW2, though it is being nursed back again, albeit slowly, and you'll never persuade me that plants designed to be incapable of reproduction are natural - seedless varieties, F whatever hybrids, registered flower brands and such like rubbish!
- There's never been a time when cottage gardening has been more relevant than it is today - it's small-scale, natural and organic, has a very positive effect on the environment and we can all do it ourselves.
- I believe that the ecological power of cottage gardens can certainly make a difference to our environment and, hopefully, enable us to leave a planet on the road to recovery for our children to lead their lives on, at the very least.

3

Garden and Landscape Design

GARDEN AND LANDSCAPE DESIGN

The development and decorative planting of gardens, yards, grounds, parks, and other types of areas. Garden and landscapedesign is used to enhance the settings for buildings and public areas and in recreational areas and parks. It is one of the decorative arts and is allied toarchitecture, city planning, and horticulture.

The vegetated landscape that covered most of the Earth's continents before humans began to build still surrounds and penetrates even the largest metropolises. Efforts to design gardens and to preserve and develop green open space in and around cities are efforts to maintain contact with the original pastoral, rural landscape. Gardens and designed landscapes, by filling the open areas in cities, create a continuity in space between structural urban landscapes and the open rural landscapes beyond. Moreover, gardens and designed landscapes have a special type of continuity in time. Buildings, paintings, and sculpture may survive longer than specific plants, but the constant cyclical growth and change in plants provide a continuous time dimension that static structures and sculpture can never achieve.

The functional aspects of landscaping, the aesthetic and physical components of design, the various kinds of private and public design, and the role and development of gardening in human history.

Functions and concerns of garden and landscape design

Aspects of landscape architecture

Garden and landscape design is a substantial part but by no means all of the work of the profession of landscape architecture. Defined as "the art of arranging land and the objects upon it for human use and enjoyment," landscape architecture also includes site planning, land planning, master planning, urban design, and environmental planning. Site planning involves plans for specific developments in which precise arrangements of buildings, roadways, utilities, landscape elements, topography, water features, and vegetation are shown. Land planning is for larger-scale developments involving subdivision into several or many parcels, including analyses of land and landscape, feasibility studies for economic, social, political, technical, and ecological constraints, and detailed site plans as needed.

Master planning is for land use, conservation, and development at still larger scales, involving comprehensive areas or units of landscape topography or comprehensive systems such as open space, park-recreation, water and drainage, transportation, or utilities. Urban design is the planning and designing of the open-space components of urbanized areas; it involves working with architects on the building patterns, engineers on the traffic and utility patterns, graphic and industrial designers on street furniture, signs, and lighting, planners on overall land use and circulation, economists on economic feasibility, and sociologists on social feasibility, needs, and desires.

Environmental planning is for natural or urbanized regions or substantial areas within them, in which the impact of development upon land and natural systems, their capacity to carry and sustain development, or their needs for preservation and conservation are analyzed exhaustively and developed as constraints upon urban design and master, land, and site planning. Within this framework of comprehensive survey, study, analysis, planning, and design of the continuous environment, garden and landscape design represents the final, detailed, precise, intensive refinement and implementation of all previous plans.

Ideally, all of these planning and design phases follow one another closely in a continuous sequential process, but this rarely happens. Various levels of planning and design are performed by different people at different times; often the more-comprehensive phases are not performed at all or are performed in an oversimplified manner. The wise gardener or landscape architect, therefore, always begins with a careful analysis of conditions surrounding the project.

Garden and landscape design deals with the treatment of land areas not covered by buildings, when those areas are considered important to visual experience, with or without utilitarian function.

Typically, these land areas are of four types: those closely related to single buildings, such as front yards, side yards, and backyards, or more-extensive grounds; those around and between groups of buildings such as campuses, civic and cultural centres, commercial and industrial complexes; those bordering and paralleling transportation and utility corridors such as parkways, freeways, waterways, power easements; and park-recreation open-space areas and systems.

These areas may be of any size, from small urban courtyards and suburban gardens to many thousands of acres of regional, state, or national parks. Although usually conceived as vegetated green spaces on natural ground, they can include also playgrounds, urban plazas, covered malls, roof gardens, and decks, which may be almost entirely formed by construction and paving.

Garden and landscape design, therefore, works with a wide range of natural and processed materials capable of holding up well in the specific local climatic conditions of the site. These materials include earth, rock, water, and plants, either existing on the site or brought in; and construction materials such as concrete, stone, brick, wood, tile, metal, and glass.

Art, science, and nature

Garden and landscape design is uniquely concerned with direct relations among art, science, and nature. It operates exactly at the frontier between people and nature, developing transitional connecting zones between the outside limits of buildings and engineering structures and the natural forms and processes that surround them. This is true for large houses and gardens in the country, for regional parks at the edges of cities, for urban and suburban gardens, for urban plazas and roof decks; it is true wherever soil exists to be treated, wherever it may be brought in to fill containers, wherever open spaces are exposed to the weather.

If garden and landscape design is concerned with the relations between humankind and nature, it is largely determined by one or the other of the conflicting philosophies about how human beings do or should relate to nature. People know that they are biologically and physiologically the products of natural evolution, yet their great technological accomplishments lead them to feel that they are above, beyond, or outside nature, that they have conquered and dominated the wilderness and have it now within their power to remake the world. Every work of garden and landscape design reflects one or the other of these conflicting attitudes. The Japanese garden, for example, is inspired by the notion of humans as a part of nature, the Renaissance garden by the idea that humans are nature's masters. Garden and landscape design thus reveals much about a culture and a period. One result of the impact of the environmental movement on design in the West in the late 20th century was the emergence of design values that sought the integration of the human and the natural rather than their separation.

Garden and landscape design is an art insofar as it creates for people experiences that uplift their spirits, expand their vision, and invigorate their lives. It is a science insofar as it develops precise knowledge of its processes and materials. And it is directly related to and expressive of nature insofar as it incorporates natural materials and scenes. When the preservation of natural landscape is primary, as in a regional park, art and science manifest themselves in the skill and sensitivity with which necessary facilities and changes are related to the natural landscape. At the other extreme, in an urban plaza, trees in boxes or openings in the paving may be the only natural elements; art and science then are manifested in the design and construction of the total plaza, including its display of trees as symbols of nature, as pleasing forms, and as sources of shade.

Art, science, and nature become most intimately interlocked in certain aspects ofhorticulture expressed in designed gardens and landscapes: in improved varieties of herbaceous and woody plants; in the cultural practices that stimulate their maximum contributions to the scene; and in the techniques and skills for directing and reshaping the forms of plants—in a range from trimmed hedges and topiary (careful sculptural cutting), through espaliered (trained to grow flat against a wall or trellis) and pollarded (cut back to the trunk to promote a dense head of foliage) trees, to ultimate refinements such as the Japanese practice of removing individual needles from pine trees.

No doubt much art recognizes, expresses, or symbolizes nature in some way. Onlythe arts of garden and landscape, however, produce works in which nature participates directly with more-processed forms and materials. As in most other arts, garden and landscape design must solve not only aesthetic but also technical and functional problems. Gardens are for horticulture as well as for viewing, parks are for active recreation as well as for passive relaxation. The surface of the earth must be covered to prevent erosion, dust in summer, and mud in winter. Water persists in running downhill, and even light garden structures must have adequate footings.

This does not mean, however, that there is an inherent or inevitable conflict between utility and beauty. Such conflicts usually develop either because the designer tries to carry out an aesthetic concept that ignores the technical and functional requirements of the problem or because the program is so demanding technically, functionally, or economically that it eliminates aesthetic considerations from the design process. In most garden and landscape design situations, it is necessary first to evaluate the technical conditions and functional demands and then to derive from them design concepts that resolve them.

DESIGN

AESTHETIC COMPONENTS

ELEMENTS

The traditional elements of design are space; mass; line, or outline; colour; light and shade; texture; scent; and time, as related to climate, season, and growth factors.

SPACE

Space is air or atmospheric volume defined by physical elements and visual imagination. Space has floors: earth, rock, grass, low planting, concrete, asphalt, stone, brick, wood, carpet, tile, linoleum. It has sides or walls: topography, rock, vegetation, vertical structures. And it has ceilings: treetops, structural coverage, or the sky. The most easily understood spaces are the rooms, terraces, patios, and gardens of private residences. A room is defined precisely and unavoidably by floor, walls, and ceiling, particularly with doors closed and windows draped.

Beyond these rooms there are the streets, squares, plazas, parks, and public buildings of the city. An urban plaza surrounded by major buildings likewise has positive floors and walls, with sky for ceiling. The fields, meadows, orchards, groves, forests, plains, lakes, river and stream valleys, hills, and mountains of the wider landscape have less precise and regular enclosures. Patios may have fences and walls, gardens hedges and trellises, but in parks there are loose spaces of many soft sizes and forms, defined by trees, ground forms, and shrubbery masses. And in the open landscape there are many different apparent space scales, from the intimate, small farming scenes of New England, Portugal, or Japan to the almost limitless panoramas of North America's Great Plains, the deserts of the American Southwest, or the Rocky Mountains. In all of these, space is defined by ground or floor surfaces below, obstacles that block vision horizontally or terminate it at the horizon, and sky overhead. The human sense of space in all of them results partly from what is visible and partly from an individual's imaginative extension, interpretation, and structuring of reality. Thus, a sand dune, a rock, and a cactus may become a "room" in the desert, while the entire Yosemite Valley can be seen as a great room housing thousands of people.

MASS

Mass is the opposite of space. They define each other and depend upon each other for visual existence. Mass may be topographical earth forms, rock outcrops and boulders, trees and shrub groups, buildings, and water forms—streams, lakes, or waterfalls. These are masses in the larger landscape, even though they also incorporate spaces within themselves. Trees, shrubs, and buildings have multiple spaces within them, even though they read as masses from outside. Water forms contain spaces for divers and aquatic life, but of a different density.

LINE

Line in the landscape may be the sharp edge of paving, structure, or rock; the boundary between two different surface materials, as grass and ivy; the edge of a shadow; or the silhouette outline of any three-dimensional form, such as a rock, plant, or building. Whatever its source, a line in the landscape plays an important role in the way one sees, interprets, and relates to the scene. A line may lead the eye into the distance, around a corner and out of the scene, or around the scene and back again, holding the viewer within it. It is similar to the role of lines in a painting, holding the viewer within or leading him out of the composition. In a landscape, however, the function of lines is vastly more complicated and difficult to predict. Thepattern—that is, the form created by lines—is three-dimensional in any given scene that is viewed. It is four-dimensional in that a spectator continues to move through the landscape over periods of time. The pattern changes throughout each day because of the changing light and shade patterns produced by the movement of the Earth around the Sun. And the pattern is never exactly the same on one day as on any previous day, because of changes in the weather, the seasons, and the elements of the landscape. Buildings, topography, and rocks may be maintained almost the same for substantial periods of time, but vegetation changes constantly, with both seasonal adjustments and annual growth. That is one reason why landscapes without vegetation seem static, lifeless, and monotonous.

COLOUR

Colour gives physical landscapes that final dimension of real life, definition, and interest. Spring blossoms and fresh green leaves, after the cold barrenness of winter, herald a new season of vitality and fun. After the deep and stable green of summer, fall colours mark a last resurgence of liveliness before the winter barrenness sets in again. The apparent sizes and forms of landscape spaces change with each such seasonal change: bright colours advance, dull colours recede, changing apparent distances.

Structural colours, too, affect the apparent sizes and forms of landscape spaces. Most obvious is the negative effect of bright billboards upon quiet landscapes. To most people billboards seem destructive and arbitrary intrusions; they do not grow out of the scene but are forced onto it. Yet man-made forms—even billboards—can be made to appear to be a part of nature to the extent that they are designed to harmonize with the existing scene.

The aim of the garden and landscape designer is to combine the strong artificial colours of paint and structure with the softer and more-subdued grays, greens, browns, and blues of nature as well as with seasonal outbursts of the purest and truest colours in the world. Colour varies by hue, the actual colour from the colour wheel; by value, the strength of the colours, bright or pale; the tone or grayness, how pure they are or how grayed by admixture with other colours; by the way that light and shade play on them; and by the texture, smooth or rough, of the surface they are on. All of these factors are taken into account by the garden and landscape designer.

LIGHT AND SHADE

Because the Sun—and, to a lesser extent, the Moon, stars, fire, and artificial lighting—has the property of casting shadows, landscape design, in placing trees, structures, and other elements on the land, must always take into consideration the light and shade resulting from such placement. Light and shade are not the same in all parts of a country or the world. Light is welcome in cool, gray, northern climates, shade in hot, bright, desert or tropical regions. In the clear air of unspoiled deserts, one can see so far that all sense of size, scale, and distance is lost; in the foggy humidity of the western coasts of Europe and North America, distances seen and objects perceived change from day to day, sometimes from hour to hour, so that one lives with a continuing sense of mystery and variety. Landscape design must, ideally, remain sensitive to and work carefully with the light and shade relations that are most desirable in each different region or subregion.

TEXTURE

Texture—the smoothness or roughness of surfaces—is another element of landscape design. It is perceived primarily by touch, although through vision one approximates the textures of different surfaces and imagines how they would feel. The surface texture of the earth may vary from fine sand or silt to coarse clods, gravel, or boulders. The texture of plant coverage may vary from fine bent grasses through coarser meadow grasses to brush, ivy, or cactus. Wall surfaces range from the smoothness of glass and plaster to the roughness of brick, stone, or rough-sawn lumber. Tactile textures must be experienced intimately. Visual textures may be experienced at any distance. Farther away, larger elements participate in texture effects; at medium distances the foliage of trees and the size of rocks create textural qualities; from an airplane or hilltop the size and arrangement of buildings, topographic forms, masses of vegetation, or water create textural effects.

SCENT

Scent is a delicate and subtle element in landscape experience, often lost to individuals in modern times because of widespread pollution of the air with foul-smelling exhaust and industrial waste gases. The fragrance of flower and fruit is one of the traditional delights of garden and park, still attainable through sensitive selection and arrangement of plants.

TIME, CLIMATE, AND SEASON

Unlike the static continuity of architectural and urban monuments, garden and landscape spaces are dependent on maintenance, which determines whether the form envisioned by the original designers will endure or change over decades or centuries. Because of continuing maintenance, the Saihô-ji garden and many others in Japan continue today in much the same form as they began. On the other hand, inadequate maintenance of Renaissance gardens designed as geometric architectural abstractions, to which plant forms were made to conform by clipping and trimming—allowed many of the larger plants to resume their natural forms. The results, however pleasant, are not what the designers envisioned. Instead of hundreds of years, the typical suburban garden in the United States has a predictable life of about five years.

Time and climate are closely interrelated in their effects on garden and landscape spaces. Because relations between temperature and moisture, light and shade,change daily throughout the year, every region and locality on Earth—in fact, every building site—has its own climate, unlike any other. Therefore, garden and landscape design for every region, locality, and site may be expected to be different. Nevertheless, climates can be generalized in certain broad categories that are similar, though not identical, over large areas of the Earth.

Climatic factors having major impact on garden and landscape design are temperature range (hot to cold), precipitation range (high to low, rain to snow), their combinations (hot, wet summers; hot, dry summers; cold, wet winters; cold, dry winters; and so on), growing season (year-round in the tropics, a few weeks in the Arctic), atmospheric humidity (clear air or clouds, fog, mist) and its effects on visibility and patterns of light and shade, and air movement (winds, breezes) and its effect on the other factors (cooling in hot weather, chilling in cold, moving clouds and fog).

The combination of all these factors affects how people see the landscape (bright, clear desert distances; soft, mysterious, changeable foggy landscapes), what they expect from design (shade from the sun, protection from the wind, shelter from rain and snow), and how gardens and landscapes are designed. The patios, cloisters, and oases of Mediterranean and Middle Eastern regions, the romantic naturalistic parks of Europe, China, and eastern North America, the esoteric garden abstractions of Japan—all of these different approaches to design were inspired partly by the particular qualities of the landscape climate in which they developed.

Time and natural light are, of course, intimately interlocked in the daily cycle of night and day, in the seasonal cycles (light is different in summer and winter because of differences in temperature and humidity), and in the annual cycles (long days in summer, short days in winter).

Time, climate, and season are all reflected in garden and landscape in the growth and change of plants. In the tropics, growth is constant and taken for granted, a problem of control. As growing seasons become shorter in the north and south or at higher elevations, they become more precious. In far northern and southern latitudes the short summer is a period of rejoicing and outdoor activity. A tree that will mature in 5 to 10 years in southern California or Florida will require 30 to 40 years in the north-central United States. Spring blossoms, fall colour, the change from summer green to winter's exposed branch structures, all of these mark the seasonal changes clearly and strongly in the eastern United States, in Europe, and in other temperate areas.

PRINCIPLES

The basic principles of design deal with the arrangement or organization of the elements, as expressed in specific materials, on a specific site. The site—a piece of land, with surface form and internal content—may in itself require reshaping. On it will be placed—or may already exist—buildings, roads, minor structures, trees, shrubs, ground-cover planting, water elements, rocks. The elements of design are contained in these individual components and in specific relations that may develop among them on a particular site. The principles of design—which deal with overall relations—are unity and variety, rhythm and balance, accent and contrast, scale andproportion, and composite three-dimensional spatial form.

UNITY AND VARIETY

Unity and variety are derived from the number of elements, or kinds of material, within a given visual area and from the way they are combined. A brick building or a rose garden is unified by concentration on one material. The difficulty of achieving a sense of unity increases as the number of elements, or kinds of material, increase. A building of six materials or a garden of 30 kinds of plants, for example, will have more variety, but unity can be achieved only by careful organization and arrangement. At a certain point, which varies with the situation and the skill of the designer, it becomes impossible to establish unity. Variety then dominates.

RHYTHM AND BALANCE

Rhythm and balance result from the three-dimensional arrangement of elements and materials on the site. Rhythm is a sequence or repetition of similar elements—as a double row of trees. It tends to emphasize direction and movement, as along anallée toward a viewpoint or terminus. Balance is the sense one gets, looking in any direction, that the elements to one's left balance those to one's right and the feeling one has that the views one has just experienced are in equilibrium with what one sees now. The most obvious examples of balance are the symmetrical axial Renaissance gardens of Europe, but these are not the only or even the most interesting ways to achieve balance.

ACCENT AND CONTRAST

Accent and contrast enliven arrangements that may be so balanced, orderly, and harmonious as to be dull. An accent is an element that differs from everything around it, as silver-gray foliage against dark green conifers, but is limited in quantity in relation to surrounding elements. Contrast is stronger: two different elements may be juxtaposed in almost equal quantity to emphasize the special qualities of each. Well-known examples are the formal palace in the informal park, the green park in the densely built-up city. Accent and contrast are more difficult to handle successfully than straightforward, simple, harmonious design. An example of the failure to handle it successfully is the common practice of lining a street with alternate specimens of two quite different trees, as pines and cherries, which merely cancel each other out.

SCALE AND PROPORTION

Scale refers to the apparent (not the actual) size of a landscape space or of the elements within it. Proportion is the determined relations among the sizes of all the parts within an element and of all the elements within a space. Thus, the proportionate sizes of the legs, arms, and back of a garden bench, for example, determine the scale of the seat. And the overall size of the seat, in proportionate relation to walk width, arbor height, lawn area, tree size, and so on, helps to determine the scale of the garden.

COMPOSITE THREE-DIMENSIONAL SPATIAL FORM

Composite three-dimensional spatial form results from the delineation of a block of air by physical elements, which enclose and frame the space and establish its relations with neighbouring spaces, distant views, and so on. A patio with paved floor and walled enclosure (with perhaps a grilled outlook) and sheltered by trees orpergola structures (arbor or trellis) is an obvious example of this form.

THE DESIGN PROCESS

The design process has been called in the past modes of composition and style or period selection. In the first quarter of the 20th century, the arts, including architectural, garden, and landscape design, were dominated by traditional, eclectic, preconceived systems of form and approach called the Beaux Arts system, after the famous school in Paris. In essence, these systems told designers what to design and where. Their only choice and their only skill lay in how to adapt preconceived systems—such as formal and informal gardens—to the particular problem at hand. Innovation consisted of timid new relationships among traditional elements.

Also in the first quarter of the 20th century there occurred what was called the modern revolt. Beginning in painting and sculpture, it soon swept through architecture and reached garden and landscape design toward the end of the quarter in Europe, reaching the United States about 1935. The essence of the modern revolt was the rejection of preconceived or traditional styles, periods, rules, regulations, or systems governing design. In place of these, systems and processes developed for analyzing problems and situations in their own terms and in terms of the modern resources available for solving them. Basic to the new theories was the idea that designed forms should arise from and express each specific situation and the contemporary industrial culture around it. By the 1970s all fields of design seemed to be dominated by these theories, but, although submerged, traditional Beaux Arts design continued to surface regularly in strange new combinations with modern forms. A form of this eclecticism emerged in the early 1970s, when architects once again designed symmetrical monumental buildings with little functional or structural expression, and traditional formal-informal concepts in garden and landscape design began to reappear.

Physical components

NATURAL

Natural integrants of garden and landscape design include earth, rock, water, and plants.

EARTH

As a base for design, earth is the floor of landscape spaces, the root medium in which half of every plant lives, the foundation for structures, the vehicle for surface and subsurface drainage of excess water, and a sculptural material in its own right.

As a floor, earth can be seen as an abstract surface. If apparently level, with just enough slope for drainage, it is ready to be covered with paving, grass, ground cover, or other planting, which is necessary to prevent dust in dry weather and mud in wet weather; if sloping or irregular, earthwork may be necessary to conform to new construction or to the design plan, to provide adequate drainage, or in order to relate properly to neighbouring topography and views.

As a root medium for plants, earth must be understood as soil. One must know the type and depth of soil before planning a garden or landscape. Soil occurs in layers: topsoil, in which there is a high percentage of organic humus and microorganisms; subsoil, which is more sterile as it gets deeper; and bedrock, which is not yet broken up. There are many variations in these layers. In the mountains there may be only a few inches of soil over rock; in old valleys the soil may be hundreds of feet deep. Most plants require one to six feet of topsoil, with good drainage, but there are plants that will grow in rock, sand, sterile soil, boggy land, shallow water, or open water. If the soil is not adequate for the planting desired or if the form of the earth is to be changed, then new soil conditions must be created.

As a foundation for structures, earth must be dry and firm. Although structures can be built in almost any soil, they become more and more expensive as the earth becomes less dry and firm. Desirable foundation conditions, the exact opposite of the loose, moist soil that is best for most plants, create many technical problems in the relations between structures and plant areas.

As a drainage vehicle, earth absorbs a high percentage of the water that falls on its surface. This absorbed water may be stored below ground, or it may move horizontally through sloping soil patterns. Surface water that is not absorbed, either because the soil is saturated or because the slope of the ground makes it run off too fast, must drain away on the surface. This creates many technical problems, especially if the surface is not covered to prevent erosion or if a great deal of land is covered by roofed structures or paved surfaces, which increase the amount of water running off because none is absorbed.

As a sculptural material, earth can be contoured to conform with functional and maintenance demands. Rolling natural hills and golf-course earth forms demonstrate the potential. Slopes must not be too steep for planting to hold, unless they are structurally retained.

ROCK

Rock is a major factor in some regions, minor in others, nonexistent in some. It varies in size from sand through pebbles, cobbles, boulders, and fixed outcrops to solid-rock mountains. It varies in form from square or jagged, newly cut or broken to rounded forms produced by the action of water. It varies also in colour and in texture. It can be used as a ground cover, dry or in cement; in vertical structures with various degrees of cutting and finishing; to simulate natural rock formations; and in sculptural groupings that emphasize the natural form of the rocks, as the Japanese do so well.

WATER

Water is essential to all gardens and landscapes, even in the desert, although amounts vary considerably. As a design element, water contributes coolness, moisture, sparkle, lightness, depth, serenity, the possibility of aquatic plants and animals, and recreation. It may run through natural stream and river channels and collect in natural ponds, lakes, and seas, or it may be kept in structural channels and pools, recirculated to avoid waste. In some soil conditions it may be necessary to seal the bottoms of natural-appearing streams and ponds to hold the water. Under natural conditions water runs downhill through naturally formed channels and collects in low spots or bowls of firm form. Water also may be pumped uphill or thrown into the air in jets and fountains. Water is used increasingly throughout countries with technically complex artificial irrigation systems, which become distinctive landscape elements.

PLANTS

Plants are considered the primary material of gardens and landscapes, by contrast with the concentration of structures in cities. They may be grouped and organized for design purposes in several ways: by size (trees, shrubs, low plants, grass); by form (vertical, horizontal, round, irregular); by texture (size, shape, and arrangement of foliage and structure); by colour (flowers, fruit, foliage, structure); by rate of growth (fast, medium, slow); by seasonal effect (spring, summer, fall, winter); by fragrance (flowers, fruit, foliage); by environmental requirements (soil, drainage, sun or shade, temperature range, pests and diseases, pruning needs). All of these properties affect the selection, arrangement, and maintenance of plants in designed landscapes.

STRUCTURAL

Structural integrants of garden and landscape include structures closely related to the earth, enclosure structures, shelter structures, engineering structures, and specialbuildings.

EARTH-RELATED STRUCTURES

Earth-related structures include paving (walks, roads, terraces, patios) and change-of-level structures (retaining walls, steps, ramps, bridges), which must be made of materials that will resist decay, such as brick, stone, concrete, asphalt. These structures provide the connections for movement and circulation and the areas for intensive gathering, social use, or active recreation. They embody a complex technology.

ENCLOSURE STRUCTURES

Enclosure structures, such as walls and fences, are designed to control vision or movement or both. They may be of various heights, 3 to 10 feet (1 to 3 metres) or more, and of many materials: brick, stone, or concrete masonry; wood; metal; sheet materials such as glass, plastic, asbestos, pressed boards. Because they are at eye level and extend and connect buildings, they are very important in intimate visual design.

SHELTER STRUCTURES

Shelter structures, designed to protect from sun, rain, or wind, may incorporate enclosure elements at the sides with overhead elements, which may be open framework pergolas or arbors carrying vines or solid opaque or translucent roofs. Among such structures are gazebos, pavilions, garden temples, summer houses, hermit huts, follies, ruins, and grottoes.

ENGINEERING STRUCTURES

Engineering structures tend to appear unexpectedly, because incongruously, in gardens and landscapes. They are usually mechanical or electrical transformers, vents, valves, siphons, drains, culverts, headwalls, dams, and many other nameless and mysterious forms. In a good landscape design, these structures are integrated into the overall plan.

SPECIAL BUILDINGS

Special buildings include many that are nearly as complete as the fully enclosed buildings that are the province of the architect: greenhouses, conservatories, orangeries, tool sheds, dovecotes, icehouses, root houses, bathhouses, playhouses, and many more. These are usually auxiliary in relation to the main house or building but relate to them in character and detail.

Shelter structures, engineering structures, and special buildings are important in garden and landscape because they introduce precise geometric forms intermediate in scale between main buildings and landscape. If scattered or designed indiscriminately, they can destroy a pleasant landscape; carefully designed, they can be so grouped or arranged as to create rhythmic connections and patterns within the overall architectural landscape design concept.

SCULPTURAL COMPONENTS AND OUTDOOR FURNISHINGS

Sculptural components of garden and landscape have traditionally been predictable forms and types: figurative sculpture, decorative urns and plaques, fountains, sundials, birdbaths, cisterns, and wells. All of these continue to appear as elements of the persistent underground Beaux Arts vocabulary. In contemporary design, however, they are eliminated or take on new forms derived from modern sculpture. The possibility now exists for the production of gardens and landscapes so completely sculptured that one cannot tell where design stops and sculpture begins.

Outdoor furnishings and equipment include all of those fixed and movable elements that tend to appear in garden or landscape after the plans are done and installed and therefore without benefit of design control. In the garden they are seats, tables, barbecues, umbrellas, plant containers, supports, and guards, as well as lights and light systems. In the public landscape they include these garden elements and many more: signs, trash containers, alarm boxes, mailboxes, newsstands, kiosks, service elements, telephone stands. If all of these elements are not predicted insofar as possible in the original design plans, incorporated in them, and carefully controlled thereafter, they can destroy carefully planned landscapes. One red oil drum for trash can dominate the visual experience of a large pastoral picnic area.

Kinds of design

The landscape is everything an observer, whether still or in motion, can see. The landscape as a work of individual art is any garden or space designed, developed, and maintained for the private experience of an individual or family, a space not accessible to others either physically or visually. The landscape as a work of collective art is everything beyond this private range: everything seen beyond the confines of private gardens or estates, all borrowed landscapes, all streetscapes, all city, metropolitan, and regional landscapes, and their accumulation in national, continental, and world landscapes. This collective art may be good or bad depending on whether it results from the accidental accumulation of individual and conflicting efforts or from controlled and planned efforts.

Private or residential design

The history of landscape design is largely the history of landscape as a work of private, individual art. Plazas (structural public open spaces not dominated by foliage), throughout Classical, medieval, and Renaissance history, were the concessions of the ruling class to the need for public meeting places, but it was not until Central Park was developed in New York City in the mid-19th century that this need reached the level of designed public green spaces. During most of its history, landscape design was of three kinds: private utilitarian farms and gardens; private gardens in which the enhancement of the quality of living was paramount; and private gardens designed to express the power and benevolence of the ruling or upper classes. The expansion in scale of private gardens beyond the needs of private living led, inexorably, first to the dedication of such spaces to public use and then to the development of public gardens and parks designed for public use.

The private garden, however, has remained the centre for private fantasy and a means of escape from the grinding and difficult world of reality. The most important aspect of the private garden is its seclusion: from the physical world, by means of distance and enclosure; from the social world, by separation and exclusion. Space and greenery are also important. The space may be very small, perhaps a tiny courtyard, and greenery limited to one or two plants, but these make possible that private world of fantasy that may make the difference between sanity and lunacy. The 20th-century mass migration to the suburbs was the latest expression of this need.

Generally, the private garden occupies a space somewhere between 20 feet (6 metres) square and one-quarter of an acre (100 feet square). The forms of private gardens range from the formalism of pure geometry or the artistic representation of natural processes through the variations of standard gardening techniques and the informalism of letting nature take its course to various manifestations of literary, poetic, historic, and subjective concepts.

When housing moves from single-family detached buildings on private lots to higher-density variations—duplexes, semidetached villas, town houses, clusters, condominiums, low- and high-rise apartments—new relationships develop. As population density increases, private design shrinks and public design increases. Somewhere between the extremes of the single-family dwelling with minimum public space and the high-rise apartment with minimum private space, there is an optimum relationship in which real needs can be expressed. Perhaps the best potential lies in town house, cluster house, and condominium developments in which there is a flexible relationship between public and private elements.

Public design

Because of fixation on the notion that the original resource of land and landscape, continuous from sea to shining sea, is best organized for private or public use by gridiron subdivision into innumerable separate parcels, public landscape design begins at the level of single buildings on single lots, with front yards and backyards. The buildings may be government offices, quasi-public companies, or private corporations, but all tend to be designed in terms of public and private spaces, as though they were private residences for the groups involved.

Campus design begins when publicly accessible buildings grow into complexes of two or more, for religious, commercial, industrial, governmental, or educational use. Instead of or in addition to simple front-yard and backyard design, there are more complex systems of spaces between buildings, which vary from courtyards and quadrangles of varying forms and dimensions to passageways connecting them in varying widths and degrees of overhead coverage. The open spaces range in character from paved architectural courtyards and cloisters to open playing fields and parklike spaces. Campus design makes possible the richest, most complex, and rewarding range of relationships between architectural and landscape design. Perhaps the best examples, in which the sequential experience of indoor and outdoor space approaches the maximum, are the religious, educational, and civic complexes of Europe, developed before the idea of gridiron subdivision fragmented environmental design.

In China and Japan there are many highly refined and sophisticated temple, shrine, palace, and castle complexes. There are also many fine examples in the United States of similar institutions that have transcended or resisted subdivision.

In the broader area of urban design, landscape architecture deals with such open-space components as public gardens, parks and playgrounds, plazas, squares, and malls. In these urban spaces, the designer attempts to meet the need for community, for play and recreation, for refreshment and relaxation, for individual withdrawal in a gregarious atmosphere.

Towns, cities, and metropolitan areas may be said to have three basic components: buildings, designed by architects or builders; open spaces, designed by landscape architects or technicians; and circulation-utility corridors—street, highway, railway, and rapid-transit systems—which are usually planned and designed by engineers.

The basic structure of urban areas consists of the open spaces together with corridors comprising a total open-space system, defined by and connecting the buildings. The corridors have usually been considered merely a utilitarian framework, connecting and servicing buildings and quality open spaces, channelling traffic and utilities throughout urban areas, and connecting them with the open country around. Modern urban thinking has begun to go beyond this concept, to see the total open-space system as the major qualitative structure of the city, which, when viewed in conjunction with overall building design, is seen to establish the city's basic character.

From this point of view the role of landscape architecture, once limited to tasteful planting of corridors designed by engineers, begins to expand. Some urban planners would expand it even further, believing that open-space corridors should be designed throughout primarily as social spaces for people and only secondarily as utilitarian passages for vehicles.

Commemorative sites—cemeteries, historic spots, battlefields—are important because they memorialize and symbolize important events in personal, local, national, or world history. Wherever they occur, these sites or areas are marked with stone or bronze memorials and often dramatized with more elaborate developments.

The designs tend to follow traditional and conservative precedents, often impressive but seldom imaginative. It is still difficult to equal Asplund's Forest Crematorium (1940) in Stockholm or the Fosse Ardeatine memorial in Rome.

GARRETT ECKBO

HISTORICAL DEVELOPMENT

Western

The earliest surviving detailed garden plan, dating from about 1400 BCE, is of a garden belonging to an Egyptian high court official at Thebes. The main entrance is aligned on a pergola (trellis-bordered) walk of vines leading directly to the dwelling. The rest of the garden is laid out with tree-lined avenues, four rectangular ponds containing waterfowl, and two garden pavilions. Although rigidly symmetrical, the garden is divided into self-contained walled enclosures, so that the symmetry of the whole could not have been apparent to the viewer. Such a highly developed pattern argues a considerable incubation period, and it is likely that similar enclosed pleasure gardens had been designed as early as 2800 BCE.

ASSYRIAN, BABYLONIAN, AND PERSIAN

The gardens of Assyria, Babylon, and Persia were of three kinds: large, enclosed game reserves, like the garden of Eden described in the Hebrew Bible (Old Testament); pleasure gardens, which were essentially places where shade and cool water could be privately enjoyed; and sacred enclosures rising in man-made terraces, planted with trees and shrubs, forming an artificial hill such as the Hanging Gardens of Babylon.

GREEK AND HELLENISTIC

The urban life of ancient Greece led to houses built around central private courtyards. Lined with colonnades that gave access to the rooms of the house, the courtyard, or peristyle, was open to the sky and insulated from the street. In the peristyle was a garden consisting of a water supply and potted plants. Much of life, however, was lived in public. The sports grounds, where exercise was taken, became popular gathering places and developed into the original academy and lyceum, which included the exercise ground, seats for spectators, porticoes for bad weather, statues of honored athletes, and groves of shade trees. These public recreation grounds set the type for the later Classical Roman villa garden and the 19th-century European public park. A third type of Greek garden was the sacred landscape, such as the Vale of Tempe or the mountain sanctuary of Delphi.

The relatively austere Greek taste was transformed in the Hellenistic Age (*c.* 323–30BCE) by the influence of the East. Luxurious pleasure grounds were made, especially at colonies such as Alexandria and Syracuse. These gardens were conspicuously luxurious in their display of precious materials and artificial in their use of hydraulic automata.

ROMAN

Roman gardens derived from the Greek, those in the seaside resorts of Pompeii and Herculaneum (1st century BCE) following the Hellenistic pattern. These small, enclosed town gardens were visually extended by landscapes painted on the walls. Throughout the imperial period, the more ambitious villa gardens flourished in many forms on sites carefully chosen for climate and aspect.

The most elaborate was that of Nero's Golden House, which covered more than 300 acres (120 hectares) in the middle of Rome and included an artificial lake (where the Colosseum now stands) and a pastoral landscape of plowland, vineyard, pasture, and wood. More influential in later times was the vast garden complex of Hadrian's Villa, of which extensive ruins can still be found near Tivoli.

MIDDLE AGES

The barbarian invasions of the 4th and 5th centuries CE destroyed Roman civilization and with it the gardens of western Europe. The Eastern Empire, centred on Constantinople, retained its hold on Greece and much of Asia Minor for another millennium, and Byzantine gardens persisted in the Hellenistic tradition, laying more emphasis on wonder-provoking apparatus than on aesthetic values. A recurrent feature of these gardens was a tree of gold or silver equipped with birds that flapped their wings and sang and branches that sprayed wine or perfume.

ISLAMIC

Beginning in the 7th century, the Arabs progressively captured much of western Asia, Egypt, the whole of the North African coast, and Spain. In the process, they spread features of Persian and Byzantine gardens across the Mediterranean as far as the Iberian Peninsula. Most characteristic of these gardens was the use of water—the ultimate luxury to desert dwellers, who appreciated it not only because it allowed plants to grow but also because it cooled the air and gratified the ear with the sound of its movement. It was commonly used in regularly shaped, often rectangular, pools.

The water was kept moving by simply designed fountains and was fed by narrow canals resembling agricultural irrigation channels. Because water was rarely abundant, the pools were shallow but increased in apparent depth by a blue tile lining.

These pools of water graced Islamic gardens—such as those of the Alhambra in Granada—that resembled the Hellenistic colonnaded courtyard. The gardens provided shade, excluded hot winds, and created the sense of being in a jewelled private world. Water mirroring the sky gave an impression of spaciousness and introduced lightness, brightness, and an air of unreality. In the Moorish Caliphate of Córdoba in Spain, in the valley of the Guadalquivir, there were said to have been 50,000 villas, all of which probably had such garden courts.

The greatest period of garden making in the Islamic world was the 14th century. In the vicinity of the conqueror Timur Lenk's capital ofSamarkand, the names of 11 royal gardens are recorded, and there were probably others belonging to his nobles. Whereas gardens of the Alhambra type were architecturally conceived within the total plan of a building, some of the more extensive Timurid gardens and their derivatives, the Mughal gardens of India, were pleasances of water, meadow, trees, and flowers, in which buildings took a subordinate place. Although these garden buildings were permanent, their subordinate role and the lightness and luxuriating frivolity of their design mark them as heirs of the casually positioned tents seasonally erected in hunting parks. There were also gardens of strictly architectural design—huge walled enclosures with corner towers, a central palace, regularly disposed avenues, and tanks of water. Deer and pheasants were kept in these gardens, which combined the quality of hunting park and of *hortus conclusus*, or closed garden. Trees were planted sometimes in regular quincuncial patterns (one in the middle and one at each corner of a square or rectangle) but more often freely. In all types of Islamic gardens, flowers were lavishly used. Their presence was even simulated in garden carpets and in the woven hangings that were used as temporary screens.

Influential on later Western practice were the parks made by the Saracen emirs of Sicily. The Normans who conquered the Saracens in the 11th century adopted the manner of life of those they had overthrown, and thus the emirs' gardens survived their makers. A large area of the Conca d'Oro, the great natural amphitheatre behind Palermo, was taken up with pleasure grounds—walled enclosures large enough to contain woods and hills, canals, artificial lakes, groves of oranges and lemons, fountains, water stairways, and wild creatures running free.

WESTERN EUROPEAN

In Europe beyond the limits of the Islamic conquest, the destruction of civilized society by the barbarian tribes had been nearly complete, but the physical remains of the past shaped the reviving future: the peristyle gardens of Roman villas became the cloisters of Christian basilicas. Security and leisure existed only in the monastic system, which also preserved some of the traditional skills of cultivation. For some time the only type of garden was the cloister, with its well, herbs, potted plants, and shaded walk. Then secular gardens began to appear, but they were usually of limited extent, confined within the fortifications of a castle and often raised well above ground level on a battlemented turret.

These gardens were rectangular, with the traditional division into four parts by paths, the quarters again subdivided according to the amount of ground available and the convenience of cultivation. At the point of principal intersection was a well, which, when elaborated, became the vertical feature of the garden. Seats—often of turf—were constructed in the walls. Many flowers were grown, but their season was short; after June and often earlier, the beds were flowerless. More extensive and elaborate gardens were rare.

In 13th-century Italy, through the influence of the Holy Roman emperor Frederick II, who had spent much of his youth in Sicily, the example of the Saracen emirs was felt in Apulia and Naples. The *Triumph of Death*, painted by the Florentine artist Andrea Orcagna (Pisa, Campo Santo), shows a garden of considerably greater extent than the cloister or battlement type. Gardens like this existed also in Lombardy, where the court ofGian Galeazzo Visconti, the founder of the great walled park of Pavia, cultivated the arts of civilized life. In describing the Royal Gardens at Naples, the writer and poet Giovanni Boccaccio speaks of statues disposed regularly around a lawn, interspersed with marble seats. Such a garden suggests that Frederick II's classicizing influence extended into the mid-14th century.

Also significant was the garden of Hesdin in Picardy, which became famous throughout France for its automata and water tricks. It was made by a Crusader who, having returned to France by way of Palermo in 1270, no doubt incorporated in his garden what he had seen of Saracenic gardens there and in Syria. Hesdin was an exotic creation without parallel in its northerly location for several centuries.

RENAISSANCE TO MODERN: 15TH TO 20TH CENTURIES

ITALIAN

The increasing prosperity of western Europe and the increasing confidence in humankind's capacity to impose order on the external world was reflected in the gardens of Italy by the mid-15th century. The change began near Florence, where the old medieval enclosures began to open up. The rectangles, which had been dissociated, were now sited one behind the other, thus prolonging the main axis, which was now aligned on the centre of the dwelling. This change inevitably introduced the idea that house and garden were a coherent, complementary whole. And, because villas were increasingly sited for amenity rather than defense, gardens became less enclosed, more susceptible first to visual, then to actual extension.

The unity of house and garden, together with the need for physical adjustment to the sloping sites favoured by Classical precedent, threw the planning of the new Renaissance garden into the hands of architects. Most influential was the garden courtyard designed by Donato Bramante at the Vatican to link the papal palace with the Villa Belvedere; the uneven site and the disparity in bulk of the two buildings was overcome with terraces and stairways. It remained an enclosed garden but one far removed from the earlier cloistral courtyards. The garden of the Belvedere combined the function of an open-air room with that of an outdoor sculpture gallery.

The ingredients of the Renaissance garden thus separately established were united in varying proportions. The typical evolved garden of the period was characterized by some openness of aspect, axial development, a tendency to prolongation, unity of concept between house and garden emphasized by a considerable "built" element of stone, lavish employment of statuary (often in the form of fountains), and the proliferation of such Classical accents as grottoes, nymphaea (Roman buildings with a fountain, plants, and sculpture), urns, and inscriptions. There is no adequate evidence that this type of garden had an exact equivalent in the Classical period, although there is evidence that each of its elements existed.

The variation in style among Italian gardens is considerable and is due to not only the date they were made, the exigencies of the site, and regional variation but also their social function. The scale of the garden compartments at the back of the Villa Gamberaia at Settignano (1610), for example, is small in contrast with the extensive view over Florence from the front and thus suggests intimate use by members of a small household. The more extensive parterregarden (an ornamental garden with paths between the beds) of the Villa Lante at Bagnaia (begun 1564) is designed neither for solitary enjoyment nor for a crowd but for a select, discerning company—as is the garden of the far more splendid Villa Farnese at Caprarola (completed 1587). The most remarkable mid-16th-century garden, that of the Villa d'Este at Tivoli (1550), is situated on a steep slope of the Sabine hills.

The river that plunges down this slope is harnessed to an astonishing variety of fountains, including a "water organ." Although the garden is designed around a central axis, the stream is not used centrally but is led about the garden in order to take maximum advantage of its force. Unlike the less copious stream of the Villa Lante garden, which quietly emphasizes the central axis, the Tivoli stream is ostentatious. The Villa d'Este is, in fact, a spectacular permanent theatricalperformance meant to astonish and impress the multitude. A different impression is given by the Boboli Gardens of the Pitti Palace at Florence (1550). Though, like the Villa d'Este gardens, they were designed for a crowd—specifically, for state functions—they are not dramatic in themselves. Unless used ceremonially, they are lifeless and arid. The ruined garden associated with, though detached from, the Orsini Castleat Bomarzo is a remarkable aberration probably influenced by accounts of visits to the Far East by a locally born traveller, Biagio Sinibaldi. Its original layout consisted of a grove in which were concealed the stone giants and strange monsters that now astonish visitors.

Flowers were extensively used in most Italian gardens, but because of the shortness of their season they could not be the principal feature. Beds were divided into decorative geometric compartments by trimmed herbs, rosemary, lavender, or box. In general, more emphasis was given to evergreens; ilex, cypress, laurel, and ivy gave shade and were an enduring contrast to stonework.

17TH- AND 18TH-CENTURY FRENCH

The French invasions of Italy in the last quarter of the 16th and first quarter of the 17th centuries introduced to France the idioms of the Italian garden. The first garden coordinated with a dwelling appeared at the château of Anet (1547–56) and was designed by the architect Philibert Delorme, but, despite its evident sophistication, it remained an inward-looking, essentially medieval garden. The first sign of prolongation and calculated extension of vision beyond the garden proper appeared in the grounds of Dampierre. There the moat that formerly surrounded French castles became an ornamental body of water on one side and a decorative canal on the other. Both aspects of the new garden design—coordination with the dwelling and extension along a central axis—were united at the château of Richelieu (1631) and later at Vaux-le-Vicomte (completed 1661), the château of Nicolas Fouquet, the minister of finance. On Fouquet's fall in the mid-17th century, his team of artists—which included the landscape designer André Le Nôtre—was taken over by the young Louis XIV, and the gardens of Versailles were begun.

The French version of the Italian garden was created in the plain of north France, which largely conditioned the manner of its development. The array of steep terraces linked by stairways, which characterized the Villa d'Este and many others, was predominant in France only at Saint-Germain-en-Laye, where the steep site permitted it. Elsewhere, grandeur on the scale that competitive pride demanded was achieved by extraordinary extension: an axial development suggesting a domain coextensive with the world. The French 17th-century garden, a manifestation ofBaroque taste, required variety as well as unlimited vista and achieved it with fountains, parterres, and lesser gardens disposed within the boscages (wooded enclosures) that flanked the central axis. These hidden gardens were the successors of the *giardini segreti* of the Italians but had a different function; they were not retreats for private contemplation or intimate conversation but the setting for ingenious theatrical entr'actes. Distinctively French was the unified and elaborate treatment of the compartmentalized garden beds, which the Italians had made in a variety of forms. These *compartiments de broderie* were arabesques, sometimes of box edging and flowers but more often of coloured stones and sand. The Persians had copied their flower gardens on carpets and taken them indoors, but the French laid out their grounds in the form of carpets. The French garden was marked by a ruthlessly logical extension of practices that had been empirically evolved in Italy.

French cultural dominance of Europe in the early 18th century led to an almost universal adoption of Versailles as the model for palatial gardens. Even at Naples, where the gardens of Poggio Reale had astonished the invading French in the late 15th century, a vast layout inspired by the axial extent of Versailles was developed at Caserta, and, as far away as Peter the Great's Peterhof in Russia, a pseudo-Versailles was laid out by the French gardener Jean-Baptiste-Alexandre Le Blond. Impressive exercises in the same manner were carried out in Germany and Austria. In Holland also, the example of the French garden was irresistible, although local conditions and national temperament led to regional variation. Because Dutch canals were busy highways, they generally flanked gardens rather than constituted the main axis. No luxury in Holland, water was less extravagantly used than in drier, hotter climates. Moreover, fountains were less common because the absence of high ground required that they be power-driven. Because stone was scarce, terraces were usually held by turf banks rather than by retaining walls, and sculpture was often of lead. Another sculpture typical of the Dutch garden was topiary: trees and shrubs were trained, cut, and trimmed into sculptural, ornamental shapes. Social conditions made the extension of a geometric garden easy, for a man-made landscape already existed in the intensively cultivated Netherlands. In Spain, aridity as well as Islamic tradition perpetuated the patio garden, a room of air and shade in the Greek peristyle tradition. Although a famous layout in the French style was made on high ground at La Granja, where the cooler air and ample water made it acceptable, the Classical extension garden remained basically alien to the Iberian Peninsula.

17TH- AND 18TH-CENTURY ENGLISH

The Italian pronouncement that "things planted should reflect the shape of things built" had ensured that gardens were essentially open-air buildings and the making of them the province of architects. Before the 18th century, geometric regularity had been applied in great details of design and in small. England was committed to a version of the French geometric extension garden but with an emphasis on English grass lawns and gravel walks. Whereas the typical French vista was along the main axis, with subordinate vistas at right angles to it, in the two most influential gardens in England, St. James's and Hampton Court, the vistas sprang like the rays of the sun from a semicircle. With the accession of William and Mary (1689–1702), Dutch influence led to widespread use of topiaried yew and box.

In 18th-century England, people became increasingly aware of the natural world. Rather than imposing their man-made geometric order on the natural world, they began to adjust to it. Literary men, notably Alexander Pope and

Joseph Addison, began to question the propriety of trees being carved into artificial shapes as substitutes for masonry and to advocate the restoration of free forms.

The man who led the revolt against the "artificial," symmetrical garden style was the painter and architect William Kent, the factotum of Richard Boyle, 3rd earl of Burlington. Together, Burlington and Kent created at Chiswick House (1734) a garden with a meandering stream and an "irregular" path. As the writer Horatio Walpole put it, Kent's "principle was that nature abhors a straight line." The process of relaxing the garden's architectural discipline advanced with speed. At Stowe, Buckinghamshire, the original enclosed geometrical garden was amended over the years until a totally different, "irregular" formality was achieved. Trees, for example, were allowed to assume their natural forms, and a large expanse of water was redesigned into two irregularly shaped lakes.

The use of the ha-ha, or sunken fence, to create and at the same time conceal the physical division between garden and contiguous park grounds (a division needed to keep grazing animals out of the garden) was a major step in the creation of the new, "natural" garden. Walpole explains the purpose of the visual unification:

> The contiguous ground of the park without the sunk fence was to be harmonized with the lawn within; and the garden in its turn was to be set free from its prime regularity, that it might assort with the wilder country without.

The face of the "country without" was altered by the rage that afflicted the English nobility for planting vast areas of trees. Much of England was covered with new parks, traversed by rides and avenues that primarily were conceived as visual extensions of the garden paths. The unification of park and garden was virtually completed by Lancelot ("Capability") Brown (1715–83) by the simple expedient of making the garden into a park. "Capability" (so-called because he always spoke of a place as having "capabilities of improvement") developed the current aesthetic that an undulating line was "natural" and that it was the "line of beauty" by using little statuary and few buildings and concentrating on designing landscapes according to nature's harmonies and gradients. His landscapes consist of expanses of grass, irregularly shaped bodies of water, and trees placed singly and in clumps.

Although the adherents of the new English school of garden design were in agreement in their abhorrence of the straight, Classical line and the geometrically ordered garden, they did not agree on what the natural garden should be. Unlike Brown, for example, the taste for the romantic and the literary led many to seek inspiration in the dramatic and the bizarre, in the remote past, and in remote, exotic places.

The Brownian style was strongly challenged, for example, by the "Picturesque" school, led by Sir Uvedale Price and the artist-parson William Gilpin, who argued, quite correctly, that the "naturalism" of the Brownians was no less unnatural than the geometric regularity of Le Nôtre's Versailles and that sudden declivities, rocky chasms, and rotting tree trunks (all deliberately designed) were more proper for the natural garden than were enormous undulating meadows accented with tight clumps of thickly planted trees. Another school of opinion created what might be called the English garden of poetic bric-a-brac. The aim in this garden was to create an air of accident and surprise and to arouse varied sensations (solemnity, sublimity, terror) in the viewer—sensations evoked by associations with the remote in time and space. Wandering through the grounds, one came upon Classical statues, urns, and temples; Gothic ruins, ivy-covered and inhabited by owls; or Chinese pagodas and bridges. After Horatio Walpole recorded the first appearance of chinoiserie at Wroxton in 1753 (a garden no doubt laid out some years before), "Chinese" and Gothic details were featured, together with Classical temples, in most fashionable grounds.

By 1760 the enthusiasm for this style had diminished in England, but in continental Europe the poetic bric-a-brac garden (*le jardin anglo-chinois*, or *le jardin anglais*, as the French called it) was almost as widely emulated as Versailles had been. In Italy, for example, Renaissance gardens were destroyed to make way for the new fashion, as at the Villa Mansi near Lucca. In France the sculpted group *Apollo Tended by the Nymphs* was removed from the Classical Grotto of Thetis on the terrace of Versailles to a secluded boscage garden, where it was housed under ornamental "Turkish" tents; eventually it was moved from there to a simulated rocky cavern in the *jardin anglais* of the Petit Trianon. The *jardin anglais* was to be found even at Queluz in Portugal and in the Potsdam garden of Frederick the Great of Prussia.

19TH CENTURY

Increasing world trade and travel brought to late 18th-century Europe a flood of exotic plants whose period of flowering greatly extended the potential season of theflower garden. Although the emphasis in Italian Renaissance gardens, in the Classical Baroque gardens of France, in the lawns and gravelled walks of 17th-century England, and in the Brownian park garden was upon design, they had rarely been totally without flowers. In most gardens flowers were grown, sometimes in great numbers and variety, but flower gardens in the modern sense were limited to cottages, to small town gardens, and to relatively small enclosures within larger gardens. The accessibility of new plants, together with avidity for new experience and a high-minded concern with natural science, not only gave renewed life to the flower garden but was the first step toward the evolution of the garden from work of art to museum of plants. A compromise between the new flower garden and the Brownian park was effected by Humphry Repton.

He was largely responsible for popularizing the open terrace overlooking the park, which frankly admitted the different functions of park and garden and also emphasized their stylistic disharmony. The plant collectors' garden, or "gardenesque" style, was most strongly advanced by J.C. Loudon in the mid-19th century. Loudon urged that garden making be taken out of the hands of the architect, the painter, and the cultivated dilettante and left to the professional plantsman.

The undiscerning use of the new palette that importation and plant breeding had made available was so patently an aesthetic disaster that by the end of the 19th century attempts were made to break its hold. The architect Sir Reginald Blomfieldadvocated a return to the formal garden, but to this, insofar as it required dressed stonework, there were economic objections. More successful and more in tune with the escapist needs of the increasing number of urban dwellers were the teaching and practice of William Robinson, who attacked both the old ceremonial garden and the collectors' garden with equal vigour and preached that botany was a science, but gardening was an art. Under his leadership a more critical awareness was brought to the planning and planting of gardens. His own garden at Gravetye Manor demonstrated that plants look best where they grow best and that they should be allowed to develop their natural forms. Adapting Robinson's principles, Gertrude Jekyll applied the cult of free forms over a substructure of concealed architectural regularity, bringing the art of the flower garden to its highest point.

In North America, where for a long time most men were preoccupied with making a world, not a garden, ornamental gardens were slow to take hold. In the gardens that did exist, the rectilinear style popular in late 17th- and early 18th-century Europe persisted well into the 18th century—perhaps because it met man's psychological need to feel he could master a world that was still largely untamed. The town gardens of Williamsburg (begun in 1698) were typical of the Anglo-Dutch urban gardens that were being attacked everywhere in 18th-century Europe except Holland. And Belmont, in Pennsylvania, was laid out as late as the 1870s with mazes, topiary, and statues, in a style that would have been popular in England about two centuries before.

Although garden improvers set up in business in the United States, there is no evidence that they prospered until the 19th century, when one hears of André Parmentier, a Belgian, who worked on Hosack's estate at Hyde Park and then of A.J. Downing, a successful protagonist of the gardenesque, who was succeeded byCalvert Vaux and Frederick Law Olmsted (the latter the originator of the title and profession of landscape architect), the planners of Central Park (begun 1857) in New York City and of public parks throughout the country.

The eclecticism of the 19th century was universal in the Western world. Besides the gardens that were fundamentally Reptonian—that is, an attempted compromise between the Brownian park garden and the Loudonian flower garden—gardens of almost every conceivable style were copied; designing teams such as Sir Charles Barry, the architect, and William Eden Nesfield, the painter, in England, for example, produced Italianate parterres as well as winding paths through thickets.

MODERN

A sense of history still played a part in 20th-century gardening. The desire to maintain and reproduce old gardens, such as the reconstruction of the 16th-century gardens of Villandry in France and the colonial gardens of Williamsburg in the United States, was not peculiarly modern (similar things were done in the 19th century), but, as humans increasingly need the reassurance of the past, the impulse may well continue. Attempts to create a distinctive modern idiom are rare. Gardens large by modern standards are still made, in styles that vary from a version of the grand early 18th-century manner at Anglesey Abbey in Cambridgeshire to an inflated Jekyllism crossed with gardenesque at Bodnant near Conway. An air either of controlled wilderness or of slightly run-to-seed orderliness is preferred. Modern public gardens, which have evolved from the large private gardens of the past, seek instant popular applause for the quantity and brightness of their flowers. In Brazil Roberto Burle Marx used tropical materials to give an air of contemporaneity to traditional modes of design. Gardens frequently reflect Japanese influence, particularly in America.

Most characteristic of the 20th century was functional planning, in which landscape architects concentrated upon the arrangement of open spaces surrounding factories, offices, communal dwellings, and arterial roads. The aim of such planning was to provide, at best, a satisfactory setting for the practical aspects of living. It was gardening only in the negative, "tidying up" sense, with little concern for the traditional garden purpose of awakening delight. So starved was the spirit of those living in heavily populated regions, however, that demands grew more insistent for gardening in the positive sense—for environmental planning with a chief goal not of facilitating economic activities but of refreshing the spirit.

Non-Western

CHINESE

Western gardens for many centuries were architectural, functioning as open-air rooms and demonstrating the Western insistence on physical control of the environment. Because of a different philosophical approach, Eastern gardens are of a totally different type.

China—which is to Eastern civilization what Egypt, Greece, and Rome are to Western—practiced at the beginning of its history an animist form of religion. The sky, mountains, seas, rivers, and rocks were thought to be the materialization of spirits who were regarded as fellow inhabitants in a crowded world. Such a belief emphasized the importance of good manners toward the world of nature as well as toward other individuals. Against this background, the Chinese philosopher Laozi taught the quietist philosophy of Daoism, which held that one should integrate oneself with the rhythms of life, Confucius preached moderation as a means of attaining spiritual calm, and the teaching of Buddha elevated the attainment of calm to a mystical plane.

Such a history of thought led the Chinese to take keen pleasure in the calm landscape of the remote countryside. Because of the physical difficulty of frequent visits to the sources of such delight, the Chinese recorded them in landscape paintings and made three-dimensional imitations of them near at hand. Their gardens were therefore representational, sometimes direct but more often by substitution, making use of similar means to recreate the emotions that choice natural landscapes evoked. The kind of landscape that appealed was generally of a balanced sort; for the Chinese had discovered the principle ofcomplementary forms, of male and female, of upright and recumbent, rough and smooth, mountain and plain, rocks and water, from which the classic harmonies were created. The principle of scroll painting, whereby the landscape is exposed not in one but in a continual succession of views, was applied also in gardens, and grounds were arranged so that one passed pleasantly from viewpoint to viewpoint, each calculated to give a different pleasure appropriate to its situation. A refined and expectant aestheticism, which their philosophy had inculcated, taught the Chinese to ignore nothing that would prepare the mind for the reception of such experiences, and every turn of path and slope of ground was carefully calculated to induce the suitable attitude. As the garden was in effect a complex of linked, related, but distinct sensations, seats and shelters were situated at chosen spots so that the pleasures that had been meticulously prepared for could be quietly savoured. Kiosks and pavilions were built at places where the dawn could best be watched or where the moonlight shone on the water or where autumn foliage was seen to advantage or where the wind made music in the bamboos. Such gardens were intended not for displays of wealth and magnificence to impress the multitude but for the delectation of the owner, who felt his own character enhanced by his capacity for refined sensation and sensitive perception and who chose friends to share these pleasures with the same discernment as he had exercised in planning his garden.

Based on natural scenery, Chinese gardens avoided symmetry. Rather than dominating the landscape, the many buildings in the garden "grew up" as the land dictated. A fanciful variety of design, curving roof lines, and absence of walls on one or on all sides brought these structures into harmony with the trees around them. Sometimes they were given the rustic representational character of a fisherman's hut or hermit's retreat. Bridges were often copied from the most primitive rough timber or stone-slab raised pathways. Rocks gathered from great distances became a universal decorative feature, and a high connoisseurship developed in connection with their colour, shape, and placement.

Although the troubled 20th century largely destroyed the old gardens, paintings and detailed descriptions of them dating from the Song dynasty (960–1279 CE) reveal a remarkable historical consistency. Nearly all the characteristic features of the classic Chinese garden—man-made hills, carefully chosen and placed rocks, meanders and cascades of water, the island and the bridge—were present from the earliest times.

Chinese gardens were made known to the West by Marco Polo, who described the palace grounds of the last Song emperors, during whose reign the arts were at their most refined. Other accounts reached Europe from time to time but had little immediate effect except at Bomarzo, the Mannerist Italian garden that had no successors. In the 17th century the English diplomat and essayist Sir William Temple, sufficiently familiar with travelers' tales to describe the Chinese principle of irregularity and hidden symmetry, helped prepare the English mind for the revolution in garden design of the second quarter of the 18th century. Chineseexample was not the sole or the most important source of the new English garden, but the account of Father Attiret, a Jesuit at the Manchu (Qing) court, published in France in 1747 and in England five years later, promoted the use of Chineseornament in such gardens as Kew and Wroxton and hastened the "irregularizing" of grounds. The famous *Dissertation on Oriental Gardening* by the English architect Sir William Chambers (1772) was a fanciful account intended to further the current revolt in England against the almost universal Brownian park garden.

Influence of the West on Chinese gardens was slight. Elaborate fountain works, Baroque garden pavilions, and mazes—all of which the Jesuits made for the imperial garden at Yuanmingyuan ("Garden of Pure Light")—took no root in Chinese culture. Not until the 20th century did European regularity occasionally become evident near the Chinese dwelling; at the same time, improved Western hybrids of plant species that had originated in the East appeared in China.

JAPANESE

Chinese culture permeated East Asia and, by way of Korea, infiltrated Japan. By the year 1000 CE Japan was already developing a distinctive national art best described as a stylized, ritualistic version of the Chinese. The typical early Japanese garden lay to the south of the dwelling and consisted of a narrow pond or lake orientated through its longer axis and containing an island. At the north end of the pond was an artificial hill from which a secondary stream descended in a cascade. These stereotyped gardens of the Heian period (794–1185 CE) show by their carefulreproduction of magical detail that they derive from a single prototype—certainly Chinese. Variation entered only through the individual particularities of the site and the detailed handling of stones and trees.

Creativity began to replace imitation in the Kamakura period (1192–1333). Although there were many subsidiary styles, gardens were broadly classified, according to terrain, as either hill or flat. The hill garden, consisting of hills and ponds, came to be associated with Mount Fuji, the mountain of ideal form. The flat garden represented a surface of water—lake or sea—with its adjacent shores and islands. Since the scale was so small—a heap of earth 30 feet (9 metres) high representing a mountain, a half-acre (0.2-hectare) pond an arm of the sea—the intention was to reproduce the spirit rather than the features of the chosen landscape. Association and symbolismthus played a major role in the creation and appreciation of these gardens.

The scaling down of landscapes to garden size was logically continued to the point where miniature gardens were made in trays as small as a foot square containing lakes, streams, islands, hills, bridges, garden houses, and real trees painstakingly cultivated to an appropriate scale. These small, portable gardens reflected the extreme of the picturesque tradition of Eastern gardening.

Two characteristic Japanese styles are the abstract garden and the tea garden. The most famous example of the former is the garden of the Ryôan-ji in Kyôto, where an area about the size of a tennis court is covered with raked sand and set with 15 stones divided into five groups. If anything is represented here, it is some rocky islets in a sea, but the appeal of the garden lies essentially in the charm of its relationships. The Japanese tea garden grew out of an esoteric ritual originated in China and connected with the taking of tea. The tea cult, which flourished from the 14th to the end of the 16th century, was calculated to instill humility, restraint, sensibility, and other cognate virtues. The gardens through which the guests approached the teahouse were governed by severe rules of design intended to create an appropriate spiritual atmosphere, such as the "lonely precincts of a secluded mountain shrine" or "a landscape in clouded moonlight, with a half-gloom between the trees" or any mood "in harmony with the spirit of tea." Even the precise number and arrangement of nails in the teahouse door were specified.

The Japanese fondness for systematization led them to classify garden treatment as well as subject. Three standard treatments were recognized: the elaborate, the moderate, and the modest. Once the degree of finish was determined, certain rules were followed to preserve consistency. The Daoist doctrine of complementary forms was at the root of much Japanese design, but the cult of stones is also central to Japanese gardening. The nine stones, five standing and four recumbent, used in Buddhist gardens weresymbols of the nine spirits of the Buddhist pantheon; the shapes and postures chosen were presumed to have a relationship with the character and history of the persons represented. Sacred associations played a part in profane gardens as well. It was regarded as inauspicious, for example, if three stones—the Guardian Stone, the Stone of Adoration, and the Stone of the Two Deities (or the Stone of Completeness)—were not present. In addition to the sacred symbols, a whole armoury of poetic associations and symbols grew up, and stones, according to their shape and use, acquired such names as Torrent-Breaking Stone, Recumbent Ox Stone, Propitious Cloud Stone, and Seagull-Resting Stone. Beyond what they represented, stones were part of an aesthetic design and had to be placed so that their positions appeared natural and their relationships harmonious. The concentration of the interest on such detail as the shape of a rock or the moss on a stone lantern led at times to an overemphatic picturesqueness and an accumulation of minor features that, to Western eyes accustomed to a more general survey, may seem cluttered and restless. Nevertheless, Japanese gardening has had and continues to have an influence on the gardens of the West, particularly in the United States. The influence appears not so much in direct imitation of Japanese themes as in the selection and presentation of detail.

INDIAN

The influence of Chinese culture throughout the East was such that other indigenous cultures usually succumbed to it, but India was an exception. Western garden styles were introduced into northern India first through contact with Iranian culture, then by the invasion of Alexander the Great and the subsequent Hellenistic influence, and, finally, by the invading Mughals, who introduced the Islamic garden.

In southern India and in Sri Lanka elaborate gardens existed before the birth of theBuddha (*c.* 6th–4th century BCE). Beneath a tree in such a garden—containing baths, lotus-covered pools, trees, and beds of flowers—the Buddha himself was said to have been born. Anciently worshipped by the Hindus, trees thus acquired an additional sanctity. Buddhist temples were associated with gardens whose purpose was to promote contemplation and whose preferred sites were therefore away from cities.

AFRICAN, OCEANIC, AND PRE-COLUMBIAN

The African cultures beyond European and Asiatic influence did not evolve pleasure gardens, although in their more-settled societies a beginning had perhaps been made. Nor is more than a love of flowers and a casual cultivation of decorative plants recorded of the Oceanic peoples. But of the Aztecs of Mexico and the Incas of Peru, the conquistadores reported elaborate gardens with terraced hills, groves, fountains, and ornamental ponds that were essentially royal pleasure grounds, reflecting a need for private solace and public display not unlike contemporary gardens in the West.

English landscape garden

The English landscape garden, also called English landscape park or simply the English garden (French: *Jardin à l'anglaise*,Italian: *Giardino all'inglese*, German: *Englischer Landschaftsgarten*, Portuguese: *Jardim inglês*, Spanish: *Jardín inglés*), is a style of "landscape" garden which emerged in England in the early 18th century, and spread across Europe, replacing the more formal, symmetrical *jardin à la française* of the 17th century as the principal gardening style of Europe. The English garden presented an idealized view of nature. It drew inspiration from paintings of landscapes by Claude Lorraine and Nicolas Poussin, and, in the Anglo-Chinese garden, from the classic Chinese gardens of the East, which had recently been described by European travellers. The English garden usually included a lake, sweeps of gently rolling lawns set against groves of trees, and recreations of classical temples, Gothic ruins, bridges, and other picturesque architecture, designed to recreate an idyllic pastoral landscape. The work ofLancelot "Capability" Brown was particularly influential. By the end of the 18th century the English garden was being imitated by theFrench landscape garden, and as far away as St. Petersburg, Russia, in Pavlovsk, the gardens of the future Emperor Paul. It also had a major influence on the form of the public parks and gardens which appeared around the world in the 19th century.

History of the English landscape garden

Castle Howard (1699-1712), a predecessor of the English garden modelled on the gardens of Versailles.

The predecessors of the landscape garden in England were the great parks created by Sir John Vanbrugh (1664–1726) andNicholas Hawksmoor at Castle Howard (1699–1712), Blenheim Palace (1705–1722), and the Claremont Landscape Garden atClaremont House (1715–1727). These parks featured vast lawns, woods, and pieces of architecture, such as the classical mausoleum designed by Hawksmoor at Castle Howard. At the center of the composition was the house, behind which were formal and symmetrical gardens in the style of the garden *à la française*, with ornate carpets of floral designs and walls of hedges, decorated with statues and fountains. These gardens, modelled after the gardens of Versailles, were designed to impress visitors with their size and grandeur.

William Kent and Charles Bridgeman

The new style that became known as the English garden was invented by landscape designers William Kent and Charles Bridgeman, working for wealthy patrons, including Richard Temple, 1st Viscount Cobham, Richard Boyle, 3rd Earl of Burlington, and banker Henry Hoare; men who had large country estates, were members of the anti-royalist Whig Party, had classical educations, were patrons of the arts, and had taken theGrand Tour to Italy, where they had seen the Roman ruins and Italian landscapes they reproduced in their gardens.

William Kent (1685–1748) was an architect, painter and furniture designer who introduced Palladian style architecture to England. Kent's inspiration came from Palladio's buildings in the Veneto and the landscapes and ruins around Rome—he lived in Italy from 1709 to 1719, and brought back many drawings of antique architecture and landscapes. His gardens were designed to complement the Palladian architecture of the houses he built.

Charles Bridgeman (1690–1738) was the son of a gardener and an experienced horticulturist, who became the Royal Gardener for Queen Anne and Prince George of Denmark, responsible for tending and redesigning the royal gardens at Windsor, Kensington Palace [1], Hampton Court, St. James's Park and Hyde Park. He collaborated with Kent on several major gardens, providing the botanical expertise which allowed Kent to realize his architectural visions.

Chiswick House

Ionic Temple at Chiswick House

Kent created one of the first true English landscape gardens at Chiswick House for Richard Boyle, 3rd Earl of Burlington. The first gardens that he laid out between 1724 and 1733 had many formal elements of a Garden à la française, including alleys forming a trident and canals, but they also featured something novel: a picturesque recreation of an Ionic temple set in a theatre of trees. Between 1733 and 1736, he redesigned the garden, adding lawns sloping down to the edge of the river and a small cascade. For the first time the form of a garden was inspired not by architecture, but by an idealized version of nature.

Rousham

Rousham House in Oxfordshire is considered by some as the most accomplished and significant of William Kent's work. The patron was General

Dormer, who commissioned Bridgeman to begin the garden in 1727, then brought in Kent to recreate it in 1737. Bridgeman had built a series of gardens, including a grotto of Venus, on the slope along the river Cherwell, connected by straight alleys. Kent turned the alleys into winding paths, built a gently turning stream, used the natural landscape features and slopes, and created a series of views and tableaus decorated with allegorical statues of Apollo, a wounded gladiator, a lion attacking a horse, and other subjects. He placed "eye-catchers," pieces of classical architecture, to decorate the landscape, and made use of the "ha-ha", a concealed ditch that kept grazing animals out of the garden while giving an uninterrupted vista from within. Finally, he added cascades modelled on those of the garden of Aldobrandini and Pratolino in Italy, to add movement and drama.

Stowe House

Stowe, in Buckinghamshire, (1730–1738), was an even more radical departure from the formal French garden. In the early 18th century, Richard Temple, 1st Viscount Cobham, had commissioned Charles Bridgeman to design a formal garden, with architectural decorations by John Vanbrugh. Bridgeman's design included an octagonal lake and a Rotunda (1720–21) designed by Vanbrugh.

In the 1730s, William Kent and James Gibbs were appointed to work with Bridgeman, who died in 1738. Kent remade the lake in a more natural shape, and created a new kind of garden, which took visitors on a tour of picturesque landscapes. It eventually included a Palladian bridge (1738); a Temple of Venus (1731), in the form of a Palladian villa; a Temple of Ancient Virtues (1737), with statues of famous Greeks and Romans; a Temple of British Worthies (1734–1735), with statues of British heroes; and a Temple of Modern Virtues, which was deliberately left in ruins, which contained a headless statue of Robert Walpole, Cobham's political rival.

The garden attracted visitors from all over Europe, including Jean-Jacques Rousseau. It became the inspiration for landscape gardens in Britain and on the Continent.

Stourhead

Stourhead, in Wiltshire (1741–80), created by banker Henry Hoare, was one of the first 'picturesque' gardens, inspired to resemble the paintings of Claude Lorrain. Hoare had travelled to Italy on the Grand Tour and had returned with a painting by Claude Lorrain. Hoare dammed a stream on his estate, created a lake, and surrounded the lake with landscapes and architectural constructions representing the different steps of the journey of Aeneas in the Aeneid by Virgil.

THE GREAT AGE OF THE ENGLISH GARDEN

Capability Brown

The most influential figure in the later development of the English landscape garden was Lancelot "Capability" Brown (1716–1783) who began his career in 1740 as a gardener at Stowe under Charles Bridgeman, then succeeded William Kent in 1748.

Brown's contribution was to simplify the garden by eliminating geometric structures, alleys, and parterres near the house and replacing them with rolling lawns and extensive views out to isolated groups of trees, making the landscape seem even larger. "He sought to create an ideal landscape out of the English countryside." He created artificial lakes and used dams and canals to transform streams or springs into the illusion that a river flowed through the garden.

He compared his own role as a garden designer to that of a poet or composer. "Here I put a comma, there, when it's necessary to cut the view, I put a parenthesis; there I end it with a period and start on another theme."

Brown designed 170 gardens. The most important were:

- Petworth (West Sussex) in 1752;
- Chatsworth (Derbyshire) in 1761;
- Bowood (Wiltshire) in 1763;
- Blenheim Palace (Oxfordshire) in 1764.

Humphry Repton

Humphry Repton (21 April 1752 – 24 March 1818) was the last great English landscape designer of the eighteenth century, often regarded as the successor to Capability Brown. Repton hit upon the idea of becoming a "landscape gardener" (a term he himself coined) after failing at various ventures and, sensing an opportunity after Brown's death, was ambitious to fill the gap and sent circulars round his contacts in the upper classes advertising his services. To help clients visualize his designs, Repton produced 'Red Books' (so called for their binding) with explanatory text and watercolors with a system of overlays to show 'before' and 'after' views.

In 1794 Richard Payne Knight and Uvedale Price simultaneously published vicious attacks on the 'meagre genius of the bare and bald', criticizing Brown's smooth, serpentine curves as bland and unnatural and championing rugged and intricate designs, composed according to 'picturesque theory' that designed landscapes should be composed like landscape paintings, with a foreground, a middle ground and a background. Early in his career, Repton defended Brown's reputation during the 'picturesque controversy'. However, as his career progressed Repton came to apply picturesque theory to the practice of landscape design. He believed that the foreground should be the realm of art (with formal geometry and ornamental planting), that the middle ground should have a parkland character of the type created by Brown and that the background should have a wild and 'natural' character. Repton re-introduced formal terraces, balustrades, trellis work and flower gardens around the house in a way that became common practice in the nineteenth century.

Repton published four major books on garden design: *Sketches and Hints on Landscape Gardening* (1795), *Observations on the Theory and Practice of Landscape Gardening* (1803), *An Inquiry into the Changes of Taste in Landscape Gardening* (1806) and*Fragments on the Theory and Practice of Landscape Gardening* (1816). These drew on material and techniques used in the Red Books. These works greatly influenced other landscape-designers including John Claudius Loudon, John Nash, Jean Charles Adolphe Alphand, Hermann Ludwig Heinrich Pückler-Muskau and Frederick Law Olmsted.

The Anglo-Chinese garden

Fig. The Kew Gardens Pagoda at the Royal Botanic Gardens at Kew,London (1761)

The Far East inspired the origins of the English Garden via Holland. In 1685, the English diplomat in The Hague and writer Sir William Temple wrote an essay Upon the garden of Epicurus (published in 1690), which contrasted European theories of symmetrical gardens with asymmetrical compositions from China, for which he introduced the Japanese term *sharawadgi*. Temple had never visited the Far East, but he was in contact with the Dutch and their discourse on irregularity in design, had spoken to a merchant who had been in the Far East for a long time, and read the works of European travellers there.

He noted that Chinese gardens avoided formal rows of trees and flower beds, and instead placed trees, plants, and other garden features in irregular ways to strike the eye and create beautiful compositions, with an understatement criticizing the formal compositions of the gardens at the Palace of Versailles of Louis XIV of France.His observations on the Chinese garden were cited by the essayist Joseph Addison in an essay in 1712, who used them to attack the English gardeners who, instead of imitating nature, tried to make their gardens in the French style, as far from nature as possible.

The novelty and exoticism of Chinese art and architecture in Europe led in 1738 to the construction of the first Chinese house in an English garden, in the garden of Stowe House. The style became even more popular thanks to William Chambers (1723–1796), who lived in China from 1745 to 1747, and wrote a book, *The Drawings, buildings, furniture, habits, machines and utensils of the Chinese*, published in 1757. In 1761 he built a Chinese pagoda, house and garden in Kew, London, as part of Kew Gardens, a park with gardens and architecture symbolizing all parts of the world and all architectural styles. Thereafter Chinese pagodas began to appear in other English gardens, then in France and elsewhere on the continent. French and other European observers coined the term *Jardin Anglo-Chinois* (Anglo-Chinese garden) for this style of garden.

The gothic revival influence on English gardens

In the 1750s, classical architecture and Chinese architecture were joined by gothic revival ruins in English gardens. This was largely the result of Horace Walpole, who introduced gothic revival features into his house and garden at Strawberry Hill in Twickenham.

At Stowe, Capability Brown followed the new fashion between 1740 and 1753 by adding a new section to the park, called Hawkwelle Hill or the gothic promenade, with a gothic revival building.

The English garden spreads to the continent

The English Grounds of Wörlitz were one of the largest English parks in 18th-century Europe.

Descriptions of English gardens were first brought to France by the Abbé Le Blanc, who published accounts of his voyage in 1745 and 1751. A treatise on the English garden, *Observations on Modern Gardening*, written by Thomas Whately and published in London in 1770, was translated into French in 1771. After the end of the Seven Years' War in 1763, French noblemen were able to voyage to England and see the gardens for themselves, and the style began to be adapted in French gardens. The new style also had the advantage of requiring fewer gardeners, and was easier to maintain, than the French garden.

One of the first English gardens on the continent was at Ermenonville, in France, built by marquis René Louis de Girardin from 1763 to 1776 and based on the ideals of Jean Jacques Rousseau, who was buried within the park. Rousseau and the garden's founder had visited Stowe a few years earlier. Other early examples were the Désert de Retz, Yvelines (1774–1782); the Gardens of the Château de Bagatelle, in the Bois de Boulogne, west of Paris (1777–1784); The Folie Saint James, in Neuilly-sur-Seine, (1777–1780); and theChâteau de Méréville, in the Essonne department, (1784–1786). Even at Versailles, the home of the most classical of all French gardens, a small English landscape park with a Roman temple was built by the Petit Trianon and a mock village, the Hameau de la reine, Versailles (1783–1789), was created for Marie Antoinette.

The new style also spread to Germany. The central English Grounds of Wörlitz, in the Principality of Anhalt, was laid out between 1769 and 1773 by Prince Leopold III, based on the models of Claremont, Stourhead and Stowe Landscape Garden. Another notable example was The Englischer Garten in Munich, Germany, created in 1789 by Sir Benjamin Thompson (1753–1814).

In the Netherlands the landscape-architect Lucas Pieters Roodbaard (1782-1851) designed several gardens and parks in this style. The style was introduced to Sweden by Fredrik Magnus Piper.

The style also spread rapidly to Russia, where in 1774 Catherine the Great adapted the new style in the park of her palace at Tsarskoe Selo, complete with a mock Chinese village and a Palladian bridge, modeled after that at Wilton House.

Characteristics of the English garden

The continental European "English garden" is characteristically on a smaller scale and more filled with "eye-catchers" than most English landscape gardens: grottoes, temples, tea-houses, belvederes, pavilions, sham ruins, bridges and statues, though the main ingredients of the landscape gardens in England are sweeps of gently rolling ground and water, against a woodland background with clumps of trees and outlier groves. The name—not used in the United Kingdom, where "landscape garden" serves—differentiates it from the formal baroque design of the garden *à la française*. One of the best-known English gardens in Europe is the Englischer Garten in Munich.

The dominant style was revised in the early 19th century to include more "gardenesque" features, including shrubberieswith gravelled walks, tree plantations to satisfy botanical curiosity, and, most notably, the return of flowers, in skirts of sweeping planted beds. This is the version of the landscape garden most imitated in Europe in the 19th century. The outer areas of the "home park" of English country houses retain their naturalistic shaping. English gardening since the 1840s has been on a more restricted scale, closer and more allied to the residence.

The canonical European *English park* contains a number of Romantic elements. Always present is a pond or small lake with a pier or bridge. Overlooking the pond is a round or hexagonal pavilion, often in the shape of a monopteros, a Roman temple. Sometimes the park also has a "Chinese" pavilion. Other elements include a grotto and imitation ruins.

A second style of English garden, which became popular during the 20th century in France and northern Europe, is the late 19th-century English cottage garden.

Landscape architecture

Landscape architecture is the design of outdoor public areas, landmarks, and structures to achieve environmental, social-behavioral, or aesthetic outcomes. It involves the systematic investigation of existing social, ecological, and soil conditions and processes in the landscape, and the design of interventions that will produce the desired outcome. The scope of the profession includes landscape design; site planning; stormwater management; environmental restoration; parks and recreation planning; visual resource management; green infrastructure planning and provision; and private estateand residence landscape master planning and design; all at varying scales of design, planning and management. A practitioner in the profession of landscape architecture is called a landscape architect.

Definition

Landscape architecture is a multi-disciplinary field, incorporating aspects of botany, horticulture, the fine arts, architecture, industrial design, soil sciences, environmental psychology, geography, and ecology. The activities of a landscape architect can range from the creation of public parks and parkways to site planning for campuses and corporate office parks, from the design of residential estates to the design of civil infrastructure and the management of large wilderness areas or reclamation of degraded landscapes such as mines or landfills. Landscape architects work on structures and external spaces with limitations toward the landscape or park aspect of the design - large or small, urban, suburban and rural, and with "hard" (built) and "soft" (planted) materials, while integrating ecological sustainability. The most valuable contribution can be made at the first stage of a project to generate ideas with technical understanding and creative flair for the design, organization, and use of spaces.

The landscape architect can conceive the overall concept and prepare the master plan, from which detailed design drawings and technical specifications are prepared. They can also review proposals to authorize and supervise contracts for the construction work. Other skills include preparing design impact assessments, conducting environmental assessments and audits, and serving as an expert witness at inquiries on land use issues.

Fields of activity

The variety of the professional tasks that landscape architects collaborate on is very broad, but some examples of project types include:

- The planning, form, scale and siting of new developments
- Parks of General design and public infrastructure
- Sustainable development
- Stormwater management including rain gardens, green roofs, groundwater recharge, Green infrastructure, and treatment wetlands
- Landscape design for educational function and site design for public institutions and government facilities
- Parks, botanical gardens, arboretums, greenways, and nature preserves
- Recreation facilities; i.e.: playgrounds, golf courses, theme parks and sports facilities
- Housing areas, industrial parks and commercial developments
- Estate and residence landscape master planning and design
- Highways, transportation structures, bridges, and transit corridors
- Urban design, town and city squares, waterfronts, pedestrian schemes, and parking lots
- Natural park, tourist destination, and recreating historical landscapes, and historic garden appraisal and conservation studies
- Reservoirs, dams, power stations, reclamation of extractive industry applications or major industrial projects andmitigation
- Environmental assessment and landscape assessment, planning advice and land management proposals.
- Coastal and offshore developments and mitigation
- Ecological Design any aspect of design that minimizes environmentally destructive impacts by integrating itself with natural processes and sustainability

Landscape managers use their knowledge of landscape processes to advise on the long-term care and development of the landscape. They often work in forestry, nature conservation and agriculture.

Landscape scientists have specialist skills such as soil science, hydrology, geomorphology or botany that they relate to the practical problems of landscape work. Their projects can range from site surveys to the ecological assessment of broad areas for planning or management purposes. They may also report on the impact of development or the importance of particular species in a given area.

Landscape planners are concerned with landscape planning for the location, scenic, ecological and recreational aspects of urban, rural and coastal land use. Their work is embodied in written statements of policy and strategy, and their remit includes master planning for new developments, landscape evaluations and assessments, and preparing countryside management or policy plans. Some may also apply an additional specialism such as landscape archaeology or law to the process of landscape planning.

Green roof designers design extensive and intensive roof gardens for storm water management, evapo-transpirative cooling, sustainable architecture, aesthetics, and habitat creation.

History of landscape architecture

Fig. Orangery at the Palace of Versailles, outside Paris

For the period before 1800, the history of landscape gardening (later called landscape architecture) is largely that of master planning and garden design for manor houses, palaces and royal properties, religious complexes, and centers of government. An example is the extensive work by André Le Nôtre at Vaux-le-Vicomte and for King Louis XIV of France at the Palace of Versailles. The first person to write of *making* a landscape was Joseph Addison in 1712. The term landscape architecture was invented by Gilbert Laing Meason in 1828, and John Claudius Loudon (1783–1843) was instrumental in the adoption of the term landscape architecture by the modern profession. He took up the term from Meason and gave it publicity in his Encyclopedias and in his 1840 book on the *Landscape Gardening and Landscape Architecture of the Late Humphry Repton*. It was first used as a professional title by Frederick Law Olmsted in 1863. Andrew Jackson Downing (1815–1852) was another early American landscape designer, and editor of *The Horticulturist* magazine (1846–52). Some scholars consider Downing to be The Father of American Landscape Architecture, although others chooseFrederick Law Olmsted. In 1841 his first book, *A Treatise on the Theory and Practice of Landscape Gardening, Adapted to North America*, was published to a great success; it was the first book of its kind published in the United States. During the latter 19th century, the term landscape architect begun to be used by professional landscapes designers, and was firmly established after Frederick Law Olmsted, Jr. andBeatrix Jones (later Farrand) with others founded the American Society of Landscape Architects (ASLA) in 1899. IFLA was founded at Cambridge, England, in 1948 with Sir Geoffrey Jellicoe as its first president, representing 15 countries from Europe and North America. Later, in 1978, IFLA's Headquarters were established in Versailles.

Relation to Urban planning

Fig. The combination of the traditional landscape gardening and the emerging city planning combined together gave landscape architecture its unique focus.Frederick Law Olmsted used the term 'landscape architecture' using the word as a profession for the first time when designing theCentral Park.

Through the 19th century, urban planning became a more important need. The combination of the tradition oflandscape gardening and emerging city planning that gave Landscape Architecture its unique focus to serve these needs.

In the second half of the century, Frederick Law Olmsted completed a series of parks which continue to have a huge influence on the practices of Landscape Architecture today. Among these were Central Park in New York City,Prospect Park in Brooklyn, New York and Boston's Emerald Necklace park system. Jens Jensen designed sophisticated and naturalistic urban and regional parks for Chicago, Illinois, and private estates for the Ford family including Fair Lane and Gaukler Point.

One of the original ten founding members of the American Society of Landscape Architects(ASLA), and the only woman, was Beatrix Farrand. She was design consultant for over a dozen universities including:Princeton in Princeton, New Jersey; Yale in New Haven, Connecticut; and the Arnold Arboretum for Harvard in Boston,Massachusetts. Her numerous private estate projects include the landmark Dumbarton Oaks in the Georgetownneighborhood of Washington, D.C.. Since that time, other architects — most notably Ruth Havey and Alden Hopkins—changed certain elements of the Farrand design.

Landscape architecture continues to develop as a design discipline, and to respond to the various movements in architecture and design throughout the 20th and 21st centuries. Thomas Church was a mid-century landscape architect significant in the profession. Roberto Burle Marx in Brazil combined the International style and native Brazilian plants and culture for a new aesthetic. Innovation continues today solving challenging problems with contemporary design solutions for master planning, landscapes, and gardens.

Ian McHarg was known for introducing environmental concerns in landscape architecture. He popularized a system of analyzing the layers of a site in order to compile a complete understanding of the qualitative attributes of a place. This system became the foundation of today's Geographic Information Systems (GIS). McHarg would give every qualitative aspect of the site a layer, such as the history, hydrology, topography, vegetation, etc. GIS software is ubiquitously used in the landscape architecture profession today to analyze materials in and on the Earth's surface and is similarly used by Urban Planners, Geographers, Forestry and Natural Resources professionals, etc.

Profession

In many countries, a professional institute, comprising members of the professional community, exists in order to protect the standing of the profession and promote its interests, and sometimes also regulate the practice of landscape architecture. The standard and strength of legal regulations governing landscape architecture practice varies from nation to nation, with some requiring licensure in order to practice; and some having little or no regulation. In North America,

Europe, Australia and New Zealand, landscape architecture is a regulated profession.

Australia

The Australian Institute of Landscape Architects (AILA) provides non statutory professional recognition for landscape architects. Once recognized by (AILA), landscape architects use the title 'Registered Landscape Architect'. Across the eight states and territories within Australia, there is a mix of requirements for landscape architects to be 'Registered', however it is not always a statutory requirement to be registered with AILA to practice use the term "Landscape Architect".

Any regulations or requirements are state based, not national. The AILA's system of professional recognition is a national system overseen by AILA's National Office in Canberra. Non (AILA) Landscape Architects are professionals who are also paid to undertake a specialised set of tasks and to complete them for a fee.

Some agencies require AILA professional recognition or registration as part of the pre-requisite for contracts. Landscape architects within Australia find that some contracts and competitions require the AILA recognition or 'registration' as the basis of demonstrating a professional status. To apply for AILA Registration, an applicant usually needs to satisfy a number of pre-requisites, including university qualification, two years of practice and a record of continuing professional practice. The application is in two stages: (1) A minimum 12 months of mentoring and assessment; and (2) oral assessment/ interview. Professional recognition includes a commitment to continue professional development. AILA Registered Landscape Architects are required to report annually on their continuing professional development.

Canada

In Canada, landscape architecture, like law and medicine, is a self-regulating profession pursuant to provincial statute. For example, Ontario's profession is governed by the Ontario Association of Landscape Architects pursuant to the *Ontario Association of Landscape Architects Act*. Landscape architects in Ontario, British Columbia, and Alberta must complete the specified components of L.A.R.E (Landscape Architecture Registration Examination) as a prerequisite to full professional standing.

Provincial regulatory bodies are members of a national organization, the Canadian Society of Landscape Architects / L'Association des Architectes Paysagistes du Canada(CSLA-AAPC), and individual membership in the CSLA-AAPC is obtained through joining one of the provincial or territorial components.

Italy

AIAPP (Italian Association of Landscape Architecture) is the Italian association of professional landscape architects formed in 1950 and is a member of IFLA and IFLA Europe (formerly known as EFLA). AIAPP is in the process of contesting this new law which has given the Architects' Association the new title of Architects, Landscape Architects, Planners and Conservationists whether or not they have had any training or experience in any of these fields other than Architecture. In Italy, there are several different professions involved in landscape architecture:

- Architects
- Landscape designers
- Doctor landscape agronomists and Doctor landscape foresters, often called Landscape agronomists.
- Agrarian Experts and Graduated Agrarian experts.

New Zealand

The New Zealand Institute of Landscape Architects (NZILA) is the professional body for Landscape Architects in NZ www.nzila.co.nz.

In April 2013, ILA jointly with AILA, hosted the 50th International Federation of Landscape Architects (IFLA) World Congress in Auckland, New Zealand. The World Congress is an international conference where Landscape Architects from all around the globe attend.

Within NZ, Members of NZILA when they achieve their professional standing, can use the title Registered Landscape Architect NZILA.

NZILA provides accreditation review of education course providers and currently there are three accredited Landscape Architecture course providers in New Zealand.

Republic of Ireland

The professional body in Ireland for landscape architects is the Irish Landscape Institute (ILI) www.irishlandscapeinstitute.com. The ILI is an affiliate body to the European Federation for Landscape Architecture (EFLA) and IFLA. The ILI was formed in 1993 to merge the disciplines of landscape architecture and landscape horticulture. It continues to promote the profession by its accreditation of the degree programme in Dublin, certification of Continuing Professional Development (CPD) for landscape architects, administration of professional practice examinations, advice on development of policy at national level and organisation of conferences, lectures and design awards. The ILI is a member institute of the Urban Forum, representing professional bodies involved in urban spatial disciplines of engineering, architecture, planning, quantity surveying and landscape architecture. The profession has gained in status and numbers due to the construction boom of the past decade and raising of standards of Irish design. There is still no registration of title in Ireland and the profession is unregulated, but there is increasing awareness of the profession and of status of the ILI. Landscape architects in Ireland work in private practice, public sector bodies at local government level and in some bodies such transport and national heritage and in the academic sector.

The demand for landscape architects is often associated with strategic infrastructure projects due to Ireland's recent major infrastructural investments. Landscape architects are employed in design of: green infrastructure, public realm, institutional/medical/industrial campuses and settings, parks, play facilities, transport (road/rail/cycle/port) corridors, retail complexes, residential estates (including plans for remediation of now-abandoned housing 'ghost' estates), village improvements, accessibility audits, graveyard restoration schemes, wind farms, wetland drainage systems and coastal zones. They are also significantly employed in preparation/review of statutory impact assessment reports on landscape, visual and ecological impacts of design proposals.

United Kingdom

The UK's professional body is the Landscape Institute (LI). It is a chartered body which accredits landscape professionals and university courses. At present there are fifteen accredited programmes in the UK. Membership of the LI is available to students, academics and professionals, and there are over 3,000 professionally qualified members.

The Institute provides services to assist members including support and promotion of the work of landscape architects; information and guidance to the public and industry about the specific expertise offered by those in the profession; and training and educational advice to students and professionals looking to build upon their experience.

In 2008, the LI launched a major recruitment drive entitled "I want to be a Landscape Architect" to encourage the study of Landscape Architecture. The campaign aims to raise the profile of landscape architecture and highlight its valuable role in building sustainable communities and fighting climate change.

United States

In most US jurisdictions such as states and municipalities, all designs for public space must be reviewed and approved by licensed landscape architects. In the United States, Landscape Architecture is regulated by individual state governments. For a landscape architect, obtaining licensure requires advanced education and work experience, plus passage of the national examination. Several states require passage of a state exam as well. In the U.S. licensing is overseen both at the state level, and nationally by the Council of Landscape

Architectural Registration Boards (CLARB). Landscape architecture has been identified as an above-average growth profession by the US Bureau of Labor Statistics and was listed in *U.S. News & World Report*'s list of Best Jobs to Have in 2006, 2007, 2008, 2009 and 2010. The national trade association for U.S. landscape architects is the American Society of Landscape Architects. The average salary for landscape architecture professionals in the U.S. is $71,000.

THE ART OF LANDSCAPING – ELEMENTS FOR GARDEN DESIGN

The Power of Line

Line is one of the most important and useful of all design elements. Everything in the garden involves line. A pathway, drive, or fence is a clear and readily accessible line in the landscape. As you plan and design your garden, always consider the line that is created by whatever you are adding.

There are four main ways to describe lines: Curves, straight, horizontal, and vertical. None is more important than the others – each has different effects.

Curved lines shape informal garden beds and add interest to pathways. Straight lines evoke a sense of order and a crispness that is more formal. Soothing horizontal lines create a sense of stability. Where wide expanse meets the sky, it creates a sense of majestic peacefulness. Vertical lines project a sense of strength and movement. No matter which types of line you use, be aware that lines lead the eye.

Light, Texture and Form

Light

Light and shade change the way colours look and how they work together. Keep in mind that light can be either natural or artificial. It is easy to add a low-voltage lighting system to extend your garden enjoyment into the evening hours. Various fixtures and their positioning create different effects. Front lighting a dark area highlights a particular feature. Backlighting silhouettes a sculpture, tree, or shrub. Side lighting, which can also produce dramatic effects, is used mostly for safety along walks and paths.

Texture

Use texture to contrast plants in groups or minimize architectural lines.

The characteristics of texture divide plants into three basic groups: coarse, medium, and fine. Coarse-textured plants, hardscaping materials, or garden structures have large or boldly tactile components, such as the leaves of rhubarb or a pergola made with brute cut posts. Fine-textured materials include many ferns and grasses or a delicate structure such as a bent-wire trellis or arbor. Medium textures fall in between.

Changes in texture can be subtle; the textures of various plants (and objects) are relative to one another. An ornamental grass, when viewed alone, may seem a fine-textured plant. However, when compared with say, Hare's-tail grass (Lagurus ovatus), which is much more finely textured, it may appear more coarse-textured.

You'll find lots of textures – smooth or prickly, rippling or frilly – and endless ways to combine them to achieve repetition, contrast, balance, and unity. All are found in a successful garden.

Form

A Landscape needs strong, contrasting forms. The form and shape of plants and other objects in the garden work to divide space, enclose areas, and provide architectural interest. Grouping plants displays their shapes and creates various effects.

Round forms, such as boxwood or barberry shrubs, for instance, add definition and stability to a mixed border. A series of mounded forms creates an undulating rhythm. Repeated, narrow verticals also add stability. Alone, an upright arborvitae or a thin cactus looks awkward. Clustered, they appear well-placed. The strong uprights of a fence add a sense of security and completeness.

Scale, Pattern and Balance

Scale

Scale, or proportion, is the size relationship of one object to another. A 30-foot tree is out of place in the middle of a small patio, but a dwarf tree makes sense. Conversely, a massive house overpowers a narrow front walk lined with strips of flowers.

Consider the ultimate size of a tree before you plant it. The most beautiful tree in the world will look awkward and out of place if it towers over the front of a house. That same tree, if placed in the back yard, may provide a pleasing frame for the house.

Pattern

Pattern is the repetition of shapes in order. Pattern creates rhythm, as well as charm. It reinforces texture and contrast. When creating patterns, think of light and shadow as part of the palette. Use pattern to draw attention to an area; be careful not to overdo bold patterns, which can overwhelm. Also apply this principle when creating backgrounds. Lay a brick herringbone pattern in walkways, patios, entryways, and driveway borders to unify your hardscape, for example. Employ pattern as a way to direct people through the garden too.

Balance

Visual balance is achieved when the elements on each side of a real or imaginary axis are equal. If too much emphasis is placed on one side of the garden, your eye will be drawn more readily there and not to the garden as a whole.

There are two basic types of balance: symmetrical (formal) and asymmetrical (informal). Formal balance doesn't always suit a home or garden style. You may prefer informal, or asymmetrical, balance. For example, a large tree on the left can be balanced by three smaller ones on the right. Or a large mass of cool colours (blues, whites and greys) on one side can balance a small mass of hot (red, orange, yellow) colours on the other side.

Accents and focal points serve to make a landscape more interesting. Use them sparingly, however, to maximize their individual impact. Often, a single, interest element added to an otherwise drab scene can make all the difference.

These focal points should stand out from the rest of the garden. Occasional accents, such as an arbour, a sculpture, or a specimen plant, help create balance in a garden between the reference points and the background.

Unity, Contrast and Colour

Unity

Unity results when all of the basic garden design principles come together in a balanced, harmonious whole. Focusing on harmony will help as you choose from an exciting and sometimes bewildering array of plants and other landscaping materials.

Make simplicity a guidepost as well, and you likely will achieve a unified design that gives you a sense of completeness. Good structure in the overall design, combined with hardscape that meets your needs for service and enjoyment, creates the perfect setting into which you can place favourite plants – trees, shrubs, groundcovers, flowers, and seasonal containers.

Contrast

Contrast emphasizes the difference between a plant or an object and its surroundings. Using contrast is the best way to avoid predictability in a garden. It also adds a pleasing sense of tension between elements. Like most garden design principles, in moderation contrast is good, but too much can be confusing and unrelaxing to the eye. You can contrast textures by varying hardscaping materials, such as bricks and gravel, or plant textures, such as a leathery leaved magnolia next to a finely needled cedar or juniper shrub. The colours of flower blossoms can create wonderful contrasts. To be most effective, the hues should be widely separated on the colour wheel. For example, red and green, purple and orange, and yellow and blue represent the highest contrast in colour. You can also contrast variegated leaves with solid colours, or green and purple.

Colour

Colour seduces the eye, evokes mood, and reflects the seasons. Cool blues, purples, and greens soothe and recede, whereas warm reds, oranges, and yellows enliven a garden. Single-colour schemes enchant with their simplicity. The real fun comes in expressing your personality by combining colours. Some colours compete for attention; others harmonize. Although flowers are the jewels of the garden, too many different colours look chaotic. Remember that a balance of subtly different colours creates a pleasing effect.

Rhythm and Variety

Rhythm and repetition come about when you correctly position or contrast features. Rhythm avoids monotony.

Gardens that may be complete in almost every sense may seem ordinary until rhythm is introduced – for instance, a stately procession of shade trees along a drive or the repetition of paves or the pickets in a fence. These elements create a clear sense of movement.

You can combine a variety of plants for compatibility.

Some pairs of plants just seem to grow well together, often because one helps repel pests from the other.

Employed by gardeners for centuries, this concept is called companion planting. For example, planting onions or sage near carrots helps repel flies that can infest the carrots. Similarly, radishes planted among cucumbers help ward off cucumber beetles. Garden books can help you find good companions for your favourite plants. Certain plants are natural botanical bodyguards, protecting just about anything nearby. Marigolds, for example, boast a natural resistance to harmful nematodes and an odour that turns off pests large and small. Other pest-repelling plants include garlic, lovage, and catnip.

You don't have to take on garden pests by yourself. Nature provides an army of allies in the form of predators that feed on insects. Your friends include birds, bees, wasps, and spiders, as well as beneficial insects such as ladybugs, green lacewings, predator mites, mealybug destroyers, ground beetles, and the wickedly named assassin bug. A birdbath and feeder will attract feathered predators to your garden, while nectar-producing flowers will draw beneficial insects. These are only the basic guide lines as preached by the likes of the Royal Horticultural Society. Nothing is better than your own on-the-ground experience and trial and error.

Principles of Landscape Design

Principles of Landscape Design

The principles of landscape design include the elements of *unity, scale, balance, simplicity, variety, emphasis,* and *sequence* as they apply to *line, form, texture*, and *color*. These elements are interconnected. Landscape design is a process of developing practical and pleasing outdoor living space.

***Unity* is the Quality of Oneness.**

Unity attracts and holds attention. It organizes view into orderly groups with emphasis. Unity starts with the *story line* developed in the *family analysis*, Step 2, in the design process.

***Line* Connects and Defines the Space, Creating Outdoor Rooms**

Fig. Notice the strong use of "line" here in the Japanese Garden at Butchart Gardens, Victoria BC. The path (primary line) invites you into the garden. Secondary lines form the beds.

Lines are a powerful design element that define rooms and connect people to the landscape.For a professional touch, use sweeping bold lines and curves rather than small zigzags and small wavy curves.

***Form* Includes the Three-Dimensional Mass.**

Form is determined by the line, direction, and arrangement of branches and twigs. The resulting mass influences the scale. For unity, repeat the topography form in plant forms.

- Horizontal and spreading forms emphasis the lateral extent and breath of space. They are comfortable because it corresponds with the natural direction of eye movement.
- Rounded forms are most common in plant materials. They allow for easy eye movement and create a pleasant undulation that leads itself to plant groupings.
- Vase-shaped trees define a comfortable "people space" beneath the canopy.
- Weeping forms lead the eye back to the ground. What is below the weeping form often becomes a focal point.
- Pyramidal forms direct the eyes upward, so use sparingly. Grouping pyramidals will soften the upward influence. They will look more natural in the surroundings with foliage to the ground.

Color Gives Greatest Appeal, and Evokes the Greatest Response.

How Does Color Speak to You?

Color is powerful in creating mood and feeling. "Color therapy" is a popular topic in our rapid paced modern world. What moods and feeling do various color create for you? What colors work for the landscape story line? What moods and feeling do you want in the garden? Is it a room for relaxation and healing or a room for action activities?

What Color Schemes Work for the Design Theme?

Scale Evokes Emotional Connection and is Closely Related to Color.

Cool Colors	**Warm Collars**
green, blue, purple	red, yellow, orange
Less conspicuous	Conspicuous
Restful	Cheerful
Recede	Stimulating
Suggest distance	Come forward
Low scale	High Scale

- Absolute scale relates the comparative value of landscape elements to a fixed structure (house).
- Relative scale relates to comparative relative sizes or "values" of objects in the landscape. Relative scale is very emotionally charged

and closely linked to color. It may create a feeling of relaxation and peacefulness or one of energy and action.

- Low scale is relaxing and calming. It is used in the home landscape to give a feeling of peace and relaxation.
- High scale promotes action. It is used around large buildings and in large spaces to fill the space. Use of high scale in small spaces makes the space feel smaller.

Balance **is Equilibrium on Left and Right Sides.**

- Formal balance repeats the same left and right, giving stability, stateliness, and dignity. It is high maintenance keep both side similar.
- Informal balance differs from left to right giving curiosity, movement, and feels alive. Total mass of plants need to balance left and right.
- Which gives the "feeling" desired by the story line and design?

Simplicity **and** ***Variety***

Simplicity and variety work together to balance each other. *Simplicity* is a degrees of repetition rather than constant change, creating unity. *Variety* is diversity and contrast in form, texture, and color preventing monotony.

- For simplicity, repeat some plant materials in sweeps and groupings.
- For variety, fill in with other plants.
- Avoid creating a horticultural zoo! (two of each)
- Zipper plantings (repeating the same pattern over and over again like red-white-red-white) lack simplicity and variety, rather creating monotony.

Emphasis **is Dominance and Subordination of Elements.**

The human mind looks for dominance and subordination in life. As we look at a landscape from any direction, we need to see dominance and subordination of various elements. If we don't find it, we withdraw from the landscape. Some gardens lack the dominant element. Others suffer with too many dominate elements screaming to be the focal point.

Emphasis can be achieved through different sizes, bold shapes, groupings, and the unusual or unexpected. What is the focal point?

Sequence **is the Change or Flow in Form, Color, Texture, and Size Giving Movement or Life.**

Sequence with Texture

Change leaf size of adjacent different plants by at least one-half. Use proportionally larger numbers of fine textured plants.

- In a flower/shrub bed, use coarser texture, larger plants in the back;

sequencing to finer textured, smaller plants in the front inside-curve.

- Texture and distance – Texture becomes finer with distance. In a distant corner, place finer textures in the corner, sequencing to coarser textures on the arms.

Sequence with Color

- There are few basic rules on how much warm and cool colors to use. However, watch that the scale does not become too commanding. More is NOT better. As a rule-of-thumb, the designs needs 90% green to set off the 10% color.

- Darkest shades and the purest intensity dominate and should be used at the focal point.

- Warm colors work best in sequence. Using cool colors in contrast is more effective than sequences.

Color Sequence

1. Decide what color(s) will be used.
2. Decide if light or dark will dominate. – The darker or more intense (pure) the color, the more it will show up and dominate the scene.
3. Calculate the number of plants of each color using this rule-of-thumb.
   a. Establish the largest amount of dark/dominant color that will be used.
   b. Select the next lighter shade and increase the number of plants by one-third.
   c. Select the next lighter shade and increase the number of plants by one-third.
   d. Continue the ratio to the lightest color.

- Grouping for best effect – Kidney or crescent shaped groupings create a natural flowing design.

Color contrasts

- Monochrome light/dark color contrasts – Use one-third one shade and two-thirds the other shade.
- Complementary color contrasts – Use one-third one color and two-thirds the complementary color.

Create effective plant combinations by paring opposites

- To create plant combinations with pizzazz, pair opposites.
- Fine/Course

- Short/Tall
- Round/Upright
- Thugs/Dainty
- Small/Large
- Color contrasts

4

The General Plan or Theory of the Place

Having now discussed the most essential elements of gardening, we may give attention to such minor features as the actual way in which a satisfying garden is to be planned and executed.

Speaking broadly, a person will get from a garden what he puts into it; and it is of the first importance, therefore, that a clear conception of the work be formulated at the outset. I do not mean to say that the garden will always turn out what it was desired that it should be; but the failure to turn out properly is usually some fault in the first plan or some neglect in execution.

Sometimes the disappointment in an ornamental garden is a result of confusion of ideas as to what a garden is for. One of my friends was greatly disappointed on returning to his garden early in September to find that it was not so full and floriferous as when he left it in July. He had not learned the simple lesson that even a flower-garden should exhibit the natural progress of the season. If the garden begins to show ragged places and to decline in late August or early September, it is what occurs in all surrounding vegetation. The year is maturing. The garden ought to express the feeling of the different months. The failing leaves and expended plants are therefore to be looked on, to some extent at least, as the natural order and destiny of a good garden.

These attributes are well exhibited in the vegetable-garden. In the spring, the vegetable-garden is a model of neatness and precision. The rows are straight. There are no missing plants. The earth is mellow and fresh. Weeds are absent. One takes his friends to the garden, and he makes pictures of it. By late June or early July, the plants have begun to sprawl and to get out of shape. The bugs have taken some of them. The rows are no longer trim and precise. The earth is hot and dry. The weeds are making headway. By August and September, the garden has lost its early regularity and freshness. The camera is put aside. The visitors are not taken to it: the gardener prefers to go alone to find the melon or the tomatoes, and he comes away as soon as he has secured his product. Now, as a matter of fact, the garden has been going through its regular seasonal growth. It is natural that it become ragged. It is not necessary that weeds conquer it; but I suspect that it would be a very poor garden, and certainly an uninteresting one, if it retained the dress of childhood at the time when it should develop the personalities of age.

There are two types of outdoor gardening in which the progress of the season is not definitely expressed,—in the carpet-bedding kind, and in the subtropical kind. I hope that my reader will get a clear distinction in these matters, for it is exceedingly important. The carpet-bedding gardening is the making of figure-beds in house-leeks and achyranthes and coleus and sanitalia, and other things that can be grown in compact masses and possibly sheared to keep them within place and bounds; the reader sees these beds in perfection in some of the parks and about florists' establishments; he will understand at once that they are not meant in any way to express the season, for the difference between them in September and June is only that they may be more perfect in September. The subtropical gardening (plates IV and V) is the planting out of house-grown stuff, in order to produce given effects, of such plants as palms, dracenas, crotons, caladiums, papyrus, together with such luxuriant things as dahlias and cannas and large ornamental grasses and castor beans; these plants are to produce effects quite foreign to the expression of a northern landscape, and they are usually at their best and are most luxuriant when overtaken by the fall frosts.

Now, the home gardener usually relies on plants that more or less come and go with the seasons. He pieces out and extends the season, to be sure; but a garden with pansies, pinks, sweet william, roses, sweet peas, petunias, marigolds, salpiglossis, sweet sultan, poppies, zinnias, asters, cosmos, and the rest, is a progress-of-the-season garden, nevertheless; and if it is a garden of herbaceous perennials, it still more completely expresses the time-of-year.

My reader will now consider, perhaps, whether he would have his garden accent and heighten his natural year from spring to fall, or whether he desires to thrust into his year a feeling of another order of vegetation. Either is allowable; but the gardener should distinguish at the outset.

I wish to suggest to my reader, also, that it is possible for the garden to retain some interest even in the winter months. I sometimes question whether it is altogether wise to clear out the old garden stems too completely and too smoothly in the fall, and thereby obliterate every mark of it for the winter months; but however this may be, there are two ways by which the garden year may be extended: by planting things that bloom very late in fall and others that bloom very early in spring; by using freely, in the backgrounds, of bushes and trees that have interesting winter characters.

THE PLAN OF THE GROUNDS

One cannot expect satisfaction in the planting and developing of a home area unless he has a clear conception of what is to be done. This necessarily follows, since the pleasure that one derives from any enterprise depends chiefly on the definiteness of his ideals and his ability to develop them. The homemaker should develop his plan before he attempts to develop his place. He must study the various subdivisions in order that the premises may meet all his needs. He should determine the locations of the leading features of the place and the relative importance to be given to the various parts of it,—as of the landscape parts, the ornamental areas, the vegetable-garden, and the fruit plantation.

The details of the planting may be determined in part as the place develops; it is only the structural features and purposes that need to be determined beforehand in most small properties. The incidental modifications that may be made in the planting from time to time keep the interest alive and allow the planter to gratify his desire to experiment with new plants and new methods.

It must be understood that I am now speaking of ordinary home grounds which the home-maker desires to improve by himself. If the area is large enough to present distinct landscape features, it is always best to employ a landscape architect of recognized merit, in the same spirit that one would employ an architect. The details, however, may even then be filled in by the owner, if he is so inclined, following out the plan that the landscape architect makes.

It is desirable to have a definite plan on paper (drawn to scale) for the location of the leading features of the place. These features are the residence, the out-houses, the walks and drives, the service areas (as clothes yards), the border planting, flower-garden, vegetable-garden, and fruit-garden. It should not be expected that the map plan can be followed in every detail, but it will serve as a general guide; and if it is made on a large enough scale, the different kinds of plants can be located in their proper positions, and a record of the place be kept.

It is nearly always unsatisfactory, for both owner and designer, if a plan of the place is made without a personal inspection of the area. Lines that look well on a map may not adjust themselves readily to the varying contours of the place itself, and the location of the features inside the grounds will depend also in a very large measure on the objects that lie outside it. For example, all interesting and bold views should be brought into the place, and all unsightly objects in the immediate vicinity should be planted out.

A plan of a back yard of a narrow city lot, showing the heavy border planting of trees and shrubs, with the skirting border of flowers. In the front are two large trees, that are desired for shade. It will readily be seen from this plan how extensive the area for flowers becomes when they are placed along such a devious border. More color effect can be got from such an arrangement of the flowers than could be secured if the whole area were planted to flower-beds.

A contour map plan of a very rough piece of ground. The sides of the place are high, and it becomes necessary to carry a walk through the middle area; and on either side of the front, it skirts the banks. Such a plan is usually unsightly on paper, but may nevertheless fit special cases very well. The plan is inserted here for the purpose of illustrating the fact that a plan that will work on the ground does not necessarily work on a map.

In charting a place, it is important to locate the points from which the walks are to start, and at which they are to emerge from the grounds. These two points are then joined by direct and simple curves; and alongside the walks, especially in angles or bold curves, planting may be inserted.

A suggestion for school premises on a four-corners, and which the pupils enter from three directions. The two playgrounds are separated by a broken group of bushes extending from the building to the rear boundary; but, in general, the spaces are kept open, and the heavy border-masses clothe the place and make it home-like. The lineal extent of the group margins is astonishingly large, and along all these margins flowers may be planted, if desired.

If there is only six feet between a schoolhouse and the fence, there is still room for a border of shrubs. This border should be between the walk and the fence,—on the very boundary,—not between the walk and the building, for in the latter case the planting divides the premises and weakens the effect. A space two feet wide will allow of an irregular wall of bushes, if tall buildings do not cut out the light; and if the area is one hundred feet long, thirty to fifty kinds of shrubs and flowers can be grown to perfection, and the school-grounds will be practically no smaller for the plantation.

One cannot make a plan of a place until he knows what he wants to do with the property; and therefore we may devote the remainder of this chapter to developing the idea in the layout of the premises rather than to the details of map-making and planting.

Because I speak of the free treatment of garden spaces in this book it must not be inferred that any reflection is intended on the "formal" garden. There are many places in which the formal or "architect's garden" is much to be desired; but each of these cases should be treated wholly by itself and be made a part of the architectural setting of the place. These questions are outside the sphere of this book. All formal gardens are properly individual studies.

All very special types of garden design are naturally excluded from a book of this kind, such types, for example, as Japanese gardening. Persons who desire to develop these specialties will secure the services of persons who are skilled in them; and there are also books and magazine articles to which they may go.

THE PICTURE IN THE LANDSCAPE

The deficiency in most home grounds is not so much that there is too little planting of trees and shrubs as that this planting is meaningless. Every yard should be a picture. That is, the area should be set off from other areas, and it should have such a character that the observer catches its entire effect and purpose without stopping to analyze its parts. The yard should be one thing, one area, with every feature contributing its part to one strong and homogeneous effect.

These remarks will become concrete if the reader turns his eye. The former represents a common type of planting of front yards. The bushes and trees are scattered promiscuously over the area. Such a yard has no purpose, no central idea. It shows plainly that the planter had no constructive conception, no grasp of any design, and no appreciation of the fundamental elements of the beauty of landscape. Its only merit is the fact that trees and shrubs have been planted; and this, to most minds, comprises the essence and sum of the ornamentation of grounds. Every tree and bush is an individual alone, unattended, disconnected from its environments, and, therefore, meaningless. Such a yard is only a nursery.

The other plan is a picture. The eye catches its meaning at once. The central idea is the residence, with a free and open greensward in front of it The same trees and bushes that were scattered haphazard over are massed into a framework to give effectiveness to the picture of home and comfort. This style of planting makes a landscape, even though the area be no larger than a parlor. The other style is only a collection of curious plants. The one has an instant and abiding pictorial effect, which is restful and satisfying: the observer exclaims, "What a beautiful home this is!" The other piques one's curiosity, obscures the residence, divides and distracts the attention: the observer exclaims, "What excellent lilac bushes are these!"

An inquiry into the causes of the unlike impressions that one receives from a given landscape and from a painting of it explains the subject admirably. One reason why the picture appeals to us more than the landscape is because the picture is condensed, and the mind becomes acquainted with its entire purpose at once, while the landscape is so broad that the individual objects at first fix the attention, and it is only by a process of synthesis that the unity of the landscape finally becomes apparent. This is admirably illustrated in photographs. One of the first surprises that the novice experiences in the use of the camera is the discovery that very tame scenes become interesting and often even spirited in the photograph. But there is something more than mere condensation in this vitalizing and beautifying effect of the photograph or the painting: individual objects are so much reduced that they no longer appeal to us as distinct subjects, and however uncouth they may be in the reality, they make no impression in the picture; the thin and sere sward may appear rather like a closely shaven lawn or a new-mown meadow. And again, the picture sets a limit to the scene; it frames it, and thereby cuts off all extraneous and confusing or irrelevant landscapes.

These remarks are illustrated in the aesthetics of landscape gardening. It is the artist's one desire to make pictures in the landscape. This is done in two ways: by the form of plantations, and by the use of vistas. He will throw his plantations into such positions that open and yet more or less confined areas of greensward are presented to the observer at various points. This picture-like opening is nearly or quite devoid of small or individual objects, which usually destroy the unity of such areas and are meaningless in themselves. A vista is a narrow opening or view between plantations to a distant landscape. It cuts up the broad horizon into portions that are readily cognizable. It frames parts of the country-side. The verdurous sides of the planting are the sides of the frame; the foreground is the bottom, and the sky is the top. It is of the utmost importance that good views be left or secured from the best windows of the house (not forgetting the kitchen window); in fact, the placing of the house may often be determined by the views that may be appropriated.

If a landscape is a picture, it must have a canvas. This canvas is the greensward. Upon this, the artist paints with tree and bush and flower as the painter does upon his canvas with brush and pigments. The opportunity for artistic composition and design is nowhere so great as in the landscape garden, because no other art has such a limitless field for the expression of its emotions. It is not strange, if this be true, that there have been few great landscape gardeners, and that, falling short of art, the landscape gardener too often works in the sphere of the artisan. There can be no rules for landscape gardening, any more than there can be for painting or sculpture. The operator may be taught how to hold the brush or strike the chisel or plant the tree, but he remains an operator; the art is intellectual and emotional and will not confine itself in precepts.

The making of a good and spacious lawn, then, is the very first practical consideration in a landscape garden.

The lawn provided, the gardener conceives what is the dominant and central feature in the place, and then throws the entire premises into subordination to this feature. In home grounds this central feature is the house. To scatter trees and bushes over the area defeats the fundamental purpose of the place,—the purpose to make every part of the grounds lead up to the home and to accentuate its homelikeness.

A house must have a background if it is to become a home. A house that stands on a bare plain or hill is a part of the universe, not a part of a home. Recall the cozy little farm-house that is backed by a wood or an orchard; then compare some pretentious structure that stands apart from all planting. Yet how many are the farm-houses that stand as stark and cold against the sky as if they were competing with the moon! We would not believe it possible for a man to live in a house twenty-five years and not, by accident, allow some tree to grow, were it not that it is so!

Of course these remarks about the lawn are meant for those countries where greensward is the natural ground cover. In the South and in arid countries, greensward is not the prevailing feature of the landscape, and in these regions the landscape design may take on a wholly different character, if the work is to be nature-like. We have not yet developed other conceptions of landscape work to any perfect extent, and we inject the English greensward treatment even into deserts. We may look for the time when a brown landscape garden may be made in a brown country, and it may be good art not to attempt a broad open center in regions in which undergrowth rather than sod is the natural ground cover. In parts of the United States we are developing a good Spanish-American architecture, perhaps we may develop a recognized comparable landscape treatment as an artistic expression.

Birds, and cats

The picture in the landscape is not complete without birds, and the birds should comprise more species than English sparrows. If one is to have birds on his premises, he must (1) attract them and (2) protect them.

One attracts birds by providing places in which they may nest. The free border plantings have distinct advantages in attracting chipping sparrows, catbirds, and other species. The bluebirds, house wrens, and martins may be attracted by boxes in which they can build.

One may attract birds by feeding them and supplying water. Suet for woodpeckers and others, grain and crumbs for other kinds, and taking care not to frighten or molest them, will soon win the confidence of the birds. A slowly running or dripping fountain, with a good rim on which they may perch, will also attract them, and it is no mean enjoyment to watch the birds at bathing. Or, if one does not care to go to the expense of a bird fountain, he may supply their wants by means of a shallow dish of water set on the lawn.

The birds will need protection from cats. There is no more reason why cats should roam at will and uncontrolled than that dogs or horses or poultry should be allowed unlimited license. A cat away from home is a trespasser and should be so treated. A person has no more right to inflict a cat on a neighborhood than to inflict a goat or rabbits or any other nuisance. All persons who keep cats should feel the same responsibility for them that they feel for other property; and they should be willing to forfeit their property right when they forfeit their control. The cats not only destroy birds, but they break the peace. The caterwauling at night will not be permitted in well-governed communities any more than the shooting of fire-arms or vicious talking will be allowed: all night-roaming cats should be gathered in, just as stray dogs and tramps are provided for.

I do not dislike cats, but I desire to see them kept at home and within control. If persons say that they cannot keep them on their own premises, then these persons should not be allowed to have them. A bell on the cat will prevent it from capturing old birds, and this may answer a good purpose late in the season; but it will not stop the robbing of nests or the taking of young birds, and here is where the greatest havoc is wrought.

It is often asserted that cats must roam in order that rats and mice may be reduced; but probably few house mice and few rats are got by wandering cats; and, again, many cats are not mousers. There are other ways of controlling rats and mice; or if cats are employed for this purpose, see that they are restricted to the places where the house rats and mice are to be found.

Many persons like squirrels about the place, but they cannot expect to have both birds and squirrels unless very special precautions are taken.

The English or house sparrow drives away the native birds, although he is himself an attractive inhabitant in winter, particularly where native birds are not resident. The English sparrow should be kept in reduced numbers. This can be easily accomplished by poisoning them in winter (when other birds are not endangered) with wheat soaked in strychnine water. The contents of one of the eighth-ounce vials of strychnine that may be secured at a drug store is added to sufficient water to cover a quart of wheat. Let the wheat stand in the poison water twenty-four to forty-eight hours (but not long enough for the grains to sprout), then dry the wheat thoroughly. It cannot be distinguished from ordinary wheat, and sparrows usually eat it freely, particularly if they are in the habit of eating scattered grain and crumbs. Of course, the greatest caution must be exercised that in the use of such highly poisonous materials, accidents do not occur with other animals or with human beings.

The planting is part of the design or picture.

If the reader catches the full meaning of these pages, he has acquired some of the primary conceptions in landscape gardening. The suggestion will grow upon him day by day; and if he is of an observing turn of mind, he will find that this simple lesson will revolutionize his habit of thought respecting the planting of grounds and the beauty of landscapes. He will see that a bush or flower-bed that is no part of any general purpose or design—that is, which does not contribute to the making of a picture—might better never have been planted. For myself, I would rather have a bare and open pasture than such a yard, even though it contained the choicest plants of every land. The pasture would at least be plain and restful and unpretentious; but the yard would be full of effort and fidget.

Reduced to a single expression, all this means that the greatest artistic value in planting lies in the effect of the mass, and not in the individual plant. A mass has the greater value because it presents a much greater range and variety of forms, colors, shades, and textures, because it has sufficient extent or dimensions to add structural character to a place, and because its features are so continuous and so well blended that the mind is not distracted by incidental and irrelevant ideas. Two pictures will illustrate all this. The former stretches along a field and makes a lawn of a bit of meadow which lies in front of it. The landscape has become so small and so well defined by this bank of verdure that it has a familiar and personal feeling. The great, bare, open meadows are too ill-defined and too extended to give any domestic feeling; but here is a part of the meadow set off into an area that one can compass with his affections.

These masses have their own intrinsic merits, as well as their office in defining a bit of nature. One is attracted by the freedom of arrangement, the irregularity of sky-line, the bold bays and promontories, and the infinite play of light and shade. The observer is interested in each because it has character, or features, that no other mass in all the world possesses. He knows that the birds build their nests in the tangle and the rabbits find it a covert.

Now let the reader turn which is a picture of an "improved" city yard. Here there is no structural outline to the planting, no defining of the area, no continuous flow of the form and color. Every bush is what every other one is or may be, and there are hundreds like them in the same town. The birds shun them. Only the bugs find any happiness in them. The place has no fundamental design or idea, no lawn upon which a picture may be constructed. This yard is like a sentence or a conversation in which every word is equally emphasized.

In bold contrast with this yard is the open-center treatment. Here there is pictorial effect; and there is opportunity along the borders to distribute trees and shrubs that may be desired as individual specimens.

The motive that shears the trees also razes the copse, in order that the gardener or "improver" may show his art. Many persons seem to fear that they will never be known to the world unless they expend a great amount of muscle or do something emphatic or spectacular; and their fears are usually well founded.

It is not enough that trees and bushes be planted in masses. They must be kept in masses by letting them grow freely in a natural way. The pruning-knife is the most inveterate enemy of shrubbery. Pictures 16 and 17 illustrate what I mean. The former represents a good group of bushes so far as arrangement is concerned; but it has been ruined by the shears.

The attention of the observer is instantly arrested by the individual bushes. Instead of one free and expressive object, there are several stiff and expressionless ones. If the observer stops to consider his own thoughts when he comes upon such a collection, he will likely find himself counting the bushes; or, at least, he will be making mental comparisons of the various bushes, and wondering why they are not all sheared to be exactly alike. How the same "artist" has treated two deutzias and a juniper. Much the same effect could have been secured, and with much less trouble, by laying two flour barrels end to end and standing a third one between them.

I must hasten to say that I have not the slightest objection to the shearing of trees. The only trouble is in calling the practice art and in putting the trees where people must see them (unless they are part of a recognized formal-garden design). If the operator simply calls the business shearing, and puts the things where he and others who like them may see them, objection could not be raised. Some persons like painted stones, others iron bulldogs in the front yard and the word "welcome" worked into the door-mat, and others like barbered trees. So long as these likes are purely personal, it would seem to be better taste to put such curiosities in the back yard, where the owner may admire them without molestation.

There is a persistent desire among workmen to shear and to trim: it displays their industry. It is a great thing to be able to allow the freedom of nature to remain. The artist often builds his structures into a native planting rather than to trust himself to produce a good result by planting on razed surfaces.

We have tried to enforce the importance of the open center in non-formal home grounds in greensward regions. Of course this does not mean that there may not be central planting in particular cases where the conditions distinctly call for it nor that there may not be trees on the lawn. If one has the placing of the trees, he may see that they are not scattered aimlessly; but if good trees are already growing on the place, it would be folly to think of removing them merely because they are not in the best ideal positions; in such case, it may be very necessary to adapt the treatment of the area to the trees. The home-maker should always consider, also, the planting of a few trees in such places as to shade and protect the residence: the more closely they can be made a part of the general design or handling of the place, the better the results will be.

The flower-growing should be part of the designs

The use of brilliant flowers and bright foliage and striking forms of vegetation; but these things are never primary considerations in a good domain. The structural elements of the place are designed first. The flanking and bordering masses are then planted. Finally the flowers and accessories are put in, as a house is painted after it is built. Flowers appear to best advantage when seen against a background of foliage, and they are then, also, an integral part of the picture. The flower-garden, as such, should be at the rear or side of a place, as all other personal appurtenances are; but flowers and bright leaves may be freely scattered along the borders and near the foliage masses.

It is a common saying that many persons have no love or appreciation of flowers, but it is probably nearer to the truth to say that no person is wholly lacking in this respect. Even those persons who declare that they care nothing for flowers are generally deceived by their dislike of flower-beds and the conventional methods of flower-growing. I know many persons who stoutly deny any liking for flowers, but who, nevertheless, are rejoiced with the blossoming of the orchards and the purpling of the clover fields. The fault may not lie so much with the persons themselves as with the methods of growing and displaying the flowers.

Defects in flower-growing

The greatest defect with our flower-growing is the stinginess of it. We grow our flowers as if they were the choicest rarities, to be coddled in a hotbed or under a bell-jar, and then to be exhibited as single specimens in some little pinched and ridiculous hole cut in the turf, or perched upon an ant-hill that some gardener has laboriously heaped on a lawn. Nature, on the other hand, grows many of her flowers in the most luxurious abandon, and one can pick an armful without offense. She grows her flowers in earnest, as a man grows a crop of corn. One can revel in the color and the fragrance and be satisfied.

The next defect with our flower-growing is the flower-bed. Nature has no time to make flower-bed designs: she is busy growing flowers. And, then, if she were given to flower-beds, the whole effect would be lost, for she could no longer be luxurious and wanton, and if a flower were picked her whole scheme might be upset. Imagine a geranium-bed or a coleus-bed, with its wonderful "design," set out into a wood or in a free and open landscape! Even the birds would laugh at it!

We should grow flowers freely when we make a flower-garden. We should have enough of them to make the effort worth the while. I sympathize with the man who likes sunflowers. There are enough of them to be worth looking at. They fill the eye. Now show this man ten feet square of pinks or asters, or daisies, all growing free and easy and he will tell you that he likes them. All this has a particular application to the farmer, who is often said to dislike flowers. He grows potatoes and buckwheat and weeds by the acre: two or three unhappy pinks or geraniums are not enough to make an impression.

Lawn flower-beds

The easiest way to spoil a good lawn is to put a flower-bed in it; and the most effective way in which to show off flowers to the least advantage is to plant them in a bed in the greensward. Flowers need a background. We do not hang our pictures on fence-posts. If flowers are to be grown on a lawn, let them be of the hardy kind, which can be naturalized in the sod and which grow freely in the tall unmown grass; or else perennials of such nature that they make attractive clumps by themselves. Lawns should be free and generous, but the more they are cut up and worried with trivial effects, the smaller and meaner they look.

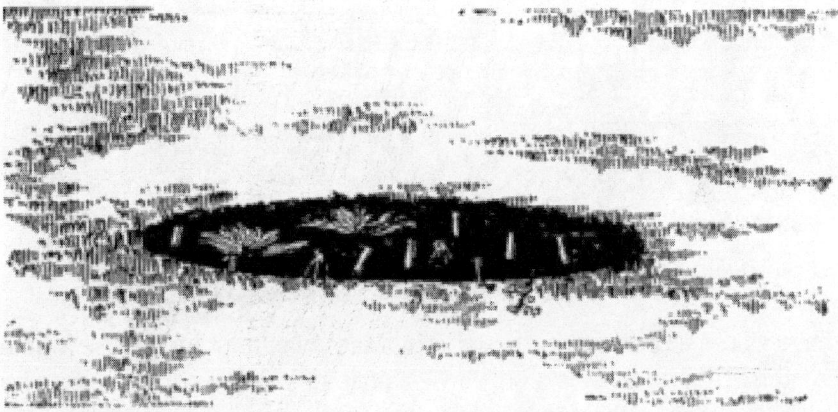

But even if we consider these lawn flower-beds wholly apart from their surroundings, we must admit that they are at best unsatisfactory. It generally amounts to this, that we have four months of sparse and downcast vegetation, one month of limp and frost-bitten plants, and seven months of bare earth I am not now opposing the carpet-beds which professional gardeners make in parks and other museums.

Flower-borders

We should acquire the habit of speaking of the flower-border. The border planting of which we have spoken sets bounds to the place, and makes it one's own. The person lives inside his place, not on it. Along these borders, against groups, often by the corners of the residence or in front of porches—these are places for flowers. Ten flowers against a background are more effective than a hundred in the open yard.

I have asked a professional artist, Mr. Mathews, to draw me the kind of a flower-bed that he likes. It is a border,—a strip of land two or three feet wide along a fence. This is the place where pigweeds usually grow. Here he has planted marigolds, gladiolus, golden rod, wild asters, China asters, and—best of all—hollyhocks.

Any one would like that flower-garden. It has some of that local and indefinable charm that always attaches to an "old-fashioned garden" with its medley of form and color.

Nearly every yard has some such strip of land along a rear walk or fence or against a building. It is the easiest thing to plant it,—ever so much easier than digging the characterless geranium bed into the center of an inoffensive lawn. The suggestions are carried further in 22 to 25.

THE OLD-FASHIONED GARDEN

Speaking of the old-fashioned garden recalls one of William Falconer's excellent paragraphs: "We tried it in Schenley Park this year. We needed a handy dumping ground, and hit on the head of a deep ravine between two woods; into it we dumped hundreds upon hundreds of wagon loads of rock and clay, filling it near to the top, then surfaced it with good soil. Here we planted some shrubs, and broadcast among them set out scarlet poppies, eschscholtzias, dwarf nasturtiums, snapdragons, pansies, marigolds, and all manner of hardy herbaceous plants, having enough of each sort to make a mass of its kind and color, and the effect was fine. In the middle was a plantation of hundreds of clumps of Japan and German irises interplanted, thence succeeded by thousands of gladioli, and banded with montbretias, from which we had flowers till frost. The steep face of this hill was graded a little and a series of winding stone steps set into it, making the descent into the hollow quite easy; the stones were the rough uneven slabs secured in blasting the rocks when grading in other parts of the park, and both along outer edges of the steps and the sides of the upper walk a wide belt of moss pink was planted; and the banks all about were planted with shrubs, vines, wild roses, columbines, and other plants. More cameras and kodaks were leveled by visitors at this piece of gardening than at any other spot in the park, and still we had acres of painted summer beds."

CONTENTS OF THE FLOWER-BORDERS

There is no prescribed rule as to what one should put into these informal flower-borders. Put in them the plants you like. Perhaps the greater part of them should be perennials that come up of themselves every spring, and that are hardy and reliable. Wild flowers are particularly effective. Every one knows that many of the native herbs of woods and glades are more attractive than some of the most prized garden flowers. The greater part of these native flowers grow readily in cultivation, sometimes even in places which, in soil and exposure, are much unlike their native haunts. Many of them make thickened roots, and they may be safely transplanted at any time after the flowers have passed. To most persons the wild flowers are less known than many exotics that have smaller merit, and the extension of cultivation is constantly tending to annihilate them. Here, then, in the informal flower-border, is an opportunity to rescue them. Then one may sow in freely of easy-growing annuals, as marigolds, China asters, petunias and phloxes, and sweet peas.

One of the advantages of these borders lying at the boundary is that they are always ready to receive more plants, unless they are full. That is, their symmetry is not marred if some plants are pulled out and others are put in. And if the weeds now and then get a start, very little harm is done. Such a border half full of weeds is handsomer than the average hole-in-the-lawn geranium bed. An ample border may receive wild plants every month in the year when the frost is out of the ground. Plants are dug in the woods or fields, whenever one is on an excursion, even if in July. The tops are cut off, the roots kept moist until they are placed in the border; most of these much-abused plants will grow. To be sure, one will secure some weeds; but then, the weeds are a part of the collection! Of course, some plants will resent this treatment, but the border may be a happy family, and be all the better and more personal because it is the result of moments of relaxation. Such a border has something new and interesting every month of the growing season; and even in the winter the tall clumps of grasses and aster-stems hold their banners above the snow and are a source of delight to every frolicsome bevy of snowbirds.

I have spoken of a weedland to suggest how simple and easy a thing it is to make an attractive mass-plantation. One may make the most of a rock or bank, or other undesirable feature of the place. Dig up the ground and make it rich, and then set plants in it. You will not get it to suit you the first year, and perhaps not the second or the third; you can always pull out plants and put more in. I should not want a lawn-garden so perfect that I could not change it in some character each year; I should lose interest in it.

It must not be understood that I am speaking only for mixed borders. On the contrary, it is much better in most cases that each border or bed be dominated by the expression of one kind of flower or bush. In one place a person may desire a wild aster effect, or a petunia effect, or a larkspur effect, or a rhododendron effect; or it may be desirable to run heavily to strong foliage effects in one direction and to light flower effects in another. The mixed border is rather more a flower-garden idea than a landscape idea; when it shall be desirable to emphasize the one and when the other, cannot be set down in a book.

The value of plants may lie in foliage and form rather than in bloom

What kinds of shrubs and flowers to plant is a wholly secondary and largely a personal consideration. The main plantings are made up of hardy and vigorous species; then the things that you like are added. There is endless choice in the species, but the arrangement or disposition of the plants is far more important than the kinds; and the foliage and form of the plant are usually of more importance than its bloom.

The appreciation of foliage effects in the landscape is a higher type of feeling than the desire for mere color. Flowers are transitory, but foliage and plant forms are abiding. The common roses have very little value for landscape planting because the foliage and habit of the rose-bush are not attractive, the leaves are inveterately attacked by bugs, and the blossoms are fleeting. Some of the wild roses and the Japanese *Rosa rugosa*, however, have distinct merit for mass effects.

Even the common flowers, as marigold, zinnias, and gaillardias, are interesting as plant forms long before they come into bloom. To many persons the most satisfying epoch in the garden is that preceding the bloom, for the habits and stature of the plants are then unobscured. The early stages of lilies, daffodils, and all perennials are most interesting; and one never appreciates a garden until he realizes that this is so.

Now let the reader, with these suggestions in mind, observe for one week the plant-forms in the humble herbs that he meets, whether these herbs are strong garden plants or the striking sculpturing of mulleins, burdocks, and jimson-weed.

Wild bushes are nearly always attractive in form and habit when planted in borders and groups. They improve in appearance under cultivation because they are given a better chance to grow. In wild nature there is such fierce struggle for existence that plants usually grow to few or single stems, and they are sparse and scraggly in form; but once given all the room they want and a good soil, they become luxurious, full, and comely. In most home grounds in the country the body of the planting may be very effectively composed of bushes taken from the adjacent woods and fields. The masses may then be enlivened by the addition here and there of cultivated bushes, and the planting of flowers and herbs about the borders. It is not essential that one know the names of these wild bushes, although a knowledge of their botanical kinships will add greatly to the pleasure of growing them. Neither will they look common when transferred to the lawn. There are not many persons who know even the commonest wild bushes intimately, and the things change so much in looks when removed to rich ground that few home-makers recognize them.

Odd and formal trees

It is but a corollary of this discussion to say that plants which are simply odd or grotesque or unusual should be used with the greatest caution, for they introduce extraneous and jarring effects. They are little in sympathy with a landscape garden. An artist would not care to paint an evergreen that is sheared into some grotesque shape.

It is only curious, and shows what a man with plenty of time and long pruning shears can accomplish. A weeping tree (particularly of a small-growing species) is usually seen to best advantage when it stands against a group or mass of foliage, as a promontory, adding zest and spirit to the border; it then has relation with the place. This leads me to speak of the planting of the

Lombardy poplar, which may be taken as a type of the formal tree, and as an illustration of what I mean to express. Its chief merits to the average planter are the quickness of its growth and the readiness with which it multiplies by sprouts. But in the North it is likely to be a short-lived tree, it suffers from storms, and it has few really useful qualities. It may be used to some advantage in windbreaks for peach orchards and other short-lived plantations; but after a few years a screen of Lombardies begins to fail, and the habit of suckering from the root adds to its undesirable features. For shade it has little merit, and for timber none. Persons like it because it is striking, and this, in an artistic sense, is its gravest fault. It is unlike anything else in our landscape, and does not fit into our scenery well. A row of Lombardies along a roadside is like a row of exclamation points!

But the Lombardy can often be used to good effect as one factor in a group of trees, where its spire-like shape, towering above the surrounding foliage, may lend a spirited charm to the landscape. It combines well in such groups if it stands in visual nearness to chimneys or other tall formal objects. Then it gives a sort of architectural finish and spirit to a group; but the effect is generally lessened, if not altogether spoiled, in small places, if more than one Lombardy is in view. One or two specimens may often be used to give vigor to heavy plantations about low buildings, and the effect is generally best if they are seen beyond or at the rear of the building.

Poplars and the like

Another defect in common ornamental planting, which is well illustrated in the use of poplars, is the desire for plants merely because they grow rapidly. A very rapid-growing tree nearly always produces cheap effects. This is well illustrated in the common planting of willows and poplars about summer places or lake shores. Their effect is almost wholly one of thinness and temporariness. There is little that suggests strength or durability in willows and poplars, and for this reason they should usually be employed as minor or secondary features in ornamental or home grounds. When quick results are desired, nothing is better to plant than these trees; but better trees, as maples, oaks, or elms, should be planted with them, and the poplars and willows should be removed as rapidly as the other species begin to afford protection. When the plantation finally assumes its permanent characters, a few of the remaining poplars and willows, judiciously left, may afford very excellent effects; but no one who has an artist's feeling would be content to construct the framework of his place of these rapid-growing and soft-wooded trees.

I have said that the legitimate use of poplars in ornamental grounds is in the production of minor or secondary effects. As a rule, they are less adapted to isolated planting as specimen trees than to using in composition,—that is, as parts of general groups of trees, where their characters serve to break the monotony of heavier forms and heavier foliage. The poplars are gay trees, as a rule, especially those, like the aspens, that have a trembling foliage. Their leaves are bright and the tree-tops are thin. The common aspen or "popple," _Populus tremuloides,_ of our woods, is a meritorious little tree for certain effects. Its dangling catkins, light, dancing foliage, and silver-gray limbs, are always cheering, and its autumn color is one of the purest golden-yellows of our landscape. It is good to see a tree of it standing out in front of a group of maples or evergreens.

Plant-forms

Before one attains to great sensitiveness in the appreciation of gardens, he learns to distinguish plants by their forms. This is particularly true for trees and shrubs. Each species has its own "expression," which is determined by the size that is natural to it, mode of branching, form of top, twig characters, bark characters, foliage characters, and to some extent its flower and fruit characters. It is a useful practice for one to train his eye by learning the difference in expression of the trees of different varieties of cherries or pears or apples or other fruits, if he has access to a plantation of them. The differences in cherries and pears are very marked. He may also contrast and compare carefully the kinds of any tree or shrub of which there are two or three species in the neighborhood, learning to distinguish them without close examination; as the sugar maple, red maple, soft maple, and Norway maple (if it is planted); the white or American elm, the cork elm, the slippery elm, the planted European elms; the aspen, large-toothed poplar, cottonwood, balm of gilead, Carolina poplar, Lombardy poplar; the main species of oaks; the hickories; and the like.

It will not be long before the observer learns that many of the tree and shrub characters are most marked in winter; and he will begin unconsciously to add the winter to his year.

Various specific examples

The foregoing remarks will mean more if the reader is shown some concrete examples. I have chosen a few cases, not because they are the best, or even because they are always good enough for models, but because they lie in my way and illustrate what I desire to teach.

A front yard example

We will first look at a very ordinary front yard. It contained no plants, except a pear tree standing near the corner of the house. Four years later sees the yard. An exochorda is the large bush in the very foreground, and the porch foundation is screened and a border is thereby given to the lawn. The length of this planting from end to end is about fourteen feet, with a projection towards the front on the left of ten feet. In the bay at the base of this projection the planting is only two feet wide or deep, and from here it gradually swings out to the steps, eight feet wide. The prominent large-leaved plant near the steps is a bramble, _Rubus odoratus,_ very common in the neighborhood, and it is a choice plant for decorative planting, when it is kept under control. The plants in this border in front of the porch are all from the wild, and comprise a prickly ash, several plants of two wild osiers or dogwoods, a spice bush, rose, wild sunflowers and asters and golden-rods. The promontory at the left is a more ambitious but less effective mass. It contains an exochorda, a reed, variegated elder, sacaline, variegated dogwood, tansy, and a young tree of wild crab. At the rear of the plantation, next the house, one sees the pear tree. The best single part of the planting is the reed overtopping the exochorda. The photograph was taken early in summer, before the reed had become conspicuous.

A ground plan of this planting. At A is the walk and B the steps. An opening at D serves as a passage. The main planting, in front of the porch, fourteen feet long, received twelve plants, some of which have now spread into large clumps. At 1 is a large bush of osier, _Cornus Baileyi,_ one of the best red-stemmed bushes. At 2 is a mass of _Rubus odoratus;_ at 5 asters and golden-rods; at 3 a clump of wild sunflowers. The projecting planting on the left comprises about ten plants, of which 4 is exochorda, 6 is arundo or reed, at the back of which is a large clump of sacaline, and 7 is a variegated-leaved elder.

Another example

A back yard. The owner wanted a tennis court, and the yard is so small as not to allow of wide planting at the borders. However, something could be done. On the left is a weedland border, which formed the basis of the discussion of wild plants on page 35. In the first place, a good lawn was made. In the second place, no walks or drives were laid in the area. The drive for grocers' wagons and coal is seen in the rear, ninety feet from the house. From I to J is the weedland, separating the area from the neighbor's premises. Near I is a clump of roses. At K is a large bunch of golden-rods. H marks a clump of yucca. G is a cabin, covered with vines on the front. From G to F is an irregular border, about six feet wide, containing barberries, forsythias, wild elder, and other bushes. D E is a screen of Russian mulberry, setting off the clothes yard from the front lawn. Near the back porch, at the end of the screen, is an arbor covered with wild grapes, making a play-house for the children. A clump of lilacs stands at A. At B is a vine-covered screen, serving as a hammock support. The lawn made and the planting done, it was next necessary to lay the walks. These are wholly informal affairs, made by sinking a plank ten inches wide into the ground to a level with the sod. The border plantings of this yard are too straight and regular for the most artistic results, but such was necessary in order not to encroach upon the central space. Yet the reader will no doubt agree that this yard is much better than it could be made by any system of scattered and spotted planting. Let him imagine how a glowing carpet-bed would look set down in the center of this lawn!

A THIRD EXAMPLE

The making of a landscape picture. The former shows a small clay field (seventy-five feet wide, and three hundred feet deep), with a barn at the rear. In front of the barn is a screen of willows. The observer is looking from the dwelling-house. The area has been plowed and seeded for a lawn. The operator has then marked out a devious line upon either border with a hoe handle, and all the space between these borders has been gone over with a garden roller to mark the area of the desired greensward.

A SMALL BACK YARD

A back yard. It is approximately sixty feet square. At present it contains a drive, which is unnecessary, expensive to keep in repair, and destructive of any attempt to make a picture of the area. The place could be improved by planting it somewhat after the manner.

A city lot

The area is fifty by one hundred, and the house occupies the greater part of the width. It is level, but the surrounding land is higher, resulting in a sharp terrace, three or four feet high, on the rear, E D. This terrace vanishes at C on the right, but extends nearly the whole length of the other side, gradually diminishing as it approaches A. There is a terrace two feet high extending from A to B, along the front. Beyond the line E D is the rear of an establishment which it is desired to hide. Since the terraces set definite borders to this little place, it is desirable to plant the boundaries rather heavily. If the adjoining lawns were on the same level, or if the neighbors would allow one area to be merged into the other by pleasant slopes, the three yards might be made into one picture; but the place must remain isolated.

There are three problems of structural planting in the place: to provide a cover or screen at the rear; to provide lower border masses on the side terraces; to plant next the foundations of the house. Aside from these problems, the grower is entitled to have a certain number of specimen plants, if he has particular liking for given types, but these specimens must be planted in some relation to the structural masses, and not in the middle of the lawn.

The owner desired a mixed planting, for variety. The following shrubs were actually selected and planted. The place is in central New York:—

Shrubs for the tall background

- 2 Barberry, *Berberis vulgaris* and var. *purpurea.*
- 1 Cornus Mas.
- 2 Tall deutzias.
- 3 Lilacs.
- 2 Mock oranges, *Philadelphus grandiflorus* and *P. coronarius.*
- 2 Variegated elders.
- 2 Eleagnus, *Eloeagnus hortensis* and *E. longipes.*
- 1 Exochorda.
- 2 Hibiscuses.
- 1 Privet.
- 3 Viburnums.
- 1 Snowball.
- 1 Tartarian honeysuckle.
- 1 Silver Bell, *Halesia tetraptera.*

These were planted on the sloping bank of the terrace, from E to D. The terrace has an incline, or width, of about three feet.

Shrubs of medium size, suitable for side plantings and groups in the foregoing example

- 3 Barberries, *Berberis Thunbergii.*
- 3 Osier dogwoods, variegated.
- 2 Japanese quinces, *Cydonia Japonica* and *C. Maulei.*
- 4 Tall deutzias.
- 1 Variegated elder.
- 7 Weigelas, assorted colors.
- 1 Rhodotypos.
- 9 Spireas of medium growth, assorted.
- 1 Rubus odoratus.
- 1 Lonicera fragrantissima.

Most of these shrubs were planted in a border two feet wide, extending from B to C D, the planting beginning about ten feet back from the street. Some of them were placed on the terrace at the left, extending from E one-fourth of the distance to A.

The plants were set about two feet apart. A strong clump was placed at N to screen the back yard. In this back yard a few small fruit trees and a strawberry bed were planted.

Low informal shrubs for front of porch and banking against house

- 3 Deutzia gracilis.
- 6 Kerrias, green and variegated.
- 3 Daphne Mezereum.
- 3 Lonicera Halliana.
- 3 Rubus phoenicolasius.
- 3 Symphoricarpus vulgaris.
- 4 Mahonias.
- 1 Ribes aureum.
- 1 Ribes sanguineum.
- 1 Rubus cratægifolius.
- 1 Rubus fruticosus var. laciniatus.

These bushes were planted against the front of the house (a porch on a high foundation extends to the right from O), from the walk around to P, and a few of them were placed at the rear of the house.

Specimen shrubs for mere ornament, for this place

- Azalea.
- Rhododendron.
- Rose.
- 2 Hydrangeas.
- 1 Snowball.
- 1 each Forsythia suspensa and F. viridissima.
- 2 Flowering almonds.

These were planted in conspicuous places here and there against the other masses.

Here are one hundred excellent and interesting bushes planted in a yard only fifty feet wide and one hundred feet deep, and yet the place has as much room in it as it had before. There is abundant opportunity along the borders for dropping in cannas, dahlias, hollyhocks, asters, geraniums, coleuses, and other brilliant plants. The bushes will soon begin to crowd, to be sure, but a mass is wanted, and the narrowness of the plantations will allow each bush to develop itself laterally to perfection. If the borders become too thick, however, it is an easy matter to remove some of the bushes; but they probably will not. Picture the color and variety and life in that little yard. And if a pigweed now and then gets a start in the border, it would do no harm to let it alone: it belongs there! Then picture the same area filled with disconnected, spotty, dyspeptic, and unspirited flower-beds and rose bushes!

Various examples

Strong and bare foundations should be relieved by heavy planting. Fill the corners with snow-drifts of foliage. Plant with a free hand, as if you meant it.

The corner by the steps is a perennial source of bad temper. The lawn-mower will not touch it, and the grass has to be cut with a butcher-knife. If nothing else comes to hand, let a burdock grow in it.

The tennis-screen may be relieved by a background, and a clump of ribbon-grass or something else is out of the way against a post.

Excellent mass effects may be secured by cutting well-established plants of sumac, ailanthus, basswood, and other strong-growing things, to the ground each year, for the purpose of securing the stout shoots.

But if one has no area which he can make into a lawn and upon which he can plant such verdurous masses, what then may he do? Even then there may be opportunity for a little neat and artistic planting. Even if one lives in a rented house, he may bring in a bush or an herb from the woods, and paint a picture with it.

Plant it in the corner by the steps, in front of the porch, at the corner of the house,—almost anywhere except in the center of the lawn. Make the ground rich, secure a strong root, and plant it with care; then wait. The little clump will not only have a beauty and interest of its own, but it may add immensely to the furniture of the yard.

About these clumps one may plant bulbs of glowing tulips or dainty snowdrops and lilies-of-the-valley; and these may be followed with pansies and phlox and other simple folk. Very soon one finds himself deeply interested in these random and detached pictures, and almost before he is aware he finds that he has rounded off the corners of the house, made snug little arbors of wild grapes and clematis, covered the rear fence and the outhouse with actinidia and bitter-sweet, and has thrown in dashes of color with hollyhocks, cannas, and lilies, and has tied the foundations of the buildings to the greensward by low strands of vines or deft bits of planting. He soon comes to feel that flowers are most expressive of the best emotions when they are daintily dropped in here and there against a background of foliage, or else made a side-piece in the place. There is no limit to the adaptations.

Presently he rebels at the bold, harsh, and impudent designs of some of the gardeners, and grows into a resourceful love of plant forms and verdure. He may still like the weeping and cut-leaved and party-colored trees of the horticulturist, but he sees that their best effects are to be had when they are planted sparingly, as borders or promontories of the structural masses.

The best planting, as the best painting and the best music, is possible only with the best and tenderest feeling and the closest living with nature. One's place grows to be a reflection of himself, changing as he changes, and expressing his life and sympathies to the last.

REVIEW

We have now discussed some of the principles and applications of landscape architecture or landscape gardening, particularly in reference to the planting. The object of landscape gardening is _to make a picture._ All the grading, seeding, planting, are incidental and supplemental to this one central idea. The greensward is the canvas, the house or some other prominent point is the central figure, the planting completes the composition and adds the color.

The second conception is the principle that _the picture should have a landscape effect._ That is, it should be nature-like. Carpet-beds are masses of color, not pictures. They are the little garnishings and reliefs that are to be used very cautiously, as little eccentricities and conventionalisms in a building should never be more than very minor features.

Every other concept in landscape gardening is subordinate to these two. Some of the most important of these secondary yet underlying considerations are as follows:— The place is to be conceived of as _a unit._ If a building is not pleasing, ask an architect to improve it. The real architect will study the building as a whole, grasp its design and meaning, and suggest improvements that will add to the forcefulness of the entire structure. A dabbler would add a chimney here, a window there, and apply various daubs of paint to the building. Each of these features might be good in itself. The paints might be the best of ochre, ultramarine, or paris green, but they might have no relation to the building as a whole and would be only ludicrous. These two examples illustrate the difference between landscape gardening and the scattering over the place of mere ornamental features.

There should be _one central and emphatic point in the picture._ A picture of a battle draws its interest from the action of a central figure or group. The moment the incidental and lateral figures are made as prominent as the central figures, the picture loses emphasis, life, and meaning. The borders of a place are of less importance than its center. Therefore:

Keep the center of the place open;

Frame and mass the sides; Avoid scattered effects.

In a landscape picture flowers are incidents. They add emphasis, supply color, give variety and finish; they are the ornaments, but the lawn and the mass-plantings make the framework. One flower in the border, and made an incident of the picture, is more effective than twenty flowers in the center of the lawn.

More depends on the positions that plants occupy with reference to each other and to the structural design of the place_ than on the intrinsic merits of the plants themselves.

Landscape gardening, then, is the embellishment of grounds in such a way that they will have a nature-like or landscape effect. The flowers and accessories may heighten and accelerate the effect, but they should not contradict it.

5

The Vegetable Garden

INTRODUCTION

SOME PLANNING HINTS

Plan the garden on paper first. Draw a map showing arrangement and spacing of crops. If you wish to keep the garden growing all season, you may need a spring, summer, and fall garden plan.

Most garden catalogs have seed available year round but they have last years seed available at the first of the year. Plan the garden and order seeds by January or February. Some plants may be started indoors as early as 12 weeks prior to being set out in the garden. See table 10.4 for temperatures and times required for growing plants for field transplanting.

In your plan, place tall and trellised crops on the north side of the garden so they won't shade the shorter vegetables.

Group plants by length of growing period. Plant spring crops together so that later crops can be planted in these areas when the early crops mature. Consider length of harvest as well as time to maturity. Place perennial crops to the side of the garden where they will not be disturbed by annual tillage.

LOCATING THE GARDEN

Vegetables grow best in a level area with loose, well-drained soil, and at least 6 hours of sun (8 to 10 hours is ideal).

Use contour rows or terraces on sloped or hillside sites to avoid erosion. South-facing slopes are warmer and less subject to damaging frosts.

Avoid placing the garden in low spots, at the base of a hill, or at the foot of a slope bordered by a solid fence. Such areas are slow to warm up in the spring, and frost settles in these places, since cold air naturally drains into low areas.

Avoid windy locations; if you must plant in a windy spot, build or grow a windbreak.

Locate near a good and easily accessible supply of water if possible.

Choose a spot near your home so it is convenient to work in the garden when you have a few minutes.

Avoid planting near trees and shrubs; they compete for nutrients and water, and may cause excessive shading.

Sites too near buildings may result in plants not receiving enough sunlight. Observe shading patterns through the growing season; if possible, before starting the garden. If you have a shaded area you wish to use anyway, plant shade-tolerant crops. Increase effective light, if needed, by providing reflective surfaces around plants.

Try not to plant vegetables from the same family in exactly the same location in the garden more often than once in 3 years. Rotation prevents the buildup of insects and disease. Use old plans as guides for rotating crops.

Avoid locations near busy roads. Airborne lead from automobile exhaust can contaminate vegetables, especially leafy types. If you must plant in a lead-prone area, try planting a hedge to trap lead in the air.

Avoid locating the garden on a site where buildings with lead paint have stood; soil lead may be present in toxic amounts. If you are unsure about your chosen location, have the soil tested for lead content, or have tissue analyses done on some leafy vegetables.

Table: Vegetable Grouped According to Family

Family	**Vegetable**
Amaryllidaceae	garlic, leek, onion
Chenopodiaceae	beet, spinach
Compositae	endive, lettuce, sunflower
Cruciferae	broccoli, Brussels sprouts, cabbage, cauliflower, Chinese cabbage, collards, kale kohlrabi, mustard, radish, rutabaga, turnip
Cucurbitaceae	cucumber, muskmelon, pumpkin, squash, watermelon
Gramineae	corn
Leguminosae	bean, pea, peanut
Liliaceae	asparagus
Malvaceae	okra
Solanaceae	eggplant, pepper, tomato
Umbelliferae	carrot, celery, parsley, parsnip

SOIL PREPARATION

The ideal vegetable garden soil is deep, friable, well-drained, and has high organic matter content. Proper soil preparation provides the basis for good seed germination and subsequent growth of garden crops. Careful use of various soil amendments can improve garden soil and provide the best possible starting ground for your crops.

Soil testing

Soil testing can be helpful if your garden is not performing as it should. Soil testing is costly for the home gardener since home test kits are of little value for Arizona soil. To obtain an accurate soil test a soil sample must be sent to a certified soils laboratory. County Extension offices have a list of labs available for your use. In general soils in Arizona will be lacking in nitrogen and phosphate. Regular applications of these two elements should prevent the majority of problems due to nutrient deficiencies.

Equipment

The type of equipment used to prepare your garden will depend on the size of the garden, your physical ability, time, and budget. Options include hand-digging with a spade or shovel, tilling with a power rotary tiller, using a small garden tractor, or a full-sized farm tractor.

Make basic nutrients and pH adjustments to the soil by spreading required fertilizers and sulfur to soils of high pH. In new garden spots, if present remove sod with a spade and use it to patch your lawn or put it in a compost pile to decay. Plow, spade, or rotary till the soil. Work only when soil moisture conditions are right. To test, pick up a handful of soil and squeeze it. If it stays in a ball it is too wet. If it crumbles freely, it should be about right. Excessively dry soil is powdery and clumpy and may be difficult to work. Take samples at the surface and at a 2 to 3-inch depth in several locations in the garden plot. If soil sticks to a shovel, or if when spading, the turned surface is shiny and smooth, it is still too wet. Working soils when excessively wet can destroy soil structure, which may take years to rebuild.

Plowing with a tractor when the soil is wet is especially damaging, causing the formation of a compaction layer that will inhibit root growth. Soils with adequate humus levels generally allow more leeway because of their improved structural qualities.

Tilling the soil

It was once assumed that gardens should be turned yearly with a moldboard plow, mostly for weed and pest control, or to incorporate nutrients or organic matter. While garden plowing is still a common practice, turning the soil completely over has been found to be detrimental in some cases, causing soil compaction, upsetting balances of microorganisms, and often causing layers of coarse organic material to be buried below the influence of insects and microbes which would otherwise cause breakdown of the material. Chisel plowing, which does not have this disruptive effect, is one alternative, but it is limited to sandy or loamy soils and many farmers who work gardens do not have chisel plows. In addition, gardeners in other-than-rural areas have trouble finding a farmer who will come to plow and disk the garden for a reasonable price (or at all). Rototilling most home gardens is sufficient, as long as plant debris accumulation is not out of hand.

Rotary tilling mixes the upper layers of soil rather than completely turning the soil over, and the effect produced are generally desirable. One possible harmful effect of rototilling is the formation of a compaction layer just beyond the reach of the tines. This also occurs when a moldboard plow is used to the same depth every year, but at a somewhat deeper level. Use of deep-rooted cover crops or double-digging can do much to prevent or alleviate this problem when it exists. Small gardens can be designed using raised beds which may be worked entirely by hand if the area is small enough.

Gardeners often wonder whether to plow/till immediately following harvest or wait until just prior to planting. Working the soil following harvest has several advantages over the traditional of plowing just prior to planting. It allows earlier planting, since the basic soil preparation is already done when planting time arrives. Turning under large amounts of organic matter is likely to result in better decomposition when done earlier, since there is more time for the process to take place.

Insects, disease organisms, and perennial weeds may be reduced by killing or inactivating them through burial or exposure to harsh weather. The physical condition of heavy clay soils may be improved by the alternate freezing and thawing, which breaks up tightly aggregated particles. Also, moisture is trapped between the hills of roughly-plowed soil, so more moisture is retained than on flat, bare ground. Incorporation of rock fertilizers in the fall gives them time to become integrated with the soil and influence spring plant growth.

After harvest plowing alone is not recommended for hillside or steep garden plots, since soil is left exposed for long periods, subjecting it to erosion when the rains come. If a cover crop is grown to improve soil and prevent erosion, the ground will have to be tilled to prepare the soil for seed, and again later to turn under the green manure. Generally, most gardens must be disked or rotary-tilled prior to planting to smooth the soil.

SEED FOR THE GARDEN

Choosing and purchasing vegetable seeds is one of the most enjoyable gardening pastimes. Thumbing through colorful catalogs and dreaming of the season's harvest is one way to make winter seem a little warmer. Seed purchased from a dependable seed company will provide a good start toward realizing that vision of bounty. Keep notes about the seeds you purchase - their germination qualities, vigor of plants, tendencies toward insects and disease, etc. From this information you can determine whether one seed company is not meeting your needs, or whether the varieties you have chosen are unsuitable for your area or gardening style. For example, if powdery mildew is a big problem on squash family plants in your area, the next year you may want to look for mildew-resistant varieties.

Saving seed

Saving your own vegetable seed is another pleasurable activity. It offers a sense of self-sufficiency and saves money. You can maintain a variety that is not available commercially, which helps to perpetuate a broad genetic base of plant materials. Breeders often search for old-time varieties when attempting to improve commercial plants, since the heirloom vegetables (as they are sometimes called) often have inbred disease- and pest-resistance or cold-hardiness. Participation in a seed-saver's exchange can be a rewarding experience. Extra seeds that you have may be traded for unusual types that are not available through other sources.

f******

There are certain considerations that should be kept in mind when saving seed, however. Hybrid varieties are not likely to be the same as the parent plants; therefore, only open-pollinated varieties should be used for home seed production. Some seed dealers have responded to the increasing interest in seed-saving by clearly marking open-pollinated varieties in their catalogs. Another consideration in saving seed is the possibility of carrying seed-borne diseases into the next year's crop. Many commercially grown seeds are grown in dry areas unsuitable to fungal, viral, and bacterial diseases which may be present in your region.

Take care to control diseases which can be carried in seed. Another weather-related factor is the speed of drying of seeds, which can be adversely affected by frequent rains and/or humidity. And finally, if you've ever saved squash seed during a season in which you had more than one type of squash planted, you have probably seen the weird results that may be obtained from cross-pollination! Saving seeds from cross-pollinated crops is not generally recommended for the novice because of problems with selection, requirements for hand pollination and isolation, biennial habits, and genetic variability.

Some common self-pollinated annual plants from which seed may be saved include lettuce, beans and peas, herbs, and tomatoes.

Saving beans and peas: Allow seed pods to turn brown on the plant. Harvest pods, dry for 1 to 2 weeks, shell, and then store in a cool (below 50° F.), dry environment in a paper bag.

On an extended trip, make special arrangements so that plants will not be frozen or damaged by cold weather. Many foliage plants will be damaged considerably if the temperature drops much below 50° F, so maintain as warm a temperature as possible around these plants when transporting them from one location to another.

Saving lettuce seed: Cut off seed stalks when fluffy in appearance, just before all the seeds are completely dried. Seeds will fall off the stalk and be lost if allowed to mature on the plant. Dry the harvested seed stalk further, shake seeds off, and then store in a cool, dry environment in an envelope or small glass jar.

Saving herb seeds: Herbs vary in the way their seeds are produced. In general, allow herb seeds to stay on the plants until they are almost completely dry. Some seed heads, such as dill, will shatter and drop their seeds as soon as they are dry. Watch the early-ripening seeds; if they tend to fall off, harvest the other seed heads before they get to that point, leaving several inches of stem attached. Hang several stems upside down, covered with a paper bag to catch falling seed, in a warm, dry place until the drying is complete. Remove seeds from the seed heads and store in envelopes or small glass jars. Some herb seeds, dill, celery, anise, cumin, coriander, and others are used for flavoring and are ready to use once dry.

Saving tomato seeds: Pick fruit from desirable plants when ripe. Cut fruit and squeeze out pulp into a container. Add a little water, then let ferment 2 to 4 days at room temperature, stirring occasionally. When seeds settle out, pour off pulp and spread seeds thinly to dry thoroughly. Store in an envelope or glass jar in a cool, dry place.

For all kinds of saved seeds, be sure to mark the storage containers clearly with permanent (preferably waterproof) ink, indicating the variety and date saved. Seeds will remain viable for some time if properly stored. To test for germination, sprout seeds between moist paper towels; if germination is low, either discard the seed or plant enough extra to give the desired number of plants.

Table: Viability of Vegetable Seeds (Average number of years seeds may be saved)

Vegetable	Years	Vegetable	Years
Asparagus	3	Leek	1
Bean	3	Lettuce	5
Beet	4	Muskmelon	5
Broccoli	4	Mustard	4
Brussels sprouts	4	Okra	2
Cabbage	4	Onion	1
Carrot	3	Parsley	2
Cauliflower	4	Parsnip	1
Celery	5	Pea	3
Chinese cabbage	4	Pepper	3
Collard	4	Pumpkin	4
Corn, sweet	1	Radish	4
Cress, water	5	Rutabaga	4
Cucumber	5	Spinach	4
Eggplant	5	Squash	4
Endive	5	Tomato	3
Kale	4	Turnip	5
Kohlrabi	4	Watermelon	5

Many types of containers can be used to start seeds. Flats or other large containers may be used; plant in rows and grow seedlings until they have one or two sets of true leaves, then transplant into other containers for growing to the size to transplant outdoors. Seedlings may also be started in pots, old cans, cut-off milk cartons, margarine tubs, egg cartons, or other throwaways. The pop-out trays found at garden centers are easy to use and re-usable. Peat pots are nice, especially for large seeds. Sow one or two large seeds directly in each peat pot.

Thin to one seedling per pot. Peat pots may be planted directly in the garden; do not allow the edges of the pot to stick out above the soil, since they will act as a wick and moisture will evaporate from this exposed surface.

Regardless of the type of container chosen, fill it 3/4 full with seed-starting mixture and sow the seeds. Cover to the specified depth and water the mix. If your home is dry, it may help to cover the containers with plastic wrap to maintain a steadier moisture level. Seeds and seedlings are extremely sensitive to drying out. They should not be kept soaking wet, however, since this condition is conducive to damping-off, a fungus disease deadly to seedlings.

Damping-off can be prevented by sprinkling milled sphagnum moss, which contains a natural fungicide, on top of the soil.

Another option is to use peat pellets or cubes, which are pre-formed and require no additional soil mix. The pellets or cubes are soaked until thoroughly wet, then seeds are planted in the holes provided. The whole pellet may then be planted without disturbing the roots. The only disadvantage to this method is the expense.

Starting seed outdoors

Many seeds may be sown directly in the garden. If garden soil is quite sandy, or is mellow with a high content of organic matter, seeds may be planted deeper. Young seedlings can emerge quite easily from a sandy or organic soil. If garden soil is heavy with a high silt and/or clay content, however, the seeds should be covered only 2 to 3 times their diameter. In such soils, it may be helpful to apply a band of sand, fine compost, or vermiculite 4 inches wide and 1/4 inch thick along the row after seeds are planted. This will help retain soil moisture and reduce crusting, making it easier for seedlings to push through the soil surface.

Soil temperature has an effect on the speed of seed germination. In the spring, soil is often cold and seeds of some plants will rot before they have a chance to sprout.

When planting the fall garden in midsummer, the soil will be warm and dry. Therefore, cover the seeds 6 to 8 times their diameter. They may need to be watered each day with a sprinkler or a sprinkling can to promote germination. Moisture can also be retained with a shallow mulch or by covering the row with a board until the seeds are up. Shading the area may be helpful to keep the soil cooler for seed germination, especially when planting cool-weather crops in summer. Seed which requires a lower germination temperature may benefit from being kept in the refrigerator for 2 weeks before planting, or from pre-sprouting indoors. Pre-sprouting is a useful technique for planting in cold soils, as well. However, seed must be handled very carefully once sprouted to prevent damaging new root tissue.

Row Planting

A string stretched between stakes will provide a guide for nice straight rows, if desired. Use a hoe handle, a special furrow hoe, or a grub hoe to make a furrow of the appropriate depth for the seed being planted. Sow seed thinly; it may help to mix very small seed with coarse sand to distribute the seeds more evenly. Draw soil over the seed, removing stones and large clods. Firming soil over seeds improves uptake of soil moisture, hastening germination. Water the seeds in to improve soil/seed contact. When plants have grown to 4 to 6 inches tall, thin according to seed packet instructions to provide adequate room for growth.

Broadcast planting

Many crops may be sown in wide rows or beds instead of in long, single rows. Crops such as spinach, beans, peas, beets, lettuce, and carrots are especially suited to this type of culture. Sow seed evenly over the area, then rake it in. Firm soil over the seeds. Thin young plants to allow room for growth.

Hill Planting

Larger vegetables such as melons, squash, corn, and cucumbers may be planted in hills. Soil is mounded to a foot or so in diameter, at the recommended spacing. Plant 4 to 6 seeds per hill, firming the soil well. Thin the seedlings to 3 to 5 plants per hill.

TRANSPLANTS FOR THE GARDEN

Most gardeners use transplants in the garden at some time or another to give long season plants a chance to grow to maturity under their preferred weather conditions, or just to lengthen the harvest season. Tomatoes would certainly have a short harvest period in all but the mid-elevation range of Arizona if started from seed in the ground, and peppers and eggplants might not produce at all if not grown from transplants. Due to the amount of time, attention and need for controlled growing conditions, many gardeners prefer to purchase plants for their gardens. However, for a larger choice in varieties and the control of plant production from seed to harvest, others choose to start their own.

Annual plants

Transplants of annual vegetables and flowers should be stocky, healthy, free from disease, and have good roots. They should not be too small or too mature (tomatoes will transplant all right with fruits already on them, but many other plants will drop flowers or fruit after transplanting). Be sure plants have been hardened-off so that they will easily adapt to environmental change, but they should not be so hardened that they are woody and yellow. Successful transplanting is achieved by interrupting plant growth as little as possible. This is one of the advantages of using peat pots or peat pellets, which do not have to be removed when transplanting.

Have garden soil prepared before transplanting. All additives which require time to break down, such as manures, sulfur, rock fertilizers, and green manures, should be incorporated several weeks before planting. Quick-acting fertilizers and well-decayed compost may be added just before planting Transplant on a shady day, in late afternoon, or in early evening to prevent wilting. It helps to water the plants several hours before transplanting; when using bare-root plants, such as sweet potato slips or plants from an old-time farm supply store, soak the roots thoroughly an hour or two before setting them out in the garden. They should not be allowed to dry out completely at any time. Handle plants carefully. Avoid disturbing the roots or bruising the stems.

Dig a hole large enough to hold the roots of the plants. Set the plants level with the ground and at recommended intervals. Tomatoes are an exception to the rule of how deep to plant; they will develop roots all along the stems, and you can plant deep enough to leave only two or three sets of leaves exposed. Press soil firmly around the roots of transplants. Pour about a cup of starter solution in the hole around the plant. Use a solution of about half the strength recommended for that type of plant during the normal growing season. Fish emulsion or dilute manure tea may also be used.

For a few days after transplanting, protect plants from wind and sun by placing newspaper or cardboard on their south sides, or by covering with jugs, baskets, or flower pots.

Water the plants once a day during the next week if there is insufficient rain. In the following weeks reduce the frequency of water, to every other day the second week and every third day the third week until established. Once established, the type of plant, soil conditions, and weather conditions will dictate how often to water and how much water to apply. Tables 10.6, 10.7 and 10.8 will help in determining irrigation timing.

Perennial plants

When buying small fruit plants and perennial crowns such as asparagus, order early or buy from reliable local outlets. Discount department stores often allow plants to dry up, so watch for this, especially if you are buying sale plants. Select varieties that will do well in your growing conditions. For perennial plants, it will pay to do some research to find out what the major disease and insect pests are and buy resistant varieties.

Dormant, bareroot plants and 1 or 2-year-old crowns are preferred. Look for roots that are full, slightly moist, and have color. Roots that are dry brown or soggy black are indicative of poor storage and will probably not give good results. Check crowns for signs of viable buds. Inspect plants for signs of insects or disease. If you receive plants by mail which are not satisfactory, do not hesitate to send them back.

Once you have the plants, keep the roots moist (but not soaking wet) by misting occasionally, and do not allow them to freeze or be exposed to high temperatures. If it is necessary to keep the crowns for more than a few days, place in cold storage (not freezing) or else heel in a trench of moist soil in a shaded location. Pack soil firmly against roots to eliminate any air pockets.

Transplant crowns according to directions, digging holes large enough to give the roots plenty of room to spread. Remove any roots which are discolored or dried out.

Perennial plants appreciate a dose of compost mixed into the bottom of the hole. Once transplanted, shade the plants if necessary and water when needed. Extra care at the beginning of their growth will result in productive, healthy plants.

Table: Transplant Production Data (Ease of transplanting)

Easily Survive Transplanting	Require Care in the Operation	Not Successfully Transplanted by Usual Methods
Broccoli	Beets	Beans
Cabbage	Carrots (young)	Corn
Cauliflower	Celery	Cucumbers
Eggplant	Chard	Peas
Lettuce	Melon (2 true leaves)	Okra
Chinese cabbage	Squash (2 true leaves)	
Sweet potato slips		
Onion (tends to bolt)		
Tomatoes		
Pepper		

IRRIGATING THE GARDEN

Adequate soil moisture is essential for good crop growth. A healthy plant is composed of 75% to 90% water, which is used for the plant's vital functions, including photosynthesis, support (rigidity), and transportation of nutrients and sugars to various parts of the plant. During the first 2 weeks of growth, plants are becoming established and must have water to build their root systems.

While growing, vegetable crops need about an inch of water per week in the form of rainwater, irrigation water, or both, from April to September. Keep a rain gauge near the garden or check with the local weather bureau for rainfall amounts, then supplement rainfall with irrigation water if needed. There are ways, however, to reduce the amount of water you have to add.

During dry periods, one thorough watering each week of 1 to 2 inches of moisture (65 to 130 gallons per 100 square feet) is usually enough for most soils. Soil should be wetted to a depth of 12 inches each time you water and not watered again until the top few inches begin to dry out. Average garden soil will store about 2 to 4 inches of water per foot of depth.

Reducing water demands

All of this water, however, may not be available to plants, particularly if the soil is a heavy clay. Clay particles hold soil moisture tightly. If, for example, there are 4 inches of water per foot of this type of soil, there may be as little as 2 inches available for plants. A relatively high level of humus in the soil, brought about by the addition and breakdown of organic matter, can improve this proportion to some extent. By causing clay particles to form aggregates or large clumps of groups of particles, humus also adds air spaces to tight clays, allowing moisture to drain to lower levels as a reserve, instead of puddling and running off the top of the soil.

The moisture-holding capacity of sandy soils is also improved by addition of organic matter. Though most soil water in sandy soil is available, it drains so quickly that plants are unable to reach water after even a few days following a rain. Humus in sandy soil gives the water something to cling to until it is needed by plants. Addition of organic matter is the first step in improving moisture conditions in the garden.

Mulching is a cultural practice which can significantly decrease the amount of water that must be added to the soil. A 4 to 6 inch organic mulch can reduce water needs by as much as 1/2 by smothering weeds (which take up and transpire moisture) and by reducing evaporation of moisture directly from the soil. Organic mulches themselves hold some water and increase the humidity level around the plant. Black or clear plastic mulch also conserves moisture but increases soil temperatures dramatically during the summer (to the detriment of some plants and the benefit of others) if not covered by other mulch materials or foliage.

Shading and the use of windbreaks are other moisture-conserving techniques. Plants that wilt in very sunny areas can benefit from partial shade during the afternoon in summer. Small plants, in particular, should be protected. Air moving across a plant carries away the moisture on the leaf surfaces, causing the plant to need more water. In very windy areas, the roots often cannot keep up with leaf demands, and plants wilt. Temporary or permanent windbreaks can help tremendously.

During those times when cultural practices simply aren't enough, when rainfall is sparse and the sun is hot, watering can benefit the garden with higher yields, or may save the garden altogether in severe drought years.

Irrigation, when properly used, can benefit the garden in many ways:

- Aids in seed emergence.
- Reduces soil crusting.
- Improves germination and plant stand

- Reduces wilting and checking of growth in transplants.
- Increases fruit size of tomato, cucumber, and melon.
- Prevents premature ripening of peas, beans, and sweet corn.
- Maintains uniform growth.
- Improves the quality and yields of most crops.

Irrigation methods

The home gardener has several options for applying water to plants - a watering sprinkler can, a garden hose with a fan nozzle or spray attachment, portable lawn sprinklers, a perforated plastic soaker hose, drip or trickle irrigation, or a semi-automatic drip system. Quality equipment will last for a number of years when properly cared for. When deciding on which type of watering equipment to use there are a number of things to consider.

Several types of drip or trickle equipment are available. The soaker hose is probably the least expensive and easiest to use. It is a fibrous hose that allows water to seep out all along its length at a slow rate. There are also hoses with holes in them that do basically the same thing; water drips out the holes. With the latter type, a flow regulator usually has to be included with the system so that water can reach the end of the hose, yet not be sprayed out at full force. A special double-wall type of irrigation hose has also been developed which helps to maintain an even flow. Finally, there is the emitter type system, best used for small raised-bed or container gardens, in which short tubes, or emitters, come off a main water supply hose; emitters put water right at the roots of the desired plants.

This is generally the most expensive form of irrigation and the most complex to set up, but it has the advantage that the weeds in the area are not watered, and evaporation from the soil is minimized. This type of system is best used in combination with a coarse mulch or black plastic. Drip systems generally have some problems with clogging from soil particles and/or mineral salts from water taken from springs or wells. New designs take into consideration the clogging problem; some include filters and self-flushing emitters. It is wise to make a complete investigation and comparison before purchasing a drip irrigation system.

IRRIGATING THE GARDEN

Adequate soil moisture is essential for good crop growth. A healthy plant is composed of 75% to 90% water, which is used for the plant's vital functions, including photosynthesis, support (rigidity), and transportation of nutrients and sugars to various parts of the plant. During the first 2 weeks of growth, plants are becoming established and must have water to build their root systems.

While growing, vegetable crops need about an inch of water per week in the form of rainwater, irrigation water, or both, from April to September. Keep a rain gauge near the garden or check with the local weather bureau for rainfall amounts, then supplement rainfall with irrigation water if needed. There are ways, however, to reduce the amount of water you have to add.

During dry periods, one thorough watering each week of 1 to 2 inches of moisture (65 to 130 gallons per 100 square feet) is usually enough for most soils. Soil should be wetted to a depth of 12 inches each time you water and not watered again until the top few inches begin to dry out. Average garden soil will store about 2 to 4 inches of water per foot of depth.

Reducing water demands

All of this water, however, may not be available to plants, particularly if the soil is a heavy clay. Clay particles hold soil moisture tightly. If, for example, there are 4 inches of water per foot of this type of soil, there may be as little as 2 inches available for plants. A relatively high level of humus in the soil, brought about by the addition and breakdown of organic matter, can improve this proportion to some extent. By causing clay particles to form aggregates or large clumps of groups of particles, humus also adds air spaces to tight clays, allowing moisture to drain to lower levels as a reserve, instead of puddling and running off the top of the soil.

The moisture-holding capacity of sandy soils is also improved by addition of organic matter. Though most soil water in sandy soil is available, it drains so quickly that plants are unable to reach water after even a few days following a rain. Humus in sandy soil gives the water something to cling to until it is needed by plants. Addition of organic matter is the first step in improving moisture conditions in the garden.

Mulching is a cultural practice which can significantly decrease the amount of water that must be added to the soil. A 4 to 6 inch organic mulch can reduce water needs by as much as 1/2 by smothering weeds (which take up and transpire moisture) and by reducing evaporation of moisture directly from the soil. Organic mulches themselves hold some water and increase the humidity level around the plant. Black or clear plastic mulch also conserves moisture but increases soil temperatures dramatically during the summer (to the detriment of some plants and the benefit of others) if not covered by other mulch materials or foliage.

Shading and the use of windbreaks are other moisture-conserving techniques. Plants that wilt in very sunny areas can benefit from partial shade during the afternoon in summer. Small plants, in particular, should be protected. Air moving across a plant carries away the moisture on the leaf surfaces, causing the plant to need more water. In very windy areas, the roots often cannot keep up with leaf demands, and plants wilt. Temporary or permanent windbreaks can help tremendously.

During those times when cultural practices simply aren't enough, when rainfall is sparse and the sun is hot, watering can benefit the garden with higher yields, or may save the garden altogether in severe drought years.

Irrigation, when properly used, can benefit the garden in many ways:

- Aids in seed emergence.
- Reduces soil crusting.
- Improves germination and plant stand
- Reduces wilting and checking of growth in transplants.
- Increases fruit size of tomato, cucumber, and melon.
- Prevents premature ripening of peas, beans, and sweet corn.
- Maintains uniform growth.
- Improves the quality and yields of most crops.

Irrigation methods

The home gardener has several options for applying water to plants - a watering sprinkler can, a garden hose with a fan nozzle or spray attachment, portable lawn sprinklers, a perforated plastic soaker hose, drip`or trickle irrigation, or a semi-automatic drip system. Quality equipment will last for a number of years when properly cared for. When deciding on which type of watering equipment to use there are a number of things to consider.

Several types of drip or trickle equipment are available. The soaker hose is probably the least expensive and easiest to use. It is a fibrous hose that allows water to seep out all along its length at a slow rate. There are also hoses with holes in them that do basically the same thing; water drips out the holes. With the latter type, a flow regulator usually has to be included with the system so that water can reach the end of the hose, yet not be sprayed out at full force. A special double-wall type of irrigation hose has also been developed which helps to maintain an even flow. Finally, there is the emitter type system, best used for small raised-bed or container gardens, in which short tubes, or emitters, come off a main water supply hose; emitters put water right at the roots of the desired plants. This is generally the most expensive form of irrigation and the most complex to set up, but it has the advantage that the weeds in the area are not watered, and evaporation from the soil is minimized. This type of system is best used in combination with a coarse mulch or black plastic. Drip systems generally have some problems with clogging from soil particles and/or mineral salts from water taken from springs or wells. New designs take into consideration the clogging problem; some include filters and self-flushing emitters. It is wise to make a complete investigation and comparison before purchasing a drip irrigation system.

Table: Plant Feeder Root Depths*

CROP	FEEDER ROOT DEPTH	CROP	FEEDER ROOT DEPTH
ALFALFA	3 to 6 feet	NUTS	3 to 6 feet
BEANS	2 feet	ONIONS	1 1/2 feet
BEETS	2 to 3 feet	ORCHARD	3 to 5 feet
BERRIES (Cane)	3 feet	PASTURE (Grasses)	1 1/2 feet
CABBAGE	1 1/2 to 3 feet	PASTURE (w/Clover)	2 feet
CARROTS	"1 1/2" to 2 feet	PEANUTS	2 feet
CORN	2 1/2 feet	PEAS	2 1/2 feet
COTTON	4 feet	POTATOES	2 feet
CUCUMBERS	1 1/2 feet	SOY BEANS	2 feet
GRAIN	2 to 2 1/2 feet	STRAWBERRIES	1 to 1 1/2 feet
GRAIN, SORGHUM	2 1/2 feet	SWEET POTATOES	3 feet
GRAPES	3 to 6 feet	TOBACCO	2 1/2 feet
LETTUCE	1 foot	TOMATOES	3 to 4 feet
MELONS	2 1/2 to 3 feet		

*Majority of Feeder Roots

**All information in this fact-sheet regarding soils, their classifications, water holding capacity, available moisture and infiltration rate; crops, as to feeder root depth, water use, etc.; climate, as to irrigation efficiency is general or for average conditions. This information is to be used only as a guide; local conditions must govern each individual design.

Some basic techniques and principles for watering:

1. Adjust the flow or rate of water application to about 1/2 inch per hour. Much faster than this will cause run-off, unless the soil has exceptionally good drainage. To determine the rate for a sprinkler, place small tin cans at various places within the sprinkler's reach, and check the level of water in the cans at 15 minute intervals.
2. When using the oscillating type of lawn sprinklers, place the sprinkler on a platform higher than the crop to prevent water from being diverted by plant leaves and try to keep the watering pattern even by frequently moving the sprinkler, overlapping about 1/2 of each pattern.
3. Do not get foliage wet in the evening; this can encourage diseases. Morning watering is preferred.

Table: Net Amount of Moisture to Apply to Various Soils Under Different Moisture Retention Conditions

Soil Type	Root Zone Depth	Field Capacity	Amount Held at Wilting Point		Available Moisture Plant Uses	Net Inches to Apply per Irrigation with Various Percent		
	FEET	INCHES	PERCENT	INCHES	INCHES	67%	50%	33%
LIGHT SANDY	1	1.25	20%	0.25	1.00	0.33	0.50	0.67
	1 1/2	1.88		0.38	1.50	0.50	0.75	1.00
	2	2.50		0.50	2.00	0.66	1.00	1.33
	2 1/2	3.13		0.63	2.50	0.83	1.25	1.67
	3	3.75		0.75	3.00	0.99	1.50	2.00
	4	5.00		1.00	4.00	1.32	2.00	2.66
MEDIUM	1	2.25	25%	0.56	1.69	0.57	0.85	1.13
	1 1/2	3.38		0.85	2.53	0.84	1.26	1.70
	2	4.50		1.12	3.38	1.11	1.69	2.26
	2 1/2	5.62		1.41	4.21	1.39	2.11	2.82
	3	6.75		1.69	5.06	1.67	2.53	3.38
	4	9.00		2.25	6.75	2.23	3.38	4.52
HEAVY	1	3.67	35%	1.28	2.39	0.79	1.20	1.59
	1 1/2	5.50		1.92	3.58	1.18	1.79	2.38
	2	7.34		2.56	4.78	1.58	2.39	3.25
	2 1/2	9.17		3.20	5.97	1.97	2.98	3.97
	3	11.0		3.84	7.17	2.36	3.58	4.77
	4	14.68		5.12	9.56	3.15	4.78	6.37

NOTE: For optimum yield of high valued shallow rooted crops maintain 67% available moisture. For lower valued deeper rooted crops maintain 50% available moisture. For low value deep rooted crops maintain 33% available moisture.

4. Perforated plastic hoses or soaker hoses should be placed with holes down (if there are holes) along one side of the crop row or underneath mulch. Water is allowed to soak or seep into the soil slowly.
5. It is best to add enough water to soak the soil to a depth of at least 12 inches once plants have become established. It takes approximately .65 to 1.3 gallons of water for each square foot or 65 to 130 gallons for 100 square feet of garden area. This varies with the nature of the soil. Frequent, light waterings will only encourage shallow rooting which will cause plants to suffer more quickly during drought periods, especially if mulches are not used. On the other hand, too much water, especially in poorly drained soils, can be as damaging to plant growth as too little water.
6. By knowing the critical watering periods for selected vegetables, you can reduce the amount of supplemental water you add. This can be

important where water supplies are limited. In general, water is most needed during the first few weeks of development, immediately after transplant, and during development of edible storage organs.

Specifically, the critical watering periods for selected vegetables are:

Asparagus	Spear production, fern development
Broccoli	Head development
Cabbage	Head development
Cauliflower	Head development
Beans	Pod filling
Carrot	Seed emergence, root development
Corn	Silking, tasseling, ear development
Cucumber	Flowering, fruit development
Eggplant	Flowering, fruiting
Lettuce	Head development; moisture should be constant
Melons	Flowering, fruit development
Peas	Pod filling
Tomato	Flowering, fruiting

7. In areas prone to repeated drought, look for drought-resistant varieties when buying seed or plants.
8. If water supplies are short in your area and you wish to use grey water (water from household uses) on your vegetable garden, a few rules should be observed:

- Do not use "black water" (any water run through the toilet) because of the possibility of contamination from fecal organisms.
- It is preferable not to use kitchen waste water that contains grease or harsh cleaners, ammonia, bleach, softeners, or non-biodegradable detergents
- If using water from the bathtub or washing machine, use only mild, biodegradable soaps. Omit softeners and bleaches. Allow wash and rinse water to mix, if possible, to dilute the soap content. Never use a borax-containing product (such as washing soda) in water to be used on a garden because of the danger of applying plant-toxic levels of boron.
- Apply greywater to the soil, not to plant leaves. Some county health departments require that grey water be discharged below ground, through a drip system or similar mechanism.

ERTILIZING THE GARDEN

The amount of fertilizer to apply to a garden depends on the natural fertility of the soil, the amount of organic matter present, the type of fertilizer used, and the crop being grown. The best way to determine fertilizer needs is to have the soil tested. Information on soil testing and a list of testing laboratories is available through your local Extension agent. Soil test kits are of little value to gardeners in Arizona. Vegetables fall into three main categories according to their fertilizer requirements: heavy feeders, medium feeders, and light feeders. It may be advantageous to group crops in the garden according to their fertilizer requirements to make application easier.

Table : Plants Grouped According to Nutrient Needs

Heavy Feeders		Light Feeders	
Asparagus	Lettuce	Carrot	Alfalfa
Beet	Okra	Garlic	Beans
Broccoli*	Parsley	Leek	Clover
Brussels sprouts*	Pepper	Mustard Greens	Peas
Cabbage*	Potato	Onion	Peanut
Cantaloupe*	Pumpkin*	Parsnip	Soybeans
Cauliflower	Radish	Rutabaga	
Celery	Rhubarb	Shallot	
Collard	Spinach	Sweet Potato	
Corn, Sweet*	Squash, Summer*	Swiss Chard	
Eggplant*	Strawberry		
Endive	Sunflower		
Kalle	Tomato*		
Kohlrabi	Watermelon*		

WEED CONTROL IN THE GARDEN

The amount of fertilizer to apply to a garden depends on the natural fertility of the soil, the amount of organic matter present, the type of fertilizer used, and the crop being grown. The best way to determine fertilizer needs is to have the soil tested. Information on soil testing and a list of testing laboratories is available through your local Extension agent. Soil test kits are of little value to gardeners in Arizona. Vegetables fall into three main categories according to their fertilizer requirements: heavy feeders, medium feeders, and light feeders. It may be advantageous to group crops in the garden according to their fertilizer requirements to make application easier.

WEED CONTROL IN THE GARDEN

The old saying, "One year's weed - seven years' seed," contains more truth than myth, as most gardeners soon learn. Weeds (some native and some introduced) are remarkably adapted to conditions in the area where they grow, usually much more so than the imported cultured vegetables we prize so highly for food. Many weeds which would otherwise not be growing in a lawn or natural area appear to spring up as if by magic when the soil is cultivated. Weed seeds may remain viable for those 7 (or more) years when conditions are not right for their growth. Then, brought to the surface by tilling, and uninhibited by sod, shade, or other factors, they germinate and become the pests that take water, nutrients, sunlight, and space from vegetable plants.

Beneficial weeds

Many plants considered weeds in the garden have positive attributes. Some, such as the Venice mallow (or flower-of-an-hour), morning glory, and even thistles, have flowers that rival those intentionally planted in flower beds. In fact, seeds of some weeds are sold by seed companies as flowering plants.

Other native plants are edible, providing nutritious variety to the regular diet: dandelions, purslane, chickweed, cress, mustards, and lamb's quarters all offer greens; blackberries produce sweet fruits; Jerusalem artichokes, or sunchokes, are nothing but the tubers of the native sunflower; and of course, there is always wild asparagus.

Before attempting to eat wild plants, be sure that you have properly identified them. A course from a person knowledgeable about wild edibles is probably the best way to learn; books often do not make fine distinctions between edible and non-edible wild plants.

Weeds are often a habitat for various insects, some of which are beneficial to the garden. They provide shelter, pollen, and nectar for such insects as bees and predators of garden pests, such as praying mantids.

Wild plants also have other virtues. Parts of some plants are used in natural dyes and other home-made products. Weeds can be a good source of nitrogenous materials for the compost pile if pulled before flowering. Many have long roots which bring elements from the subsoil into their above-ground tissues; when the weeds are pulled or tilled and allowed to decay in the garden, these elements are made available to other plants. Finally, the presence of some native plants can indicate certain soil problems, e.g., deficiencies, pH changes, soil compaction, etc. A small number of books are available with detailed information on this subject.

Control methods

Despite all this goodness, most gardeners won't tolerate weeds in their vegetable plots. Perhaps it is an overreaction to the first garden he or she allowed to go completely to weeds or perhaps it's the unruly appearance of weeds. This may be a sensible approach. If one doesn't have time to ruthlessly destroy morning glory vines after enjoying the first few flowers and before they go to seed, the garden will soon become one glorious display of morning glories and little else.

Cultivation:

There are several ways to rid the garden of most problem plants. Since mature weeds extract large quantities of moisture and nutrients from the soil, it is more beneficial (and easier) to remove weeds when they are young and tender. Hand-pulling and digging are okay for small gardens and raised beds. Those with larger spaces usually prefer at least a hoe.

There are manual-powered rotary cultivators that do a good job on long rows and pathways as long as the soil is not too wet or dry and the weeds are small. In large gardens, a rotary tiller of appropriate size makes the work easy and fast, but it is not the most pleasant chore to get behind a smoky, noisy engine on a hot summer day.

Manual and powered rotary cultivators are usually unable to turn under weeds very close to vegetable plants without damaging the vegetables. Hand-pulling or hoeing with a light touch are best for removing weeds near vegetable plants. Deep cultivation with any instrument is likely to damage roots or stems of crop plants.

Turning under weeds, especially before they flower, provides organic matter to the soil. Hand-pulled weeds, except for rhizomatous grasses, may be laid on top of the soil to dry out and will eventually have the same effect. However, if rain is predicted in the area within a day or two, it's best to collect the weeds and add them to the compost pile; rain will wash soil around the roots and some weeds will survive. If weeds have started to go to seed, leaving them in the garden is not a good idea.

Composting may not destroy weed seeds if the pile doesn't heat up enough after the weeds are added. Grasses that spread by rhizomes or stolons also present a problem if not completely dried up. In these cases, despite their potential value as organic material, it's better to let the trash collectors take the weeds, or burn them and spread the ashes in the garden (if local ordinances permit). Reducing weed growth around the garden by mowing or other means will also help prevent the spread of weeds and seeds to the garden area.

Cultivation is best done when the soil is somewhat moist, but not wet. Working wet soil will change the structure, especially of heavy soils. When it is too dry, weeds are difficult to pull and hoeing is also hard. A day or two after a rain or irrigation is probably the best time to cultivate. If you have a choice, remember that the work will be much more pleasant in the cool temperatures of early morning or evening. On hot summer afternoons, you are likely to fatigue more easily, get a sunburn, or suffer from sun poisoning, heat exhaustion, or sunstroke. Wear protective clothing if you must work when it's sunny, and stop frequently for rest and refreshment.

Mulching

Mulching can be an alternative to weeding if you have a reliable source of mulching materials. Thick layers of organic mulch will not allow most annual weeds to poke through, and those that do are usually easily pulled. Weeds with runners are often not so easily controlled, and black plastic may be a better choice where these prevail. For paths, newspaper, old carpeting, or other such materials, covered with sawdust, will provide excellent weed suppression. However, sawdust is not recommended for use right around plants because of its tendency to crust.

The bacteria that breaks down sawdust takes nitrogen from the soil, and thus from vegetables. Mulch can also be used to modify soil temperatures. Inorganic mulches (plastic sheeting, weed mats, etc.) warm up the soil, while organic mulches (sawdust, compost, straw, newspaper, grass clippings, etc.) cool the soil. Plant growth can be enhanced by matching the right mulch to the type of crop and weather. Inorganic mulch can be used early in the season to heat up the soil then an organic mulch can be applied later on to cool the soil as summer temperatures raise.

Close Spacing:

Once vegetable plants are established, if they have been planted close enough to each other, they will shade the soil and prevent the growth of many weed seedlings. This is the effect achieved by a well-planned raised bed, in which plants are spaced so that the foliage of adjacent plants touches and forms a closed canopy at a mature growth stage.

Other Practices:

Some gardeners are experimenting with various types of no-till gardening to reduce weed problems and prevent erosion and moisture loss. The standard farm no-till practice of sowing a fall cover crop and then killing it with a herbicide, and planting vegetables in the dead sod, after a recommended waiting period, is one method. However, there are no herbicides recommended for use in established home vegetable gardens to kill emerged weeds at the present time. Use of weed-killers normally recommended for lawns or other areas is not advised, and until a safe herbicide is available for growing weeds, this type of no-till practice is unsafe for growing vegetables in the home garden. One alternative is the use of a living sod, mowed regularly, which has many of the benefits of no-till and does not necessitate the use of herbicides. This practice works best with raised beds, so that only the paths need to be mowed. The use of cover crops over several seasons or years in a particularly weedy section can also reduce weed problems. However, this method requires leaving that part uncultivated, reducing gardening space. Cover crops must also be mown or harvested regularly, which can be time-consuming and/or difficult without appropriate tools. Investigate crop rotations thoroughly before using them to control weeds. All of the above techniques are still in the experimental stage for home gardeners. Try them in small sections of the garden to determine their effectiveness.

Herbicides:

As mentioned before, herbicides may be used in and around the home garden, but special care must be used to insure it is applied safely. They should always be used according to label instructions and only for crops listed on the label. The wrong herbicide can destroy a garden's productivity for years. Even when used properly, drift from herbicide sprays used on lawns or in areas surrounding the garden can cause damage to vegetable plants, so take care to spray on windless days and erect barriers to protect plants if necessary. Drift from pre-emergence herbicides does not damage growing plants, but may prevent seeds from germinating. Be aware that treatment with an herbicide for one type of weed may result in the area being colonized by other weeds which are tolerant to the chemical. Finally, never use a herbicide in the same sprayer used for insect and disease control. Keep a separate sprayer for plant-killers only.

VEGETABLE GARDEN: VEGETABLE PLANTING GUIDE AND RECOMMENDED PLANTING DATES

INTENSIVE GARDENING METHODS

The purpose of an intensively grown garden is to harvest the most produce possible from a given space. More traditional gardens consist of long, single rows of vegetables spaced widely apart. Much of the garden area is taken by the space between the rows. An intensive garden reduces wasted space to a minimum. The practice of intensive gardening is not just for those with limited garden space; rather, an intensive garden concentrates work efforts to create an ideal plant environment, giving better yields with less labor.

Though its benefits are many, the intensive garden may not be for everyone. Some people enjoy the sight of long, straight rows in their gardens. Others prefer machine cultivation to hand weeding; though there is often less weeding to do in intensive plantings because of fewer pathways and closely spaced plants, the weeding that must be done is usually done by hand or with hand tools. Still other gardeners like to get their gardens planted in a very short period of time and have harvests come in all at once. The intensive ideal is to have something growing in every part of the garden at all times during the growing season.

A good intensive garden requires early, thorough planning to make the best use of time and space in the garden. Interrelationships of plants must be considered before planting, including nutrient needs, shade tolerance, above- and below-ground growth patterns, and preferred growing season. Using the techniques described below, anyone can develop a high-yielding intensive garden.

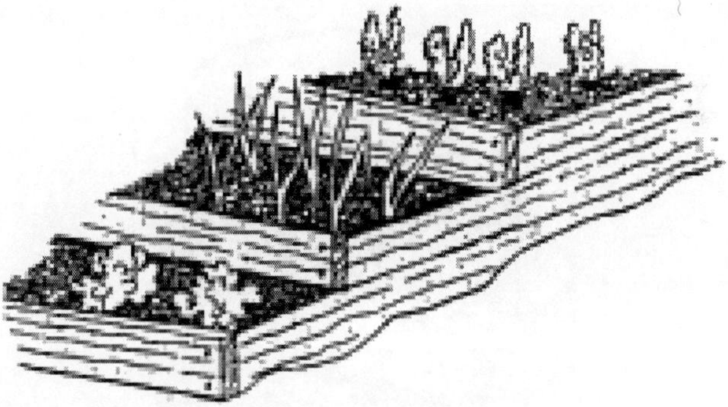

The raised bed

The raised bed or growing bed is the basic unit of an intensive garden. A system of beds allows the gardener to concentrate soil preparation in small areas, resulting in effective use of soil amendments and creating an ideal environment for vegetable growth. Raised beds warm-up more quickly in the spring. This is a major advantage when growing vegetables in the spring, giving them a head start. Because raised beds warm up faster and to a higher temperature by mid summer they dry out more quickly. In the hottest parts of Arizona raised beds may become too hot and use very high amounts of water. In the hot regions, gardeners should consider using lowered beds. With lowered beds, soil improvements are made below the natural grade rather than above and below but the other principles discussed are the same as for raised beds.

Beds are generally 3 to 4 feet wide and as long as desired. The gardener works from either side of the bed, reducing the incidence of compaction caused by walking on the soil.

Soil preparation is the key to successful intensive gardening. To grow so close together, plants must have adequate nutrients and water. Providing extra synthetic fertilizers and irrigation will help, but there is no substitute for deep, fertile soil high in organic matter. Humus-rich soil will hold extra nutrients, and existing elements that are "locked up" in the soil are released by the actions of earthworms, microorganisms and acids present in a life-filled soil, making them available for plant use.

If your soil is not deep, double-dig the beds for best results. Remove the top 12 inches of soil from the bed. Insert a spade or spading fork into the next 10 to 12 inches of soil and wiggle the handle back and forth to break up compacted layers. Do this every 6 to 8 inches in the bed. Mix the top soil with a generous amount of compost or manure, and return the mixture to the bed. It should be somewhat fluffy and may be raised slightly. To create a true raised bed, take topsoil from the neighboring pathways and mix it in as well.

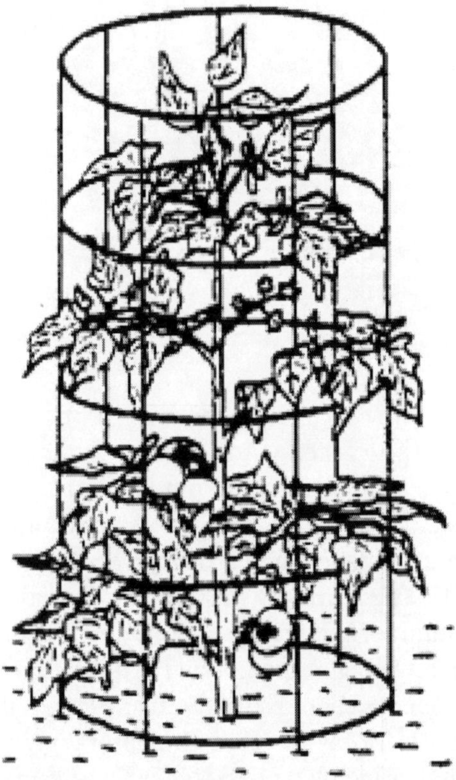

This is a lot of work! Try it in one or two beds for some of your most valuable plants; if you like the results you can proceed to other beds as you have time. One nice thing about raised bed gardening is that it breaks work into units. Instead of gazing desperately at a garden full of weeds, thinking you'll never have time to clean it up, you can look at each bed and say, "I can do that in half an hour today!" Other chores are accomplished with the same ease. By their nature, raised beds are a form of wide-bed gardening, a technique by which seeds and transplants are planted in wide bands of several rows or broadcast in a wide strip. In general, the goal is to space plants at equal distances from each other on all sides, such that leaves will touch at maturity. This saves space, and the close plantings reduce moisture loss from surrounding soil.

Vertical gardening

The use of trellises, nets, strings, cages, or poles to support growing plants constitutes vertical gardening. This technique is especially suited, but not limited, to gardeners with a small garden space. Vining and sprawling plants, such as cucumbers, tomatoes, melons, and pole beans are obvious candidates for this type of gardening. Some plants entwine themselves onto the support, while others may need to be tied. Remember that a vertical planting will cast a shadow, so beware of shading sun-loving crops, or take advantage of the shade by planting shade-tolerant crops near the vertical ones. Plants grown vertically take up much less space on the ground, and though the yield per plant may be (but is not always) less, the yield per square foot of garden space is much greater. Because vertically growing plants are more exposed, they dry out faster and may need to be watered more frequently than if they were allowed to spread over the ground. This fast drying is also an advantage to those plants susceptible to fungus diseases. A higher rate of fertilization may be needed, and soil should be deep and well-drained to allow roots to extend vertically rather than compete with others at a shallow level.

Interplanting

Growing two or more types of vegetables in the same place at the same time is known as interplanting. Proper planning is essential to obtain high production and increased quality of the crops planted. This technique has been practiced for thousands of years, but is just now gaining widespread support in this country. To successfully plan an interplanted garden the following factors must be taken into account for each plant: length of the plant's growth period, its growth pattern (tall, short, below or above ground), possible negative effects on other plants (such as the allelopathic effects of sunflowers and Jerusalem artichokes on nearby plants), preferred season, and light, nutrient and moisture requirements. Interplanting can be accomplished by alternating rows within a bed (plant a row of peppers next to a row of onions), by mixing plants within a row, or by distributing various species throughout the bed. For the beginner, alternating rows may be the easiest to manage at first.

Long-season (slow to mature) and short-season (quick to mature) plants like carrots and radishes, respectively, can be planted at the same time. The radishes are harvested before they begin to crowd the carrots. An example of combining growth patterns is planting smaller plants close to larger plants, radishes at the base of beans or broccoli. Shade tolerant species like lettuce, spinach, and celery may be planted in the shadow of taller crops. Heavy feeders, such as cabbage family crops, should be interplanted with less gluttonous plants.

Interplanting can help keep insect and disease problems under control. Pests are usually fairly crop-specific; that is, they prefer vegetables of one type or family. Mixing families of plants helps to break up large expanses of the pest-preferred crop, helping to contain early pest damage within a small area, thus giving the gardener a little more time to deal with the problem. One disadvantage is that when it does come time to spray for pests, it's hard to be sure that all plants are protected.

Spacing

Individual plants are closely spaced in a raised bed or interplanted garden. An equidistant spacing pattern calls for plants to be the same distance from each other within the bed; that is, plant so that the center of one plant is the same distance from plants on all sides of it. In beds of more than two rows, this means that the rows should be staggered so that plants in every other row are between the plants in adjacent rows. The distance recommended for plants within the row on a seed packet is the distance from the center of one plant to the center of the next. This results in an efficient use of space and leaves less area to weed and mulch. The close spacing tends to create a nearly solid leaf canopy, acting as a living mulch, decreasing water loss, and keeping weed problems down. However, plants should not be crowded to the point at which disease problems arise or competition causes stunting.

Succession and relay planting

Succession planting is an excellent way to make the most of an intensive garden. To obtain a succession of crops, plant something new in spots vacated by spent plants. Corn after peas is a type of succession.

Planting a spring, summer, and fall garden is another form of succession planting. Cool season crops (broccoli, lettuce, peas) are followed by warm season crops (beans, tomatoes, peppers), and where possible, these may be followed by more cool-season plants, or even a winter cover crop.

Relaying is another common practice, consisting of overlapping plantings of one type of crop. The new planting is made before the old one is removed. For instance, sweet corn may be planted at 2-week intervals for a continuous harvest. This requires some care, though; crops planted very early are likely to get a slower start because of low temperatures. In the case of corn, it can be disastrous to have two varieties pollinating at the same time, as the quality of the kernels may be affected. Give early planted corn extra time to get started, for best results. Another way to achieve the same result is to plant, at once, various varieties of the same vegetable; for example, you can plant an early-season, a mid-season, and a late-season corn at the same time and have a lengthy harvest. Starting seeds indoors for transplanting is an important aspect of intensive gardening. To get the most from the garden plot, a new crop should be ready to take the place of the crop being removed. Several weeks may be gained by having 6-inch transplants ready to go into vacated areas. Don't forget to recondition the soil for the new plants.

Planning an intensive garden

Begin planning your garden early, pull out last-year's garden records and dig into the new seed catalogs. As with any garden, you must decide what crops you want to grow based on your own likes and dislikes, as well as how much of each you will need. An account of which cultivars were most successful or tasted best is helpful in making crop choices. Use the charts below, and your own experience, to determine which crops are likely combinations.

Table: Intensive Spacing Guide

Plant	Inches	Plant	Inches
Asparagus	15 - 18	Lettuce, head	10 - 12
Beans, lima	4 - 6	Lettuce, leaf	4 - 6
Beans, pole	6 - 12	Melons	18 - 24
Beans, bush	4 - 6	Mustard	6 - 9
Beets	2 - 4	Okra	12 - 18
Broccoli	12 - 18	Onion	2 - 4
Brussels sprouts	15 - 18	Peas	2 - 4
Cabbage	15 - 18	Peppers	12 - 15
Cabbage, Chinese	10 - 12	Potatoes	10 - 12
Carrots	2 - 3	Pumpkins	24 - 36
Cauliflower	15 - 18	Radishes	2 - 3
Cucumber	12 - 18	Rutabaga	4 - 6
Chard, Swiss	6 - 9	Southern pea	3 - 4
Collards	12 - 15	Spinach	4 - 6
Endive	15 - 18	Squash, summer	18 - 24
Eggplant	18 - 24	Squash, winter	24 - 36
Kale	15 - 18	Sweet corn	15 - 18
Kohlrabi	6 - 9	Tomatoes	18 - 24
Leeks	3 - 6	Turnip	4 - 6

Note: To determine spacing for interplanting, add the inches for the two crops to be planted together, and divide the sum by 2. For example, if radishes are planted next to beans, add 2 inches + 4 inches = 6 inches, then divide 6 inches by 2 inches = 3 inches. The radishes should be planted 3 inches from the beans.

Good gardening practices such as watering, fertilizing, crop rotation, composting, and sanitation are especially important in an intensive garden. An intensive garden does require more detailed planning, but the time saved in working the garden and the increased yields make it well worthwhile. Use your imagination and have fun!

Economic value of crops

It is difficult to evaluate the economic value of crops grown in the vegetable garden due to the different lengths of time they require for maturity and harvest, the availability of varieties and vegetables types not generally found in the marketplace, and the lack of comparison values for vegetables that are not acceptable by commercial standards (cracked tomatoes, crooked cucumbers, etc.), but which are perfectly usable by the gardener. Nevertheless, several studies have attempted to determine which crops bring the most value per square foot of garden space, partly to aid small-space gardeners in making decisions about what to plant.

Of course, if no one in the family likes beets, there is no point in growing them just because they are economically valuable, but this list may help you determine which vegetables to plant and which to buy. Perennial crops are not on the list below because each of the studies was on a one-season basis. Asparagus, rhubarb, horseradish, and other perennial crops do also have considerable economic worth. Fruit trees and shrubs are also valuable producers, especially considering the long-term.

Top 15 Vegetables in Economic Value:

Tomatoes	Beets
Green bunching onions	Carrots
Leaf lettuce	Cucumbers
Turnip (green + roots)	Peppers
Summer squash	Broccoli
Edible pod peas	Head lettuce
Onion storage bulbs	Swiss chard
Beans (pole, bush)	

Values based on pounds produced per square foot, retail value per pound at harvest time, and length of time in the garden.

Low-Value Crops (not recommended for small spaces):

Corn	Squash
Melons	Pumpkins

Miniature varieties or trellising may increase value per square foot.

CONTAINER GARDEN

If you don't have space for a vegetable garden, or if your present site is too small, consider raising fresh, nutritious, homegrown vegetables in containers. A window sill, patio, balcony, or doorstep can provide sufficient space for a productive container garden. Problems with soil-borne diseases, nematodes, or poor soil can also be overcome by switching to container gardening.

Grow vegetables that take up little space, such as carrots, radishes and lettuce, or crops that bear fruits over a period of time, such as tomatoes and peppers, for best use of space and containers. Dwarf or miniature varieties often mature and bear fruit early, but most do not produce as well overall as standard varieties. With increasing interest in container gardening, plant breeders and seed companies are working on vegetables specifically bred for container culture. These varieties are not necessarily miniature or dwarf and may produce as well as standard types if properly cared for.

The amount of sunlight that your container garden spot receives may determine which crops can be grown. Generally, root crops and leaf crops can tolerate partial shade, but vegetables grown for their fruits generally need at least 5 hours of full, direct sunlight each day, and perform better with 8 to 10 hours. Available light can be increased somewhat by providing reflective materials around the plants, e.g., aluminum foil, white-painted surfaces, marble chips.

Container gardening lends itself to attractive plantscaping. A dull patio area can be brightened by the addition of baskets of cascading tomatoes or a colorful herb mix. Planter boxes with trellises can be used to create a cool shady place on an apartment balcony. Container gardening presents opportunities for many innovative ideas.

Containers

There are many possible containers for gardening. Clay, wood, plastic, metal are some of the suitable materials. Containers for vegetable plants must:

1. be big enough to support plants when they are fully grown
2. hold soil without spilling
3. have adequate drainage
4. never have held products that would be toxic to plants or people.

Consider using barrels, cut-off milk and bleach jugs, window boxes, baskets lined with plastic (with drainage holes punched in it), even pieces of drainage pipe or cement block. If you are building a planting box out of wood, you will find redwood and cedar to be the most rot-resistant, but bear in mind that cedar trees are much more plentiful than redwoods. Wood for use around plants should never be treated with creosote or pentachlorophenol (Penta) wood preservatives. These may be toxic to plants and harmful to people as well.

Some gardeners have built vertical planters out of wood lattice lined with black plastic and then filled with a lightweight medium; or out of welded wire, shaped into cylinders, lined with sphagnum moss, and filled with soil mix. Depending on the size of your vertical planter, 2-inch diameter perforated plastic pipes may be needed inside to aid watering. Whatever type of container you use, be sure that there are holes in the bottom for drainage so that plant roots do not stand in water. Most plants need containers at least 6 to 8 inches deep for adequate rooting.

As long as the container meets the basic requirements described above it can be used. The imaginative use of discarded items or construction of attractive patio planters is a very enjoyable aspect of container gardening. For ease of care, dollies or platforms with wheels or casters can be used to move the containers from place to place. This is especially useful for apartment or balcony gardening so that plants can be moved to get maximum use of available space and sunlight, and to avoid destruction from particularly nasty weather.

Media

A fairly lightweight potting mix is needed for container vegetable gardening. Soil straight from the garden usually cannot be used in a container because it may be too heavy, unless your garden has sandy loam or sandy soil. Clay soil consists of extremely small (microscopic) particles. In a container, the bad qualities of clay are exaggerated. It holds too much moisture when wet, resulting in too little air for the roots, and it pulls away from the sides of the pot when dry. Container medium must be porous in order to support plants, because roots require both air and water. Packaged potting soil available at local garden centers is relatively lightweight and may make a good container medium. Soilless mixes such as peat-lite mix are generally too light for container vegetable gardening, not offering enough support to plant roots. If the container is also lightweight, a strong wind can blow plants over, resulting in major damage.

Also, soilless mixes are sterile and contain few nutrients, so even though major fertilizers are added, no trace elements are available for good plant growth. Add soil or compost if you wish to use a sterile mix. For a large container garden, the expense of prepackaged or soilless mixes may be quite high. Try mixing your own with one part peat moss, one part garden loam, and one part clean, coarse (builder's) sand, and a slow-release fertilizer (14-14-14) according to container size.

Planting

Plant container crops at the same time you would if you were planting a regular garden. Fill a clean container to within an inch of the top with the slightly damp soil mixture. Peat moss in the mix will absorb water and mix much more readily if soaked with warm water before putting the mix in the container. Sow the seeds or set transplants according to instructions on the seed package. Put a label with the name, variety, and date of planting on or in each container. After planting, gently soak the soil with water, being careful not to wash out or displace seeds. Thin seedlings to obtain proper spacing when the plants have two or three leaves. If cages, stakes, or other supports are needed, provide them when the plants are very small to avoid root damage later.

Watering

Pay particular attention to watering container plants. Because the volume of soil is relatively small, containers can dry out very quickly, especially on a concrete patio in full sun. Daily or even twice daily watering may be necessary. Apply water until it runs out the drainage holes. On an upstairs balcony, this may mean neighbor problems, so make provisions for drainage of water. Large trays filled with coarse marble chips work nicely. However, the soil should never be soggy or have water standing on top of it. When the weather is cool, container plants may be subject to root rots if maintained too wet. Clay pots and other porous containers allow additional evaporation from the sides of the pots and watering must be done more often. Small pots also tend to dry out more quickly than larger ones. If the soil appears to be getting excessively dry (plants wilting every day is one sign), group the containers together so that the foliage creates a canopy to help shade the soil and keep it cool. On a hot patio, you might consider putting containers on pallets or other structures that will allow air movement beneath the pots and prevent direct contact with the cement. Check containers at least once a day, and twice on hot, dry, or windy days. Feel the soil to determine whether or not it is damp. Mulching and windbreaks can help reduce water requirements for containers. If you are away a lot, consider an automatic drip emitter irrigation system.

Fertilizing

If you use a soil mix with fertilizer added, then your plants will have enough nutrients for 8 to 10 weeks. If plants are grown longer than this, add a water-soluble fertilizer at the recommended rate. Repeat every 2 to 3 weeks. An occasional dose of fish emulsion or compost will add trace elements to the soil. Do not add more than the recommended rate of any fertilizer, since this may cause fertilizer burn and kill the plants. Container plants do not have the buffer of large volumes of soil and humus to protect them from over-fertilizing or over-liming. Just because a little is good for the plants does not guarantee that a lot will be better.

General care

Vegetables grown in containers can be attacked by the various types of insects and diseases that are common to any vegetable garden. Plants should be periodically inspected for the presence of foliage-feeding and fruit-feeding insects as well as the occurrence of diseases. Protect plants from very high heat caused by light reflection from pavement. Move them to a cool spot or shade them during the hottest part of the day. Plants should be moved to a sheltered location during severe rain, hail, or wind storms, and for protection from early or late frosts.

Indoor container gardening with vegetables

If you want fresh, home-grown vegetables over the winter, or if you don't have an outdoor space in which you can place containers, it is worth trying some indoor container gardening. Of course you cannot have a full garden in the house, but a bright, sunny window can be the site for growing fresh food all year. Some small-fruited tomatoes and peppers, several types of lettuce, radishes, and many herbs are among the plants you can include in the indoor garden.

Follow directions given above for preparing pots and for watering, fertilizing, etc. However, note that plants will dry out less quickly indoors and will also grow more slowly, needing less fertilizer. To make watering easy it is wise to set the pots in large trays with an inch or two of decorative stones in them. Not only will this prevent your having to move the plants in order to water them, which may discourage you from watering when you should, but it will also provide humidity, which is a major requirement, especially during winter when the house is warm and dry.

As mentioned before, a sunny window, preferably south-facing, is almost a must for indoor vegetable growing. Fruiting vegetables such as tomatoes and peppers will also need supplemental light, such as a combination warm-white/cool-white fluorescent fixture, during winter months. Insufficient light will result in tall, spindly plants and failure to flower and set fruit.

Herbs are a first choice for many indoor gardeners. Many are less demanding than vegetable plants, and cooks find it pleasant to be able to snip off a few sprigs of fresh parsley or chop some chives from the windowsill herb garden. Chives grow like small onions with leaves about 6 inches tall. These plants prefer cool conditions with good light, but will grow quite well on a windowsill in the kitchen. One or two pots of chives will provide leaves for seasoning salads and soups. Plant seeds in a 6-inch pot. The plants should be about 1 inch apart over the entire surface area. It will require about 12 weeks from the time seeds are planted until leaves can be cut. For variety, try garlic or Chinese chives, which grow in a similar fashion, but have a mild garlic flavor.

Parsley seeds can be planted directly into 6-inch pots, or young, healthy plants can be transplanted from the garden. One vigorous plant per pot is enough. Standard parsley develops attractive, green, curly leaves about 6 or 8 inches tall. Italian, or flat-leaved, parsley has a slightly stronger flavor and is a favorite for pasta dishes. Leaves can be clipped about 10 to 12 weeks after planting the seeds.

Cilantro, or the leaves of the young coriander plant, can be grown in the windowsill garden. Cilantro is used in Oriental and Mexican dishes, but it is not available in most grocery stores and must be used fresh. Grow cilantro as you would parsley. Thyme and other herbs will also grow well indoors if given the right conditions.

The small-fruited varieties of tomatoes such as Tiny Tim, Small Fry, and the paste tomato, Roma, may be raised quite satisfactorily in the home. They will challenge your gardening ability, and supply fruits which can be eaten whole, cooked, or served with salad. The Tiny Tim tomato grows to a height of about 12 to 15 inches. Small Fry, which is about 3 feet tall, and Roma will need more space and should be located on an enclosed porch or in a sun room. Several varieties have been developed for hanging baskets; they may be worth experimenting with.

Some of the small-fruited peppers may be grown as indoor plants. Like tomatoes, they require warm, bright conditions in order to grow well indoors. Fruits will be ready to harvest from peppers and tomatoes about ten weeks after planting. Whiteflies and aphids may present a problem on indoor tomato and pepper plants. Keep a close watch for these pests so they do not get a good start in your planting. Yellow sticky traps, either purchased or homemade, are effective in trapping whiteflies. Insecticidal soap or other pesticide approved for vegetable plants can be used to control aphids. Fortunately, you will be less likely to experience problems with such outdoor pests as tomato hornworms, corn earworm (in peppers), and late blight than you would if plants were outside.

For a quick-growing crop, try radishes. These must be grown very rapidly if they are to be crisp and succulent. Scatter radish seeds on moist soil in a 6-inch pot. Cover with 1/4 inch of soil and place a piece of glass or plastic wrap over the pot to conserve moisture until the seeds germinate. Carrots are slower, but can be grown in the same way; use the small-rooted varieties, such as Little Finger, for best results indoors.

Experiment with various types of lettuce. Leaf lettuce and the miniature Tom Thumb butterhead are some to try. Space them according to package directions. Keep lettuce moist and in a very sunny spot.

If light is limited, an old standby for fresh taste and high food value is sprouted seeds. Almost any seeds can be sprouted: corn, barley, alfalfa, lentils, soybeans, rye, peas, radish, mung beans, sunflowers, etc. Use only special seeds for sprouting available from health food or grocery stores to avoid the possibility of getting seeds treated with pesticide.

Use any wide-mouthed container such as a Mason or mayonnaise jar. Soak seeds overnight, drain, and place in the container. Cover with a double cheesecloth layer held with rubber bands, or a sprouting lid. Set the container in a consistently warm spot and rinse and drain seeds two or three times daily. In 3 to 5 days, sprouts will be 1 to 3 inches long and ready for harvesting.

VEGETABLE GARDENING IN THE FALL (WINTER IN THE HOTTER REGIONS)

PLANTING FOR A FALL HARVEST

By planning and planting a fall/winter vegetable garden it is possible to have fresh vegetables up to and even past the first frosts. At the time when retail vegetable prices are on the rise, you can be reaping large and varied harvests from your still-productive garden site.

Many varieties of vegetables can be planted in midsummer to late summer for fall/winter harvests. Succession plantings of warm season crops, such as corn and beans, can be harvested until the first killing frost. Cool season crops, such as kale, turnips, mustard, broccoli, cabbage, etc., grow well during the cool fall/winter days and withstand light frosts. Timely planting is the key to a successful fall garden.

To determine the time to plant a particular vegetable for the latest harvest in your area, you need to know the average date of the first killing frost and the number of days to maturity for the variety grown. Choose earliest maturing varieties for late plantings. The formula below for determining the number of days to count back from the first frost will help determine when to start your fall garden.

Number of days from seeding or transplanting outdoors to harvest

+ Number of days from seed to transplant if you grow your own
+ Average harvest period
+ Fall Factor (about 2 weeks)
+ Frost Tender Factor (if applicable)

= Days to count back from first frost date

The Frost Tender Factor is added only for those crops that are sensitive to frost (corn, beans, cucumbers, tomatoes, squash), as these must mature 2 weeks before frost in order to produce a reasonable harvest. The Fall Factor takes into account the slower growth that results from cooler weather and shorter days in the fall, and amounts to about 2 weeks. This time can be reduced from 2 to 5 days by presprouting seeds. Almost any crop that isn't grown for transplants can benefit from presprouting. Sprout seeds indoors, allowing them to reach a length of up to an inch. Sprouted seeds may be planted deeper than normal to help prevent drying out, and they should be watered well until they break the soil surface. Care should be taken not to break off the sprouts when planting them.

When planting fall crops, prepare the soil by restoring nutrients removed by spring and summer crops. A light layer of compost or aged manure, or a small application of complete chemical fertilizer will boost soil nutrients in preparation for another crop.

Dry soil may make working the soil difficult and inhibit seed germination during the midsummer period. Plant fall vegetables when the soil is moist after a rain, or water the area thoroughly the day before planting. Seeds may be planted in a shallow trench to conserve moisture. Cover the seeds about twice as deeply as you do in the spring. An old-time trick for germinating seeds in midsummer is to plant the seeds, water them in well, and then place a board over the row until the sprouts just reach the soil surface; at that time remove the board. Plastic will also work, but must be completely anchored so the soil does not dry out underneath or the plastic blow away. Plastic, especially black plastic, may cause the soil to get too hot. An organic mulch on top will help keep soil cool. Mulching between rows can also help keep soil cool and decrease soil drying. In severe hot weather a light, open type of mulch, such as loose straw or pine boughs, may be placed over the seeded row. This must be removed as soon as seedlings are up so that they receive full sun. Starting transplants in a shaded coldframe or in a cool indoor area is another possibility.

Once young plants are established, a heavier mulch may be used to hold moisture and control weeds. Irrigate when necessary so the young plants have sufficient moisture. Fall plantings often have few insect problems, as they avoid the peak insect activity period of midsummer. However, some insects, such as cabbageworm and corn earworm, may be even worse late in the year than in summer; vigilance is still required! Avoid some pests and diseases by planting crops of different families than were originally in that section of the garden.

Some of the best quality vegetables are produced during the warm days and cool nights of the fall season. These environmental conditions add sugar to sweet corn and crispness to carrots. Parsnips and Jerusalem artichokes are examples of crops that are very much improved by a touch of frost.

Protection of vegetable plants during cold periods may extend your season even further. Though in the hot days of summer the last thing you want to think about is planting more crops to take care of, look ahead to the fall garden, which offers its own satisfaction through prolonged harvest of fresh vegetables, savings in food costs, and the knowledge that you're making full use of your gardening space and season.

Care of fall crops

The beginning of fall garden care comes when the weather and the radio station announce the first arrival of frost. Your main concern then should be to harvest all ripe, tender crops. Tomatoes, summer squash, melons, eggplant, cucumbers, peppers, and okra are some of the crops that cannot withstand frost and should be picked immediately. Store the vegetables in a place where they can be held until needed for eating or processing. If the frost warning is mild, predicting no lower than a 30 F., try covering tender plants in your garden that still hold an abundance of immature fruit. Baskets, burlap, boxes, blankets, or buckets help protect them from the frost. Warm days after the frost will still mature some of the fruit as long as the plants have this nightly frost protection. Much will depend on the garden's microclimate. If your spot is low and unsheltered, it is likely to be a frost pocket. Gardens sheltered from winds and on the upper side of a slope are less susceptible to early frost damage.

When using a cold frame to extend the harvest season, be sure to close the top on frosty nights to protect the plants from the cold. When the sun comes out the next morning and the air warms, open the cold frame again; leave it closed if daytime temperatures are low.

Cool-season crops such as cabbage, cauliflower, broccoli, spinach, and Brussels sprouts can withstand some cold. In fact, their flavor may be enhanced after a frost. They cannot stay in the garden all winter, but do not need to be picked immediately when frost comes. Kale, spinach, evergreen bunching onions, lettuce, parsley, parsnips, carrots, and salsify are some crops that may survive all winter in the garden. Mulch these overwintering vegetables with 8 inches of mulch to prevent heaving of the soil. Most of these vegetables can be dug or picked as needed throughout the winter or in early spring.

Now is the time to prepare perennial vegetables for winter, too. Most will benefit from a topdressing of manure or compost and a layer of mulch, which reduces damage from freezing and thawing. Dead leaf stalks of perennial vegetables such as asparagus and rhubarb should be cut to the ground after their tops are killed by frost, though some people prefer to leave asparagus stalks until late winter to hold snow over the bed.

When tender crops have been harvested and overwintering crops cared for, pull up all stakes and trellises in the garden except those stakes that are clearly marking the sites of overwintering plants. Clean stakes and trellises of remnants of plant materials and soil. Hose them down and allow to dry. Tie stakes in bundles and stack them so that they won't get lost over the winter. If possible, roll up wire trellises and tie them securely. Store these items inside your attic, barn, or shed in an area where they are out of the way, and where rodents and other animals cannot get to them to use as winter nests.

Preparing soil for winter

Now you are ready to prepare the soil for winter. Pull up all dead and unproductive plants and place this residue on top of the soil to be tilled under, or in the compost heap. Remove any diseased or insect-infested plant material from the garden that may shelter overwintering stages of disease and insect pests. If this plant material is left in the garden, you are leaving an inoculum of diseases and insects which will begin to reproduce the next spring and add to your pest problems.

The best thing to do is to remove infested plant material from the garden or burn it. Burning will kill any diseases or insects that may be in plant wastes. Spread the ashes on the garden to get the benefit of mineral nutrients. Check laws in your area before burning anything; you may need a permit. If you live near a wooded area, burning may be too risky. In this case, haul the diseased material away.

Clean-up also gives you the chance to add compost to the garden. Compost contains highly nutritious, decomposed plant material and beneficial organisms, and is an excellent soil-builder. By spreading compost and other wastes on the soil and plowing them in, you are adding nutrients to the soil for next year's crop. The beneficial insects and microorganisms in the compost will help integrate the compost with the soil, and the added humus will improve soil structure.

Don't overlook other excellent sources of organic material available during the fall. Leaves are abundant, and neighbors will usually be glad to give their leaves away. Put some on the garden now and store some for next year's mulch.

Leaves will mat if put on in too thick a layer, and will not decompose quickly. You can help leaves break down more easily by running a lawn mower back and forth over the pile. Put the shredded leaves directly onto the garden or compost them. Many farms and stables want to get rid of manure piles before winter sets in. All these sources of organic matter will benefit soil conditions. If you wait until just before planting to add organic material to the garden, it may not have time to decompose and add its valuable nutrients to the soil by the time you are ready to plant, and you may have to delay planting to a later date. Hot (very fresh) manure can also burn young seedlings. By adding these materials after harvest, you give them plenty of time to decompose and blend into the soil before planting time. If you don't have enough organic material for the entire garden, try to cover those areas that you want especially rich for the next gardening season.

If the weather stays dry enough before the ground freezes, you can plow or rototill in the fall. Turning under vegetation after harvest allows earlier planting the next season and is especially good for heavy soils, since they may be exposed to the freezing and thawing that takes place during the winter. This helps to improve soil structure. If you have a rainy fall, or if the garden is steep and subject to erosion, you may decide you'd rather plant a cover crop to protect the garden. A cover crop decreases erosion of the soil during the off season, adds organic material when it is incorporated prior to planting, improves soil tilth and porosity, and adds valuable nutrients. Off season cover crops should be planted early enough to make some growth before hard frost kills them. Where you have fall/winter crops growing, you can sow cover crop seed between rows a month or less before expected harvest. This way the cover crop gets a good start, but will not interfere with vegetable plant growth.

Prepare the soil for cover crop seed by tilling under plant wastes from the last crop. Ask at the seed store what the best type of cover crop for your area is and at what rate (pounds per 100 square feet) to plant it. Broadcast the seed, preferably before a rain, and rake it evenly into the soil. Planting may be delayed somewhat by the practice of cover cropping, since time must be allowed for the green manure to break down. If you have crops that need to be planted very early, you may prefer to leave a section of the garden bare or with a stubble mulch.

When time or weather conditions prohibit either tilling or cover cropping, you may wish to let your garden lie under a mulch of compost, plant wastes, or leaves all winter to be plowed or tilled under before planting. However, if you want to plant early, a mulch of heavy materials such as whole leaves may keep the soil cold long enough to delay planting. In this case, chop them fine enough that they will break down during the off season. The addition of fertilizer high in nitrogen will also help break down organic matter more quickly.

Care of garden equipment

Clean-up of tools and equipment is another important practice related to the garden which should not be ignored in the fall. Proper clean-up of tools now will leave them in top shape and ready to use when spring comes. Clean, oil, and repair all hand tools. Repaint handles or identification marks that have faded over the summer. Sharpen all blades and remove any rust. Power tools should be cleaned of all plant material and dirt. Replace worn spark plugs, oil all necessary parts, and sharpen blades. Store all tools in their proper place indoors, never outdoors where they will rust over the winter.

Unless you are lucky enough to live in a warm area where a cold frame will protect vegetables all winter, you will need to clean up the frame when all vegetables have been harvested. Remove all remaining plant material and spread it on the cold frame soil. Spade the plant refuse and any other organic material into the soil in the cold frame as thoroughly as possible. Do not leave the top on the cold frame over the winter, as the cold air or the weight of snow may crack or break the glass. Remove the top, wash it thoroughly, and store it on its side in a protected indoor area where it will not get broken.

Successful gardening doesn't stop when frost comes, but continues throughout the fall and early winter months. When following good garden care practices during this time, your garden will be ready for the growth of healthy vegetables next spring.

SEASON EXTENDERS

To get the most out of a garden, you can extend the growing season by sheltering plants from cold weather both in early spring and during the fall. Very ambitious gardeners harvest greens and other cool-weather crops all winter by providing the right conditions. There are many ways to lengthen the growing season, and your choice depends on the amount of time and money you want to invest.

Cold frames and hot beds

Cold frames, sun boxes, and hot beds are relatively inexpensive, simple structures providing a favorable environment for growing cool-weather crops in the very early spring, the fall, and even into the winter months. Some are elaborate and require a large investment, but are reasonable for those who are serious about having fresh vegetables during the winter.

Dutch Light

Cold frames and sun boxes have no outside energy requirements, relying on the sun for their source of heat. Hot beds are heated by soil heating cables, steam-carrying pipes, or fresh strawy manure buried beneath the rooting zones of the plants. Heat is collected by these frames when the sun's rays penetrate the sash, made of clear plastic, glass, or fiberglass. The ideal location for a coldframe is a southern or southeastern exposure with a slight slope to ensure good drainage and maximum solar absorption. A sheltered spot with a wall or hedge to the north will provide protection against winter winds. Sinking the frame into the ground somewhat will also provide protection, using the earth for insulation. To simplify use of the frame, consider a walkway to the front, adequate space behind the frame to remove the sash, and perhaps weights to make raising and lowering of glass sashes easier. Some gardeners make their cold frames lightweight enough to be moved from one section of the garden to another. Another possibility is the Dutch light, which is a large but portable greenhouse-like structure which is moved around the garden.

Solar Pod

New designs in cold frames include passive solar energy storage. For example, barrels painted black and filled with water absorb heat during the day and release it at night. The solar pod, shown here, is one design which provides for this type of heat storage. Other new cold frames are built with a very high back and a steep glass slope and insulated very well; these may also include movable insulation that is folded up during the day and down at night or during extremely cold weather.

In early spring, a cold frame is useful for hardening-off seedlings which were started indoors or in a greenhouse. This hardening-off period is important, as seedlings can suffer serious setbacks if they are moved directly from the warmth and protection of the house to the garden. The cold frame provides a transition period for gradual adjustment to the outdoor weather. It is also possible to start cool-weather crops in the cold frame and either transplant them to the garden or grow them to maturity in the frame.

Spring and summer uses of the coldframe center around plant propagation. Young seedlings of hardy and half-hardy annuals can be started in a frame many weeks before they can be started in the open. The soil in a portion of the bed can be replaced with sand or peat moss or other medium suitable for rooting cuttings and for starting sweet potato slips.

Fall is also a good time for sowing some cool-weather crops in frames. If provided with adequate moisture and fertilization, most cool-season crops will continue to grow through early winter in the protected environment of the cold frame. Depending on the harshness of the winter and whether or not additional heating is used, your frame may continue to provide fresh greens, herbs, and root crops throughout the cold winter months.

Growing frames can be built from a variety of materials; wood and cement block are the most common. If you use wood, choose wood that will resist decay, such as a good grade of cypress or cedar, or use pressure-treated wood. Never use creosote-treated wood or wood treated with pentachlorophenol, since these substances are harmful to growing plants. Wood frames are not difficult to build. Kits may also be purchased and easily assembled; some kits even contain automatic ventilation equipment.

There is no standard-sized cold frame. The dimensions of the frame will depend on amount of available space, desired crops, size of available window sash, and permanency of the structure. Do not make the structure too wide for weeding and harvesting; 4 to 5 feet is about as wide as is convenient to reach across. The sash of the frame should be sloped to the south to allow maximum exposure to the sun's rays.

Insulation may be necessary when a sudden cold snap is expected. A simple method is to throw burlap sacks filled with leaves over the sash on the frame at night to protect against freezing. Or, bales of straw or hay may be stacked against the frame.

Ventilation is most critical in the late winter, early spring, and early fall on clear, sunny days when temperatures rise above 45 degrees. The sash should be raised partially to prevent the buildup of extreme temperatures inside the frame. Lower or replace the sash each day early enough to conserve some heat for the evening.

In summer, extreme heat and intensive sunlight can damage plants. This can be avoided by shading with lath or old bamboo window blinds. Watering should be done early so that plants dry before dark, to help reduce disease problems.

You may convert your cold frame to a hotbed. For a manure-heated bed: dig out to 2 feet deep (deeper to add gravel for increased drainage); add an 18-inch layer of strawy horse manure; cover with 6 inches of good soil. For an electric heated bed: dig out area 8 inches deep; lay down thermostatically controlled electric cable in 6 to 8-inch long loops, evenly spacing cable, but never crossing; cover with 2 inches of sand or soil; lay out hardware cloth to protect cable; cover with 4 to 6 inches of good soil.

Cloches and row covers

The cloche (pronounced klosh) was originally a bell-shaped glass jar set over delicate plants to protect them from the elements. The definition has expanded, however, to include many types of portable structures which shelter plants from drying winds and cold air. The idea is to provide a greenhouse-like atmosphere for seeds and small plants in order to get an early start on the season, or to extend the fall garden as long as possible. Cloches are set out over individual plants or are made into tunnels for whole rows. They trap solar radiation and moisture evaporating from the soil and plants. The hotkap and the cut-off plastic jug are simple forms. More elaborate ones are fiberglass tunnels, special plastic cloches, or row covers with slits in them to allow some aeration, and panes of glass connected by specially designed hinges to form a tent. There are a variety of forms on the market now, some which work and some which don't, and some are easily constructed from materials around the home. Cloches are generally lightweight, portable, and reusable. It is preferable to have a design which can be closed completely at night to prevent frost damage and opened or completely removed during the day for good air circulation. Cloches should be anchored, or heavy enough that they don't blow away.

Greenhouses

There is an almost overwhelming selection of greenhouses on the market, and plans for building even more types are available. If you intend to purchase or build a greenhouse, it is wise to investigate the alternatives thoroughly, preferably visiting as many operating home greenhouses as possible. List your needs and wants ahead of time and determine the uses you will put your greenhouse to. Then compare on that basis. Many companies will send free specifications and descriptions of the greenhouses they offer; look in gardening magazines for their ads.

The conservation-minded person may find an attached solar greenhouse desirable. The initial cost is generally higher for a solar greenhouse than for the simpler free-standing, uninsulated types, but for maximum use with lower heating bills, one can insulate north and side walls, provide liberal glass area for winter sun-catching, and make use of some type of solar radiation storage. When attached to a house, these greenhouses can be used for supplementary household heating, but there is a trade-off between heating the home and growing plants (especially heat-loving ones) in the greenhouse. Some researchers have concluded that a good compromise is to forget winter tomatoes and grow cool-weather crops during the winter in a solar attached greenhouse.

Shading

It is not always easy to start seeds or young plants for fall crops in the hot and dry conditions of August in Arizona. One simple way to provide shade in otherwise exposed conditions is to build a portable shade frame for placing over rows after seeds are sown or transplants are set out. This can be the same type of frame used for starting early seeds, but using lath strips or an old bamboo shade instead of plastic.

6

Gardening Techniques

SQUARE FOOT GARDENING

Square Foot Gardening is the practice of planning small but intensively planted gardens. The phrase "square foot gardening" was popularized by Mel Bartholomew. The practice combines concepts from other organic gardening methods, including a strong focus on compost, closely planted raised beds and biointensive attention to a small, clearly defined area. Proponents claim that the method is particularly well-suited for areas with poor soil, beginning gardeners or as adaptive recreation for those with disabilities.

BASIC METHOD

The original square-foot-gardening method used an open-bottomed box to contain a finite amount of soil, which was divided with a grid into sections. To encourage variety of different crops over time, each square would be planted with a different kind of plant, the number of plants per square depending on an individual plant's size. A single tomato plant might take a full square, as might herbs such as oregano, basil or mint, while most strawberry plants could be planted four per square, with up to sixteen radishes per square. Tall or climbing plants such as maize or pole beans might be planted in a northern row so as not to shade other plants, and supported with lattice or netting. The logic behind using smaller beds is that they are easily adapted, and the gardener can easily reach the entire area, without stepping on and compacting the soil. In the second edition, Bartholomew suggests using a "weed barrier" beneath the box, and filling it completely with "Mel's mix," a combination by volume of one third of decayed Sphagnum "peat moss", one-third expanded vermiculite and one-third blended compost. For accessibility, raised boxes may have bottoms to sit like tables at a convenient height, with approximately 6" of manufactured soil per square foot.

RATIONALE

In this method, the garden space is divided into beds that are easily accessed from every side. A 4' x 4', 16 sq ft or 120 cm x 120 cm, 1.4 m^2 garden is recommended for the first garden, and a path wide enough to comfortably work from should be made on each side of the bed, if possible, or if the bed must be accessed by reaching across it, a narrower one should be used so that no discomfort results from tending the garden. Each of the beds is divided into approximately one square foot units and marked out with sticks, twine, or sturdy slats to ensure that the square foot units remain visible as the garden matures.

Different seeds are planted in each square, to ensure a rational amount of each type of crop is grown, and to conserve seeds instead of overplanting, crowding and thinning plants. Common spacing is one plant per square for larger plants, four plants per square for medium large plants like lettuce, nine plants per square for medium-small plants like spinach, and sixteen per square for small plants such as onions and carrots. Plants that normally take up yards of space as runners, such as squash or cucumbers, are grown vertically on sturdy frames that are hung with netting or string to support the developing crops. Ones that grow deep underground, such as potatoes or carrots, are grown in a square foot section that has foot tall sides and a planting surface above the ground, so that a foot or more of framed soil depth is provided above the garden surface rather than below it.

The beds are weeded and watered from the pathways, so the garden soil is never stepped on or compacted. Because a new soil mixture is used to create the garden, and a few handfuls of compost are added with each harvest to maintain soil fertility over time, the state of the site's underlying soil is irrelevant. This gardening method has been employed successfully in every region, including in deserts, on high arid mountain plateaus, in cramped urban locations, and in areas with polluted or high salinity soils. It is equally useful for growing flowers, vegetables, herbs and some fruits in containers, raised beds, on tabletops or at ground level, in only 4 to 6 inches of soil. A few seeds per square foot, the ability to make compost, to water by hand, and to set up the initial garden in a sunny position or where a container, table or platform garden may be moved on wheels to receive light is all that is needed to set up a square foot garden.

BENEFITS OF SQUARE FOOT GARDENING

- *Much less work*: Conventional gardening requires heavy tools to loosen the soil, whereas in this method, the soil is never compacted and it remains loose and loamy. Weeding takes only seconds to minutes, due to the light soil, raised beds, and easily accessed plants. Harvests per foot of garden are increased due to the rich soil mixture, well-spaced plants, and lack of weeds produced when following Mel Bartholomew's method.

- *Water Savings*: The soil mixture that is advised has water-holding capacities, so that the garden needs water less frequently, and in much smaller quantities than when using other gardening methods. Water is also spared by hand-watering directly at the plant roots, so that there is very little waste and tender young plants and seedlings are preserved.
- *Very little weeding*: One benefit of this close planting is that the vegetables form a living mulch, and shade out many weed seeds before they have a chance to germinate.
- *Pesticide/Herbicide Free*: Natural insect repellent methods like companion planting become very efficient in a close space and thus, pesticides are not necessary. The large variety of crops in a small space also prevents plant diseases from spreading easily.
- *Accessibility*: A plywood bottom can be attached to the bottom of a box, which can then be placed on a tabletop or raised platform for those who wish to garden without bending or squatting, or to make gardening easy for wheelchair, cane or walker users.

SUCCESSION PLANTING

Succession planting is done so garden space is put to its most efficient use. With this method, there is never an unplanted area in the vegetable plot. As soon as one crop is harvested, the space is immediately replanted with a different crop. This method of succession planting uses groupings of cool-season and warm-season crops. In the simplest plan, succession planting involves planning for spring, summer and fall crops.

Another method is to make several plantings of a vegetable. Bush beans can be planted every 2 weeks from mid-May to the beginning of August. A third type of succession planting involves a single planting of several different cultivars with varying maturity dates. This method works well for cabbage and corn. These methods allow for a continuous harvest over a longer period.

Vegetable harvest can be extended into the fall by growing the faster growing, cool-season crops. The quality of many of the cool-season crops is exceptional when they mature in the fall. Plant so there is adequate time for the crop to mature.

When planting seeds for a fall crop, you must water the seeds more often than in the spring because the summer soil is usually warm and dry. Provide some shade to help retain moisture. Cover the seedbed with cardboard or newspaper. Check the seedbed daily and remove the covering when the first seed sprouts. Keep the bed consistently watered until all the seedlings are established. Pre-sprouting also ensures good germination of cool-season crops in the hot, dry soil of August.

WEED CONTROL

Weed control is the botanical component of pest control, using physical and chemical methods to stop weeds from reaching a mature stage of growth when they could be harmful to domesticated plants and livestock. In order to reduce weed growth, many "weed control" strategies have been developed in order to contain the growth and spread of weeds.

The most basic is ploughing which cuts the roots of annual weeds. Today, chemical weed killers known as herbicides are widely used.

THE EFFECTS OF WEEDS ON OTHER PLANTS

Weeds can compete with productive crops or pasture, or convert productive land into unusable scrub. Weed are also often poisonous, distasteful, produce burrs, thorns or other damaging body parts or otherwise interfere with the use and management of desirable plants by contaminating harvests or excluding livestock.

Weeds tend to thrive at the expense of the more refined edible or ornamental crops. They provide competition for space, nutrients, water and light, although how seriously they will affect a crop depends on a number of factors. Some crops have greater resistance than others- smaller, slower growing seedlings are more likely to be overwhelmed than those that are larger and more vigourous. Onions are one of the crops most susceptible to competition, for they are slow to germinate and produce slender, upright stems. Quick growing, broad leafed weeds therefore have a distinct advantage, and if not removed, the crop is likely to be lost. Broad beans however produce large seedlings, and will suffer far less profound effects of weed competition other than during periods of water shortage at the crucial time when the pods are filling out. Transplanted crops raised in sterile seed or potting compost will have a head start over germinating weed seeds.

Weeds also differ in their competitive abilities, and can vary according to conditions and the time of year. Tall growing vigourous weeds such as fat hen can have the most pronounced effects on adjacent crops, although seedlings of fat hen that appear in late summer will only produce small plants. Chickweed, a low growing plant, can happily co-exist with a tall crop during the summer, but plants that have overwintered will grow rapidly in early spring and may swamp crops such as onions or spring greens.

The presence of weeds does not necessarily mean that they are competing with a crop, especially during the early stages of growth when each plant can find the resources it requires without interfering with the others. However, as the seedlings' size increases, their root systems will spread as they each begin to require greater amounts of water and nutrients. Estimates suggest that weed and crop can co-exist harmoniously for around three weeks, therefore it is important that weeds are removed early on in order to prevent competition occurring. Weed competition can have quite dramatic effects on crop growth. Harold A Roberts cites research carried out with onions wherein "Weeds were carefully removed from separate plots at different times during the growth of the crop and the plots were then kept clean. It was found that after competition had started, the final yield of bulbs was being reduced at a rate equivalent to almost 4% per day. So that by delaying weeding for another fortnight, the yield was cut to less than half that produced on ground kept clean all the time." He goes on to record that "by early June, the weight of weeds per unit area was twenty times that of the crop, and the weeds had already taken from the soil about half of the nitrogen and a third of the potash which had been applied".

Perennial weeds with bulbils, such as lesser celandine and oxalis, or with persistent underground stems such as couch grass or creeping buttercup are able to store reserves of food, and are thus able to grow faster and with more vigour than their annual counterparts. There is also evidence that the roots of some perennials such as couch grass exude allelopathic chemicals which inhibit the growth of other nearby plants.

Weeds can also host pests and diseases that can spread to cultivated crops. Charlock and Shepherd's purse may carry clubroot, eelworm can be harboured by chickweed, fat hen and shepherd's purse, while the cucumber mosaic virus, which can devastate the cucurbit family, is carried by a range of different weeds including chickweed and groundsel.

However, at times the role of weeds in this respect can be over-rated. As far as insect pests are concerned, often the species that live on weeds are not the same as those that attack vegetable crops; "Tests with the common cruciferous weeds such as shepherds purse have shown that they do not act as hosts for the larvae of the cabbage root fly. One exception was found to be the wild radish, but this is not usually a weed of established vegetable gardens". However pests such as cutworms may first attack weeds then move on to cultivated crops.

While charlock, a common weed in southeastern USA, may be considered a weed by row crop growers, it is highly valued by beekeepers, who seek out places where it blooms all winter, thus providing pollen for honeybees and other pollinators. Its bloom is resistant to all but a very hard freeze, and even that will only kill it back briefly. By feeding an array of pollinators during a seasonal dearth, it can redound to the farmer's advantage. Many weeds are likewise highly beneficial to pollinators.

METHODS

In domestic gardens, methods of weed control include covering an area of ground with several layers of wet newspaper or one black plastic sheet for several weeks. In the case of using wet newspaper, the multiple layers prevent light from reaching all plants beneath, which kills them. Saturating the newspaper with water daily speeds the decomposition of the dead plants.

Any weed seeds that start to sprout because of the water will also be deprived of sunlight, be killed, and decompose. After several weeks, all germinating weed seeds present in the ground should be dead. Then the newspaper can be removed and the ground can be planted. The decomposed plants will help fertilise the plants or seeds planted later.

In the case of using the black plastic sheet, the greenhouse effect is used to kill the plants beneath the sheet. A 5-10 cm layer of wood chip mulch on the ground will also prevent most weeds from sprouting. Also, gravel can be spread over the ground as an inorganic mulch. In agriculture, irrigation is sometimes used as a weed control measure such as in the case of paddy fields. Many people find that although the black plastic sheeting is extremely effective at preventing the weeds in areas where it covers, in actual use it is difficult to achieve full coverage.

Knowing how weeds reproduce, spread and survive adverse conditions can help in developing effective control and management strategies. Weeds have a range of techniques that enable them to thrive;

Annual and biennial weeds such as chickweed, annual meadow grass, shepherd's purse, groundsel, fat hen, cleaver, speedwell and hairy bittercress propagate themselves by seeding. Many produce huge numbers of seed several times a season, some all year round. Groundsel can produce 1000 seed, and can continue right through a mild winter, whilst Scentless Mayweed produces over 30,000 seeds per plant. Not all of these will germinate at once, but over several seasons, lying dormant in the soil sometimes for years until exposed to light. Poppy seed can survive 80-100 years, dock 50 or more. There can be many thousands of seeds in a square foot or square metre of ground, thus and soil disturbance will produce a flush of fresh weed seedlings.

"STALE SEED BED" TECHNIQUE

One technique employed by growers is the'stale seed bed', which involves cultivating the soil, then leaving it for a week or so.

When the initial flush of weeds has germinated, the grower will lightly hoe off before the desired crop is planted. However, even a freshly cleared bed will be susceptible to airborne seed from elsewhere, as well as seed brought in by passing animals which can carry them on their fur, or from freshly imported manure. The organic solution to the problem of spreading annual weeds lies in regular, properly timed weeding, preferably just before flowering.

This technique is also quite often used by farmers who let weeds germinate then return the soil before crop sowing.

Perennial weeds also propagate by seeding; the airborne seed of the dandelion and the rose-bay willow herb are parachuted far and wide. But they also have an additional range of vegetative means of spreading that gives them their pernicious reputation. Dandelion and dock put down deep tap roots, which, although they do not spread underground, are able to regrow from any remaining piece left in the ground. Removal of the complete tap root is the only sure remedy.

The most persistent of the perennials are those that spread by underground creeping rhizomes that can regrow from the tiniest fragment. These include couch grass, bindweed, ground elder, nettles, rosebay willow herb, Japanese knotweed, horsetail and bracken, as well as creeping thistle, whose tap roots can put out lateral roots. Other perennials put out runners that spread along the soil surface. As they creep along they set down roots, enabling them to colonise bare ground with great rapidity. These include creeping buttercup and ground ivy. Yet another group of perennials propagate by stolons- stems that arch back into the ground to reroot. Most familiar of these is the bramble.

All of the weeds can be very difficult to eradicate- thick black plastic mulches can be effective to a degree, although will probably need to be left in place for at least two seasons. In addition, hoeing off weed leaves and stems as soon as they appear can eventually weaken and kill the plants, although this will require persistence in the case of plants such as bindweed. Nettle infestations can be tackled by cutting back at least three times a year, repeated over a three year period. Bramble can be dealt with in a similar way. Some plants are said to produce root exudates that suppress herbaceous weeds. Tagetes minuata is claimed to be effective against couch and ground elder, whilst a border of comfrey is also said to act as a barrier against the invasion of some weeds including couch.

Use of Herbicides

The methods of weed control avoid using chemicals. They are often used by farmers. However, these methods may damage a fragile soil by restructuring it, hence are not always used. They are those preferred by the organic gardener or organic farmer.

However weed control can also be achieved by the use of herbicides. Selective herbicides kill certain targets while leaving the desired crop relatively unharmed. Some of these act by interfering with the growth of the weed and are often based on plant hormones.

Herbicides are generally classified as follows:

- Contact herbicides destroy only that plant tissue in contact with the chemical spray. Generally, these are the fastest acting herbicides. They are ineffective on perennial plants that are able to re-grow from roots or tubers.
- Systemic herbicides are foliar-applied and are translocated through the plant and destroy a greater amount of the plant tissue. Modern herbicides such as glyphosate are designed to leave no harmful residue in the soil.
- Soil-borne herbicides are applied to the soil and are taken up by the roots of the target plant.
- Pre-emergent herbicides are applied to the soil and prevent germination or early growth of weed seeds.

In agriculture large scale and systematic weeding is usually required, often by machines, such as liquid herbicide sprayers, or even by helicopter, to eliminate the massive amount of weeds present on farming lands.

However there are a number of techniques that the organic farmer can employ such as mulching and carefully timed cutting of weeds before they are able to set seed.

Organic Methods

Typically a combination of methods are used in organic situations:

- *Drip irrigation*: Rubber hoses and other methods are used to bring water directly to the roots of the desired plants. This limits weed access to water.
- *Manually pulling weeds*: Labourers are used to pull weeds at various points in the growing process.
- *Mechanically tilling around plants*: Tractors are used to carefully till weeds around the crop plants at various points in the growing process. Besides tilling, other mechanical weed control methods also exist
- *Ploughing*: Ploughing includes tilling of soil, intercultural ploughing and summer ploughing. Ploughing through tilling of soil uproots the weeds which causes them to die. In summer ploughing is done during deep summers. Summer ploughing also helps in killing pests.
- *Crop rotation*: Rotating crops with ones that kill weeds by choking them out, such as hemp, Mucuna pruriens, and other crops, can be a very effective method of weed control. It is a way to avoid the use of herbicides, and to gain the benefits of crop rotation.
- *Weed mat*: A weed mat is an artificial mulch, fibrous cloth material,

bark or newspaper laid on top of the soil preventing weeds from growing to the surface.

WOOD

Besides those kinds of weeds which are of an herbaceous nature, there are others which are woody, and grow to a very considerable size; such as broom, furze and Lantanas. The first may be destroyed by frequent ploughing and harrowing, in the same manner as other perennial weeds are. Another method of destroying broom is by pasturing the field where it grows with grazers.

The best method of extirpating furze is to set fire to it in frosty weather, for frost has the effect of withering and making them burn readily. The stumps must then be cut over with a hatchet, and when the ground is well softened by rain it may be ploughed up, and the roots taken out by a harrow adapted to that purpose. If the field is soon laid down to grass, they will again spring up; in this case, pasturing with grazers is an effectual remedy. The thorn, or bramble, can only be extirpated by ploughing up the ground and collecting the roots.

In June, weeds are in their most succulent state, and in this condition, after they have lain a few hours to wither, cattle will eat almost every species. There is scarcely a hedge, border, or a nook, but what at that season is valuable.

MANAGING INTERCROPS

Many combinations of crops have been grown or experimented with as mixed or relay intercrops. Some of these include sunflowers grown with black lentils, wheat with flax, and canola with flax.

Other combinations include cucumbers, beans, celery, and chives in China; upland rice, corn, and cassava in Indonesia, and in various parts of the tropics corn and cassava, corn and peanut, sorghum and millet, and sorghum and pigeonpeas.

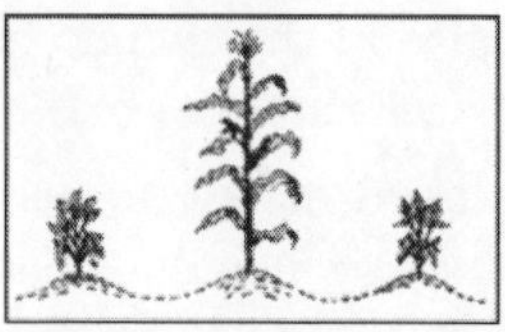

Fig. Sweetcorn and Southern Pea Planting Pattern.

Frequently these cropping combinations involve a short and a tall crop both planted at the same time. In many cases the tall crop is harvested first. Corn grown with a shorter plant would be harvested first, then peanut or sweet potato would be harvested later. Another pattern would be planting two tall crops with different growth rates. In relay intercrops, different planting dates are used so that one crop might mature sooner. Corn or sorghum, requiring three months to mature, can be grown with pigeonpea, requiring 10 months to maturation.

John Bowen and Bernard Kratky, researchers and instructors at the University of Hawaii, tell us that there are five distinct aspects to successful multiple cropping.

These are:

- Detailed planning,
- Timely planting of each crop,
- Adequate fertilization at the optimal times,
- Effective weed and pest control,
- Efficient harvesting.

Before any fieldwork is begun, adequate planning should be done. Planning covers selection of crop species and appropriate cultivars, water availability, plant populations and spacing, labor requirements throughout the season, tillage requirements, and predicted profitability of the intercrop. These and other parametres need to be evaluated before spending money on inputs.

With any crop, seed germination and seedling establishment are the most critical phases of the entire season. A good seedbed is needed to get a good stand. Delayed planting may reduce yield, since crop development may not coincide with the optimal growth periods.

Planning fertilization for intercrops can be challenging, as the full needs of both crops must be met. Generally, there is little information available on how to go about this. One possibility would be to ask for soil test results for each crop separately, then formulate a recommendation that will cover the needs of both crops to be grown. Such recommendations are generally 10% to 30% higher than rates for individual crops.

As with any crop, also accounting for residual or carryover fertility from past crops saves money. Carryover fertility from intercrops may well be lower than that of pure stands because of the two crops having different root types and feeding habits.

Weed and pest controls need in intercrops will likely be different from those in pure stands. Some disease incidence, such as soybean or mung bean rusts, may increase when aggravated with high corn populations and overfertilization. Any disease or pest that prospers in shady conditions could increase under a taller crop such as corn or sunflowers. In many cases, insect pest populations are lower when two or more crops are grown together. More on pest management will be found later in this publication.

Harvesting of mixed intercrops has been a major limitation to their adoption in mechanized farming. If the crops cannot be harvested by animals, or all together as feed, you're left with hand harvesting. Some crops such as flax and wheat have been harvested together and mechanically separated. Any other mechanized harvest efforts must get one crop without damaging the other. One example would be harvesting wheat over the top of a young stand of soybeans growing beneath the grain heads. All intercropping strategies— especially mixed intercropping—require advanced planning and keen management. Success will likely be the reward for such efforts.

EXAMPLES OF INTERCROP SYSTEMS

TRADITIONAL CORN-BEAN-SQUASH MIXED INTERCROPS

Farmers throughout Central America traditionally grow an intercrop of corn, beans and squash. Grown together, these three crops optimize available resources. The corn towers high over the other two crops, and the beans climb up the corn stalks. The squash plants sprawl along the ground, capturing light that filters down through the canopy and shading the ground. The shading discourages weeds from growing.

This mixture was compared to the individual crops grown separately in a study near Tabasco, Mexico. In the study, corn yields were considerably higher in the mixture than in a pure stand planted at optimum densities. Bean and squash yields suffered considerable yield reductions when grown in mixture.

In this example if corn were the most important crop, it was beneficial to grow it in a mixture with squash and beans. The beans and squash were just a bonus. The LER for the whole mixture was considerably higher than any of the pure stands.

Table. Yields of Corn, Beans and Suash Grown Alone or in a Mixture

Crop (pounds/acre)	Pure Stand (pounds/acre)	Intercrop
Corn	1096	1533
Beans	544	98
Squash	383	71

Corn and Soybean Mixed Intercrops

Canadian researchers have worked with several corn-soybean intercrop seeding rates to determine their economic advantages as silage. Pure stands of corn and soybeans were grown for comparison at 24,000 corn seed per acre and 200,000 soybean seed per acre.

Results showed that intercrops were more cost effective than pure stands over both years the study was conducted. The study featured five experimental intercrop seeding rates with two planting arrangements The researchers concluded that a planting rate of 16,000 corn seed per acre with 135,000 soybean seed per acre planted within the same rows along with 53 lbs. of N/acre gave the highest economic returns.

This mixture gave an LER of 1.14 over pure stand yields. The crude protein level of the intercrop silage was considerably higher than that of pure corn silage. A slightly higher yield was achieved from full stands of both corn and beans in alternate rows, but the cost of production was higher, thus offsetting the improved yields.

Corn and Sorghum Mixed Intercrops

Frank Cawrse, Jr., of Lebanon, Oregon, intercrops forage sorghum into his silage corn. He first plants the corn at 28,000 seed per acre, then goes back over the field with a drill with enough drop tubes closed off to plant 8 pounds of sorghum on 32-inch rows in between the corn. He also plants two different maturities of corn, a 95-day and a 75-day, to even out the silage moisture content. He harvests a mix of corn in hard dent and soft dent, and sorghum in the milk stage.

Strip Cropping Corn/Soybeans/Small Grains

South Dakota farmer Tod Intermill plants alternating strips of corn, soybeans, and spring wheat on his farm. The strips are six rows wide in a ridge-till system. All the crop plantings are adapted to existing equipment widths. Regular herbicide treatments can be applied using a ground sprayer of strip width. Even the wheat is drilled on ridges, using a drill with individual depth gauges on each opener. Intermill orients his rows east and west to minimize the shading effects of taller crops like corn. The crops are planted in a wheat-corn-soybean pattern, with soybeans on the north side of the corn. This arrangement reduces the effect of corn shading often associated with a straight corn-soybean pattern, since the wheat is mature before the corn has a chance to shade it. Corn gains the greatest benefit from the additional sunlight interception on the outside rows of the corn strip.

Iowa farmer Tom Frantzen strip-crops oats, corn, and soybeans on ridge-till rows. He views his strips as a crop rotation in one field. His rows are oriented generally east and west on the contour. His 1989 strip-crop corn yields were 166 bushels per acre, compared to 130 for his farm average. Stripped soybean yields were two bushels lower than farm average. His oat yields were 109 bushels stripped and 100-bushel farm average. Tom was not surprised at the increase in corn yields. The outer strip rows captured more sunlight. His average corn border row yielded 198 bushels per acre next to the soybeans and 177 bushels next to oats. The soybean yields were 37 bushels, even with the increased shading on the border rows. This loss was made up in the middle rows with yields of 44 bushels per acre. Oats showed a 107-bushel yield on the soybean side, a 103-bushel yield on the corn side, and 99 bushels in the middle. Tom says the strip intercropping is no more labor intensive than monocrop fields. His profits were $76 per acre for the stripped fields and $55 for the same crops grown in monoculture.

Rick Cruse, an Iowa State University agronomist, has observed several characteristics that narrow strips offer. The strips accommodate the pest management and soil building advantages of rotations and the yield boost of border rows. With proper management the border effect can pay off; managed improperly, it can cost yield. With oat and corn strips, the early-maturing oats are nearly mature before corn can pose much of a shade and competition problem. The corn can also provide wind protection for the oats. When the oats are harvested, more sunlight is available to the corn. In times of low moisture, oats may rob the corn border rows of water. In his field trials, Cruse found a 5% increase in oat yields on their borders while corn realised a 12 to 15% increase.

Soybean yields dropped by 10% on their border rows, but the yields in the soybean middle rows were higher than they would be in a solid field, possibly representing a windbreak effect.

Some have experimented with a shorter corn variety in the border row to minimize shading. One farmer tried planting six rows of corn and doubling his soybean strips to 12 rows to eliminate the impact of corn shading on the beans. This same farmer found that corn strips wider than eight rows did not provide adequate results. Using a 12-row planter, it's easy to establish the 6-row strips by filling the middle six hoppers with corn and the outer three hoppers with beans. Some farmers plant higher corn populations and add higher nitrogen rates in the border rows to take advantage of the extra sunlight exposure. Most farmers agree that strip cropping corn, soybeans, and oats works best with ridge-till or no-till. When the field is tilled, it's difficult to gauge where the rows should go in order to get the strips even.

UK LEGISLATION CONCERNING WEEDS

The Weeds Act, 1959 is described as"Preventing the spread of harmful or injurious weeds", and is mainly relevant to farmers and other rural settings rather than the allotment or garden scale grower. There are five'injurious' weeds covered by the provisions of the Weeds Act.

These are:

- Spear thistle

- Creeping or field thistle
- Curled Dock
- Broad leaved dock
- Common ragwort.

The Department for Environment, Food and Rural Affairs provides guidance for the treatment removal of these weeds from infested land. Much of this is oriented towards the use of herbicides, the majority of which may not be acceptable to the organic producer but in most cases there are manual techniques that can be used such as digging out the roots, mulching out or carefully timed cutting before seeds are able to spread.

Primary responsibility for weeds control rests with the occupier of the land on which the weeds are growing, therefore it is important to be alert to potential weed problems and to take prompt action. However, it should be remembered that most common farmland weeds are not"injurious" within the meaning of the Weeds Act, and many such plant species have conservation and environmental value. When dealing with complaints under the Weeds Act, DEFRA has a duty in law to try and achieve a reasonable balance between different interests. These include agriculture, countryside conservation and the public in general. Constructive discussion about problems caused by weeds can often result in effective solutions and avoid the need for DEFRA to take official action. In addition to those weeds covered by the 1959 act, under section 14 of the Wildlife and Countryside Act 1981, it can be an offence to plant or grow certain specified plants in the wild including Giant Hogweed and Japanese Knotweed. Problems involving these plants can be referred to the local authority for the area where those weeds are growing as some local authorities have bye-laws controlling these plants. There is no statutory requirement for landowners to remove these plants from their property.

STALE SEED BED

A false or stale seed bed is a useful organic weed control technique which involves creating a seedbed some weeks before seed is due to be sown. Preparation of such seedbed makes sure that any weed seeds that have been disturbed and brought to the soil surface during cultivation will thus have a chance to germinate, and can then be hoed off before sowing of the actual crop is carried out.

XERISCAPING

Xeriscaping and xerogardening refers to landscaping and gardening in ways that reduce or eliminate the need for supplemental irrigation. It is promoted in areas that do not have easily accessible supplies of fresh water, and is gaining acceptance in other areas as climate patterns shift. The word xeriscaping is a portmanteau of xeros and landscape.

Plants whose natural requirements are appropriate to the local climate are emphasized, and care is taken to avoid losing water to evaporation and run-off. While many Denver Water employees helped coin the term xeriscape, Xeriscape and the xeriscape logo are not registered trademarks of Denver Water, the water department of Denver, Colourado. They were created by the Front Range Xeriscape Task Force of Denver Department in 1978. The specific plants used in xeriscaping depend upon the climate. Some common plants used in Western xeriscaping are agave, cactus, lavender, juniper, sedum and thyme.

In some areas, terms such as water-conserving landscapes, drought-tolerant landscaping, zeroscaping, and smart scaping are used instead.

ADVANTAGES

- Lower water consumption
- More water available for other uses and other people
- Less time and work needed for maintenance, making gardening simpler and less stressful
- Little or no lawnmowing
- Xeriscape plants along with proper bed design tends to take full advantage of rainfall
- When water restrictions are implemented, xeriscape plants will tend to survive, while more traditional plants may be unable to adapt.

GREYWATER

Greywater is wastewater generated from domestic activities such as laundry, dishwashing, and bathing which can be recycled on-site for uses such as landscape irrigation and constructed wetlands. Greywater differs from water from the toilets which is designated sewage or blackwater to indicate it contains human waste.

Greywater composes 50–80% of residential wastewater generated from all of the house's sanitation equipment.

Greywater gets its name from its cloudy appearance and from its status as being neither fresh, nor polluted. Wastewater containing significant food residues or high concentrations of toxic chemicals from household cleaners, etc., may be considered "dark grey".

CHALLENGES

In recent years, concerns over dwindling reserves of groundwater and overloaded or costly sewage treatment plants have generated much interest in the reuse or recycling of greywater, both domestically and for use in commercial irrigation.

A lack of knowledge and experience with modern greywater systems has led to some concern over potential health and environmental risks.

If properly designed a greywater system will lower sewage costs, at the same time reducing water usage for irrigation and water quality can be increased to better than the government supplied initially. Less water enters the city sewage systems saving the government from building new treatment plants. Some jurisdictions demand highly intensive treatment systems for legal reuse of greywater whereas some encourage greywater use. Oregon, on June 12, 2009, passed a law which legalizes and encourages the use of greywater. Despite many obstacles, greywater is often reused for irrigation legally and illegally.

Anyone, including those in droughtzones or areas hit by hose pipe bans can harvest greywater by manual bucketing shower or sink water and using them to flush toilets. In the third world, reuse of greywater is often unregulated and is common. At present, the recycling of greywater is poorly understood by many compared with elimination.

ELIMINATION OF GREYWATER

Domestic wastewater is usually combined at the sewer, so that grey- and blackwaters are removed together using a shared sewerage system in a process called elimination.

Sewage water can then be treated to limit pollution and health risks, before being returned to the environment at large. Most greywater ends up as effluent in rivers and oceans in this way.

There are other alternatives to eliminating greywater that allow for efficient use; using it to irrigate plants is a common practice. The plants use contaminants of greywater, such as food particles, as nutrients in their growth. However, salt and soap residues can be toxic to microbial and plant life alike, but can be absorbed and degraded through constructed wetlands and aquatic plants such as sedges, rushes, and grasses.

RECYCLING

Most greywater is easier to treat and recycle than blackwater, because of lower levels of contaminants. While all greywater contains micro-organisms, the health hazards associated with greywater from a multiple-dwelling source should be considered differently from that of a single dwelling greywater source.

One may recycle greywater at home by putting a bucket in the shower or sink and using the water to flush the toilet. If collected using a separate plumbing system from blackwater, domestic greywater can be recycled directly within the home, garden or company and used either immediately or processed and stored. Recycled greywater of this kind is never safe to drink, but a number of stages of filtration and microbial digestion can be used to provide water for washing or flushing toilets. Some greywater may be applied directly from the sink to the garden or container field, receiving further treatment from soil life and plant roots. Given that greywater may contain nutrients, pathogens, and is often discharged warm, it is very important not to store it before use in irrigation purposes, unless it is properly treated first.

Systems

At present, several water recycling systems exist which can be used to:

- Recycle the water without purifying it
- Recycle the water while purifying or decontaminating it

Water recycling without purification is used in certain agricultural companies and dwellings for applications where potable water is not required. It may also be used in dwellings when the greywater is already fairly clean to begin with and/or has not been polluted with non-degradable chemicals such as non-natural soaps.

Water purification/decontamination systems then again are used for applications where potable water is required.

Water Recycling Systems Without Purification

Water Diversion Systems

The simplest greywater system is to simply divert the water directly to the garden. Regulations change by country and region, but common guidelines for safe usage include not storing the greywater for more than 24 hours, ensuring it cannot pool or run off, and depositing it with subsurface irrigation.

Greywater diversion systems can be both designed-in to new homes, or retrofitted to many existing homes. When systems are fully designed, manufactured and installed to relevant standards such as the Australian Watermark standards. Water diversion systems tend to be highly efficient, effective and safe for simple applications where potable water is not required.

Diversion systems can be as basic as running the outlet hose from a washing machine out a window to the garden, or can be designed as a permanent part of the home plumbing. Fully engineered systems incorporate a sump pump and surge tanks and deliver the water through sub-surface irrigation.

Greywater from the shower or bath is generally good quality water for the garden. The soap levels at the dilutions typical are actually good for the garden as they are a wetting agent. When laundry greywater is diverted to the garden then the laundry products must be chosen carefully to ensure phosphate and salt levels are low, and the pH balance is neutral. Basic guidelines are also available from system suppliers. It is essential that greywater is diverted to sewer when garden-unfriendly products are being used.

Water Recycling with Purification

For filtering the water to become potable, there are numerous systems based on soft processes.

These include natural biological principles such as:

- Mechanical systems
- Biological systems and Bio reactors or compact systems as activated sludge systems, biorotors, aerobic and anaerobic biofilters, submerged aerated filters, biorolls

Finally, also used for creating potable water are the "hard", direct processes, such as distillation. There seem to be no commercially available "hard" greywater recovery devices suitable for on-site use in the individual household, even though a number of such technologies exist.

In order to purify the potable water adequately, several of these systems are usually combined to work as a whole. Combination of the systems is done in two to three stages, knowingly a primary and a secondary purification. Sometimes a tertiary purification is also added.

Some municipal sewerage systems recycle a certain amount of grey- and blackwaters using a high standard of treatment, thus providing reclaimed water for irrigation and other uses.

APPLICATION OF RECYCLED GREYWATER

IRRIGATION

Greywater typically breaks down faster than blackwater and has lower levels of nitrogen and phosphorus. However, all greywater must be assumed to have some blackwater-type components, including pathogens of various sorts. Greywater should be applied below the surface where possible and not sprayed, as there is a danger of inhaling the water as an aerosol.

Long-term research on greywater use on soil has not yet been done and it is possible that there may be negative impacts on soil productivity. If you are concerned about this, avoid using laundry powders; these often contain high levels of salt as a bulking agent.

In any greywater system, it is essential to put nothing toxic down the drain—no bleaches, bath salts, artificial dyes, cleansers, and no products containing boron. It is crucial to use all-natural, biodegradable soaps whose ingredients do not harm plants. Most powdered detergents, and some liquid detergents, are sodium-based, which can inhibit seed-germination and destroy the structure of clay soils.

"Natural" body products often contain substances toxic to humans, including parabens, stearalkonium chloride, phenoxyethanol, polyethelene glycol, and synthetic fragrances.

Indoor Reuse

Recycled greywater from showers and bathtubs can be used for flushing toilets in most European and Australian jurisdictions and in United States jurisdictions that have adopted the International Plumbing Code.

Such a system could provide an estimated 30% reduction in water use for the average household.

The danger of biological contamination is avoided by using:

- A cleaning tank, to eliminate floating and sinking items
- An intelligent control mechanism that flushes the collected water if it has been stored long enough to be hazardous; this completely avoids the problems of filtration and chemical treatment

The Uniform Plumbing Code, adopted in some United States jurisdictions, prohibits greywater use indoors.

Extreme Living Conditions

Greywater use promotes the ability to build in areas unsuitable for conventional treatment, or where conventional treatment is costly. The Mars Desert Research Station uses greywater recycling, and might be used on trips to Mars to reduce water consumption and increase oxygen generation.

Heat Reclamation

Devices are currently available that capture heat from residential and industrial greywater, through a process called drainwater heat recovery, greywater heat recovery, or hot water heat recycling. Rather than flowing directly into a water heating device, incoming cold water flows first through a heat exchanger where it is pre-warmed by heat from greywater flowing out from such activities as dishwashing, or showering. Typical household devices receiving greywater from a shower can recover up to 60% of the heat that would otherwise go to waste.

Ice Rinks

Lee Valley Ice Centre in Leyton, London, is the first example of the use of a greywater system in an ice arena context, a concept which reduces the otherwise considerable water use associated with such activities.

ECOLOGY

Because greywater use, especially domestically, reduces demand on conventional water supplies and pressure on sewage treatment systems, its use is very beneficial to local waterways. In times of drought, especially in urban areas, greywater use in gardens or toilet systems helps to achieve the goals of ecologically sustainable development.

Benefits

The potential ecological benefits of greywater recycling include:

- Lower fresh water extraction from rivers and aquifers
- Less impact from septic tank and treatment plant infrastructure
- Topsoil nutrification
- Reduced energy use and chemical pollution from treatment
- Groundwater recharge
- Increased plant growth
- Reclamation of nutrients
- Greater quality of surface and ground water when preserved by the natural purification in the top layers of soil than generated water treatment processes

In the U.S. Southwest and the Middle East where available water supplies are limited, especially in view of a rapidly growing population, a strong imperative exists for adoption of alternative water technologies.

Potential Downsides of Greywater Recycling

The Southern Nevada Water Authority has expressed concern that greywater recycling for use in residential washing machines and for watering xeriscapes could encourage greater water use, and reduce the amount of water returned to Lake Mead, a reservoir currently experiencing a drought. Greywater users and advocates dispute these claims.

GOVERNMENTAL REGULATION

Government regulation governing domestic greywater use for landscape irrigation is still a developing area and continues to gain wider support as the actual risks and benefits are considered and put into clearer perspective.

'Greywater' is considered in some jurisdictions to be'sewage' but in the U.S. states that adopt the International Plumbing Code, it can be used for sub surface irrigation and for toilet flushing, and in states that adopt the Uniform Plumbing Code, it can be used in underground disposal fields that are akin to shallow sewage disposal fields. Wyoming allows surface and subsurface irrigation and other non specific use of greywater under a Department of

Environmental Quality policy enacted in March, 2010. California, Utah, New Mexico and some other states allow true subsurface drip irrigation with greywater.

Where greywater is still considered sewage, it is bound by the same regulatory procedures enacted to ensure properly engineered septic tank and effluent disposal systems are installed for long system life and to control spread of disease and pollution.

In such regulatory jurisdictions, this has commonly meant domestic greywater diversion for landscape irrigation was either simply not permitted or was discouraged by expensive and complex sewage system approval requirements. Wider legitimate community greywater diversion for landscape irrigation has subsequently been handicapped and resulted in greywater reuse continuing to still be widely undertaken by householders outside of and in preference to the legal avenues.

However, with water conservation becoming a necessity in a growing number of jurisdictions, business, political and community pressure has made regulators seriously reconsider the actual risks against actual benefits.

It is now recognized and accepted by an increasing number of regulators that the microbiological risks of greywater reuse at the single dwelling level where inhabitants already had intimate knowledge of that greywater are in reality an insignificant risk, when properly managed without the need for complex, expensive and onerous red tape approval processes. This is reflected in the NSW Government Department of Water and Energy's newly released greywater diversion rules, and the recent passage of greywater legislation in Montana. In the 2009 Legislative Session, the state of Montana passed a bill expanding greywater use into multi-family and commercial buildings. The Department of Environmental Quality has already drafted rules and design guidelines for greywater re-use systems in all these applications. Existing staff would review systems proposed for new subdivisions in conjunction with review of all other wastewater system components.

UNDERUTILIZED CROPS

Neglected and underutilized crops are plant species that are used traditionally for their food, fibre, fodder, oil or medicinal properties, but have yet to be adopted by large-scale agriculturalists. They may have the potential to contribute to food security, nutrition, health, income generation and environmental services. For a variety of reasons, some economic and some cultural, they have been neglected or underutilized.

Just three crops - maize, wheat and rice - account for about half of the world's consumption of protein and calories. 95% of the world's food needs are provided for by just 30 species of plants. In stark contrast, an estimated 7,500 species are considered edible in the world today. Underutilized and neglected plants are those that could be - and, in many cases, historically have been - used for food on a larger scale.

Alongside their commercial potential, many of the underutilized crops also provide important environmental services, as they are adapted to marginal soil and climate conditions.

To be considered as an "underutilized crop", a plant must meet three criteria:

1. It must have a proven food or energy value;
2. It must be proven able to be cultivated, either:
   - By having been widely cultivated in the past, or
   - By only being cultivated in a limited geographical area; and,
3. It must be currently cultivated less than other comparable plants.

AQUAPONICS CULTIVATION

Aquaponics is the symbiotic cultivation of plants and aquatic animals in a recirculating environment. Aquatic animal effluent accumulates in water as a by-product of keeping them in a closed system or tank. The effluent-rich water becomes high in plant nutrients but this is correspondingly toxic to the aquatic animal.

Plants are grown in a way that enables them to utilize the nutrient-rich water. The plants take up the nutrients, reducing or eliminating the water's toxicity for the aquatic animal. The water, now clean, is returned to the aquatic animal environment and the cycle continues. Aquaponic systems do not discharge or exchange water. The systems rely on the relationship between the aquatic animals and the plants to maintain the environment. Water is only added to replace water loss from absorption by the plants, evaporation into the air, or the removal of biomass from the system. Aquaponic systems vary in size from small indoor units to large commercial units. They can use fresh or salt water depending on the type of aquatic animal and vegetation.

HISTORY

Ancient Roots

Some consider Aztec chinampas to be the first example of aquaponics. Others refer to ancient Egypt. Either way, it is clear that aquaponics have ancient roots. "Integrated vegetable growing and fish farming polyculture systems have long been used in Far Eastern countries such as China and Thailand. Farm wastes are commonly added as feed to fish ponds and fish are often cultured in flooded rice paddies."

Aquaponics in the United States

Many institutions and enterprises followed on the efforts at North Carolina State University; notably by the University of Arizona Environmental Research Labs, NASA/CELSS, SandS Aquafarms, The Freshwater Institute, University of Arkansas, Bioshelters, Inc, Global Aquatics, Inslee Fish Farms and others who carried out 'research and development' of aquaponics.

From the 1980s to present day the two distinct aquaponic systems are:

- "Deep Water" or "Raft Culture" aquaponics which is the primarily research carried out at the University of the Virgin Islands under the guidance of Dr. James Rakocy and;
- Reciprocating aquaponics based on the techniques developed by Mark McMurtry, et al. at NCSU

The University of the Virgin Islands Aquaculture Program has developed an aquaponic system through over 20 years of research into its design and operation. The system can produce over 10,000 lbs. of tilapia annually and a variety of vegetables that are harvested weekly in staggered production or as needed by other fruiting crops The aquaculture program promotes several principles of aquaponics that can be applied to any size system, from hobby-scale to commercial-scale.

These principles include:

- System design that balances feed input to vegetable growing area,
- Constant input of feed by staggering fish stocking,
- Constant nutrient uptake by staggering vegetable production,
- Continuous water flow and
- Maintaining pH of 7.0. Other guidelines also apply and lead farmers to productive and profitable enterprises.

The University of the Virgin Islands teaches a course each June, the "International Aquaponics and Tilapia Aquaculture Course" to participants from around the globe. These individuals return home to develop their own commercial enterprises based on the aquaponic principles taught in the course.

In 1997 Rebecca Nelson and John Pade began publishing the Aquaponics Journal. The Aquaponics Journal was the first publicaiton to bring the research and various applications of aquaponics to people around the globe. Nelson and Pade also began offering training and internships at their facility in Mariposa, CA during the 1990s. In 2004 they produced the first video on aquaponics and in 2008, they wrote and published the first comprehensive book on aquaponics, "Aquaponic Food Production." They are known throughout the industry as leaders for offering training, consulting and sytstems. Nelson and Pade work closely with Dr. Rakocy of the University of the Virgin Islands to bring the research on aquaponics into mainstream agriculture. Now located in Montello,

WI, they are expanding their business and are the only full-spectrum provider of aquaponic systems, supplies, training and consulting in the US.

A graduate of the 2007 University of the Virgin Islands Short Course in Aquaponics, Tim Mann and his wife and partner Susanne started an aquaponics farm in Hawaii in 2007. This was the first aquaponics farm in the USA to have its produce USDA Organic certified and Food Safety Certified, and is currently shipping 1,600 pounds of its organic lettuce mix and 300 pounds of white tilapia per month. Friendly Aquaponics teaches the "Commercial Aquaponics Training" twice a year to participants worldwide. Attendees have developed their own commercial and educational enterprises based on the information provided in the course.

Aquaponics Research in Canada

The first aquaponics research in Canada was a small system added onto existing aquaculture research at a research station in Lethbridge. Later, a larger set-up was built in Brooks, Alberta. Scientists, especially Dr. Nick Savidov, at this research station have made some interesting findings related to rapid root growth in aquaponics systems.

Dr. Savidov's research is unusual for aquaponics as it is based out of a plant science background. His team took the system developed at the University of Virgin Islands and adapted it into a system in an Alberta greenhouse. One of the interesting adaptations that he made was to run his system at a low pH level, rather than a system that is half-way between the ideal pH for plants and neutral to high pH for fish. He found that even with a lower pH, the fish could survive nicely because of other advantages in the system over traditional aquaculture.

Commercial Aquaponics in Canada

Many of the pioneers of aquaponics in Canada are no longer in production. ounded in 1998, Future Aqua Farms in Nova Scotia is widely considered the first commercial aquaponics project in Canada. North Atlantic Aquaponics Ltd., in Newfoundland apparently grew eels in their aquaponic system., Agua Aquaponics Greenhouses International, in Manitoba is another early project that is no longer operational.

Other aquaponic systems tried aquaponics and then switched toward pure aquaculture. MDM farms in Alberta switched from a small aquaponics system back to a pure aquaculture system. Greenview farms also in Alberta, switched from aquaponics to a pure aquaculture system at the same time that it changed its name to Aquagrow Enterprises International Ltd. Only a few commercial aquaponics systems continue operations in Canada. Cultures Aquaponiques M.L.

Inc, in Quebec is an early aquaponics system in Canada, and an unusual one in that it combines trout and floating lettuce production. Circle M Trout Farm, in Alberta also uses trout, but does not recirculate their water because they use it to produce fruiting vegetable crops. They run the trout water through the greenhouse in pipes to warm it up and then into the plant beds. After the plants have taken the nutrients out of the water, the water is too warm to recirculate and it is taken out of the system. Floating Gardens Ltd., in Saskatchewan won an award for their business plan using aquaponics and advertise a start-up date of summer 2009. They plan to grow tilapia and various vegetables for the Saskatchewan market.

Aquaponics in the Barbados

The easternmost Caribbean island nation of Barbados is considered to be the most developed of the Caribbean states, having one of the highest per capita incomes in the region.The densely populated island nation of Barbados has limited resources required for a prosperous agricultural industry. This high population density and seasonal influx of foreign tourists - over 570,000 tourists stayed in Barbados in 2007 and over 600,000 cruise ship passengers visited the country that same year – places stress on the country's key national resources. Barbados is known as the 15th most water scarce country in the world and freshwater withdrawal per capita is 333 m3/year.

The long history of intensive plantation-style monoculture production over the past 300 years in Barbados has made extensive contributions to soil quality problems in Barbados. These include the erosion of topsoil, a decrease in soil fertility, and the consequent application of large amounts of fertilizer and pesticides in order to maintain productivity. The colonial history of Barbados has left behind a reliance on monocrop, plantation-style agriculture which focuses on the production of a single cash crop in large amounts. The agricultural industry in Barbados therefore still consists primarily of sugar cane cultivation and the sugar, rum and molasses production industry.Production of food crops in the country is quite low as Barbados imports around 80% of its food, including large amounts of fruits and vegetables.

Only 10% of the labour force in Barbados is involved in agricultural activities as agriculture must compete with more profitable industries and forms of land use such as the growing tourism and real-estate sector. The reliance on outside factors and world markets associated with such high levels of food importation place the country in a position of dependency and hinders progress towards self-sufficiency in terms of food production.

Traditionally, small-scale farming faces challenges regarding the necessity to incorporate high-input technologies into their production in order to be able to compete on the global market. These technologies involve high costs and significant initial investments that cannot be afforded by all rural food producers and which increase production costs and therefore the cost of locally produced crops. This makes small farmers uncompetitive against cheaper imported items.

Aquaponics has the potential to lessen the challenges associated with small scale farming in Barbados and generally in the Caribbean. The system requires minimal land and water resources, and no soil resources, which is desirable for highly populated and arid regions such as Barbados. Aquaponic systems provide a source of protein as well as fresh fruits, vegetables or herbs. As meat on the island is relatively expensive, protein in the form of freshwater fish would provide a healthy alternative and reduce stress on dwindling saltwater and freshwater fish supplies.

In late 2009 the project "Aquaponic island" was started with joint funding by the United Nations Development Program, the Food and agriculture organization,Ministry of Agriculture, 4H movement, Inter-American Institute for the Cooperation on Agriculture, Bellairs Research Institute And Baird's Village Aquaponic Association. The aim of the project is to educate the island population about the advantages of aquaponics. A commercial size system was set up at Baird's Village and extensive research and development was done adapting the technology to the island climate the next phase is to put aquaponic systems in many of the island schools.

ADVANTAGES

The unique advantages of aquaponic systems are:

- Conservation through constant water reuse and recycling.
- Organic fertilization of plants with natural fish emulsion.
- The elimination of solid waste disposal from intensive aquaculture.
- The reduction of needed cropland to produce like crops.
- The overall reduction of environmental footprint for crop production.
- Small efficient commercial installations can be built close to markets therefore reducing food miles.

DISADVANTAGES

Some conceivable disadvantages with aquaponics are:

- Initial expense for housing, tank, plumbing, pump/s, and grow beds.
- The infinite number of ways in which a system can be configured lends itself to equally varying results, conflicting research, and successes or failures.
- Some Aquaponic installations rely heavily on man-made energy, technology solutions, and environmental control to achieve

recirculation and water/ambient temperatures but a system designed with energy conservation in mind can be extremely energy efficient.

- Whilst careful design can minimize the risk, Aquaponics systems can have multiple'single points of failure' where problems such as an electrical failure or pipe blockage can lead to a complete loss of fish stock.
- Like all aquaculture based systems, stock feed usually consists of fish meal derived from lower value species. Ongoing depletion of wild fish stocks makes this practice unsustainable. There are now, however, organic fish feeds available which may prove to be a viable alternative and negate this concern. Other alternatives include growing duckweed with an Aquaponics system that feeds the same fish grown on the system, as well as growing Black Soldier Fly larva to feed to the fish using composting grub growers.

MORE USES

Aquaponic systems can be used to replicate controlled wetland conditions that are useful for reclaiming potable water from typical household sewage, in addition to generating a continual supply of food with minimal fertilizer use. Aquaponics takes advantage of synergy between self-organizing biological systems, emphasizing the one element/many functions principle of permaculture as a natural solution for water treatment.

FISH

In practice, tilapia are the most popular fish chosen for home and commercial projects that are intended to raise edible fish. Most green leafy vegetables grow well in the hydroponic filter. Although sometimes selected minerals or nutrients such as iron are added, the main source of nutrients for the plants is the fish waste. In Australia, due to a ban on Tilapia in all states bar W.A., natives are the most popular fish, including Silver Perch, Jade Perch, Sleepy Cod, Murray cod and Barramundi. Rainbow and brown trout while not native to Australia are also in use - along with fresh water crayfish such as yabby and redclaw.

COMPANION PLANTING

Many plants have natural substances in their roots, flowers, leaves etc. that can alternately repel and/or attract insects depending on your needs. In some situations they can also help enhance the growth rate and flavour of other varieties. Experience shows us that using companion planting through out the landscape is an important part of integrated pest management. In essence companion planting helps bring a balanced eco-system to your landscape, allowing nature to do its' job. Nature integrates a diversity of plants, insects, animals, and other organisms into every ecosystem so there is no waste. The death of one organism can create food for another, meaning symbiotic relationships all around. We consider companion planting to be a holistic concept due to the many intricate levels in which it works with the ecology.

By using companion planting, many gardeners find that they can discourage harmful pests without losing the beneficial allies. There are many varieties of herbs, flowers, etc. that can be used for companion plants. Be open to experimenting and find what works for you. Some possibilities would be using certain plants as a border, backdrop or interplanting in your flower or vegetable beds where you have specific needs. Use plants that are native to your area so the insects you want to attract already know what to look for! Plants with open cup shaped flowers are the most popular with beneficial insects.

Companion planting can combine beauty and purpose to give you an enjoyable, healthy environment. Have fun, let your imagination soar. There are many ways you can find to incorporate these useful plants in your garden, orchard, flower beds etc.

PLANT GUIDE

Alfalfa: zPerennial that roots deeply. Fixes the soil with nitrogen, accumulates iron, magnesium, phosphorous and potassium. Withstands droughts with it's long taproot and can improve just about any soil! Alfalfa has the ability to break up hard clay soil and can even send its' roots through rocks! Now that is a tenacious plant! Alfalfa is practically pest and disease free. It needs only natural rainfall to survive.

Amaranth: A tropical annual that needs hot conditions to flourish. Good with sweet corn, it's leaves provide shade giving the corm a rich, moist root run. Host to predatory ground beetles. Eat the young leaves in salads.

Anise: Licorice flavoured herb, good host for predatory wasps which prey on aphids and it is also said to repel aphids. Deters pests from brassicas by camouflaging their odor. Improves the vigour of any plants growing near it. Used in ointments to protect against bug stings and bites. Good to plant with coriander.

Asparagus Friends: Aster family flowers, dill,coriander, tomatoes, parsley, basil, comfrey and marigolds. Avoid: Onions, garlic and potatoes.

Basil: Plant with tomatoes to improve growth and flavour. Basil also does well with peppers, oregano, asparagus and petunias. Basil can be helpful in repelling thrips. It is said to repel flies and mosquitoes. Do not plant near rue or sage.

Bay Leaf: A fresh leaf bay leaf in each storage container of beans or grains will deter weevils and moths. Sprinkle dried leaves with other deterrent herbs in garden as natural insecticide dust. A good combo: Bay leaves, cayenne pepper, tansy and peppermint.

Beans: All bean enrich the soil with nitrogen fixed form the air. In general they are good company for carrots, celery, chards, corn, eggplant, peas, potatoes, brassicas, beets, radish, strawberry and cucumbers. Beans are great for heavy nitrogen users like corn and grain plants because beans fix nitrogen from the air into the soil so the nitrogen used up by the corn and grains are replaced at the end of the season when the bean plants die back. French Haricot beans, sweet corn and melons are a good combo. Summer savory deters bean beetles and improves growth and flavour. Keep beans away from the alliums.

Bee Balm: Plant with tomatoes to improve growth and flavour. Great for attracting beneficials and bees of course. Pretty perennial that tends to get powdery mildew.

Beet: Good for adding minerals to the soil. The leaves are composed of 25% magnesium making them a valuable addition to the compost pile if you don't care to eat them. Beets are also beneficial to beans with the exception of runner beans. Runner or pole beans and beets stunt each other's growth. Companions for beets are lettuce, onions and brassicas. Beets and kohlrabi grow perfectly together. Beets are helped by garlic and mints. Garlic improves growth and flavour. Rather than planting invasive mints around beets use your mint clippings as a mulch.

Borage: Companion plant for tomatoes, squash, strawberries and most plants. Deters tomato hornworms and cabbage worms. One of the best bee and wasp attracting plants. Adds trace minerals to the soil and a good addition the compost pile. The leaves contain vitamin C and are rich in calcium, potassium and mineral salts. Borage may benefit any plant it is growing next to via increasing resistance to pests and disease. It also makes a nice mulch for most plants. Borage and strawberries help each other and strawberry farmers always set a few plants in their beds to enhance the fruits flavour and yield. Plant near tomatoes to improve growth and disease resistance. After you have planned this annual once it will self seed. Borage flowers are edible.

Brassica: Benefit from chamomile, peppermint, dill, sage, and rosemary. They need rich soil with plenty of lime to flourish. Avoid planting with mustards, nightshades.

Buckwheat: Accumulates calcium and can be grown as an excellent cover crop aka green manure. Buckwheat's shallow white blossoms attract beneficial insects that control or parasitize aphids, mites and other pests. The beneficials it attracts include the following: hover flies, predatory wasps, minute pirate bugs, insidious flower bugs, tachinid flies and lady beetles. Flowering may start within three weeks of planting and continue for up to 10 weeks. Buckwheat will take up phosphorus and some minor nutrients that are otherwise unavailable to plants. These nutrients are released as the residue of the buckwheat breaks down and are then available for later crops. The fine roots makes topsoil loose and friable with only minimal tillage.

Cabbage: Celery, dill, onions and potatoes are good companion plants. Celery improves growth and health. Clover interplanted with cabbage has been shown to reduce the native cabbage aphid and cabbageworm populations by interfering with the colonization of the pests and increasing the number of predatory ground beetles. Plant Chamomile with cabbage as it Improves growth and flavour. Cabbage does not get along with strawberries, tomatoes, peppers, eggplants, rue, grapes and pole beans.

Caraway: Good for loosening compacted soil with it's deep roots so it's also compatible next to shallow rooted crops. Plant it with strawberries. Caraway can be tricky to establish. The flowers attract a number of beneficial insects especially the tiny parasitic wasps. Keep it away from dill and fennel.

Carrots: Their pals are leaf lettuce, onions and tomatoes. Plant dill and parsnips away from carrots. Flax produces an oil that may protect root vegetables like carrots from some pests. One drawback with tomatoes and carrots: tomato plants can stunt the growth of your carrots but the carrots will still be of good flavour.

Catnip: Deters flea beetles, aphids, Japanese beetles, squash bugs, ants and weevils. We have found it repels mice quite well: mice were wreaking havoc in our outbuildings, we spread sprigs of mint throughout and the mice split! Use sprigs of mint anywhere in the house you want deter mice and ants. Smells good and very safe.

Celery: Companions: Bean, cabbage family, leek, onion, spinach and tomato. Flowers for celery: cosmos, daisies and snapdragons.

Foe: Corn.

Chamomile, German: Annual. Improves flavour of cabbages, cucumbers and onions. Host to hoverflies and wasps. Accumulates calcium, potassium and sulfur, later returning them to the soil. Increases oil production from herbs. Leave some flowers unpicked and German chamomile will reseed itself. Roman chamomile is a low growing perennial that will tolerate almost any soil conditions. Both like full sun. Growing chamomile of any type is considered a tonic for anything you grow in the garden.

Chards: Companions: Bean, cabbage family and onion.

Chervil: Companion to radishes, lettuce and broccoli for improved growth and flavour. Keeps aphids off lettuce. Said to deter slugs. Likes shade.

Chives: Improves growth and flavour of carrots and tomatoes. A friend to apples, carrots, tomatoes, brassica and many others.

Keeps aphids help to keep aphids away from tomatoes, mums and sunflowers. Chives may drive away Japanese beetles and carrot rust fly. Planted among apple trees it helps prevent scab and among roses it prevents black spot. You will need patience as it takes about 3 years for plantings of chives to prevent the 2 diseases. A tea of chives may be used on cucumbers and gooseberries to prevent downy and powdery mildews. Avoid planting near beans and peas.

Chrysanthemums: C. coccineum kills root nematodes. It's flowers along with those of C. cineraruaefolium have been used as botanical pesticides for centuries. White flowering chrysanthemums repel Japanese beetles. To the right is a picture of the painted daisy from which pyrethrum is extracted.

Clover: Long used as a green manure and plant companion and is especially good to plant under grapevines. Attracts many beneficials. Useful planted around apple trees to attract predators of the woolly aphid. Clover interplanted with cabbage has been shown to reduce the native cabbage aphid and cabbageworm populations by interfering with the colonization of the pests and increasing the number of predator ground beetles.

Comfrey: Accumulates calcium, phosphorous and potassium. Likes wet spots to grow in. Comfrey is beneficial to avocado and most other fruit trees. Traditional medicinal plant. Good trap crop for slugs. More on comfrey.

Coriander: Repels aphids, spider mites and potato beetle. A tea from this can be used as a spray for spider mites. A partner for anise.

Corn: Amaranth, beans, cucumber, white geranium, lamb's quarters, melons, morning glory, parsley, peanuts, peas, potato, pumpkin, soybeans, squash and sunflower. A classic example is to grow climbing beans up corn while inter-planting pumpkins.

The corn provides a natural trellis for the beans, pumpkins smother the weeds and helps corn roots retain moisture. Corn is a heavy feeder and the beans fix nitrogen from air into the soil. The beans do not feed the corn will it is growing but when the bean plants die back they return nitrogen to the soil that was used up by the corn. A win-win situation. Another interesting helper for corn is the weed Pig's Thistle which raises nutrients from the subsoil to where the corn can reach them. Keep corn away from celery and tomato plants.

Costmary: This 2-3 foot tall perennial of the chrysanthemum family helps to repel moths.

Cucumbers: Cucumbers are great to plant with corn and beans. The three plants like the same conditions warmth, rich soil and plenty of moisture. Let the cucumbers grow up and over your corn plants. A great duet is to plant cukes with sunflowers. The sunflowers provide a strong support for the vines. Cukes also do well with peas, beets, radishes and carrots. Radishes are a good deterrent against cucumber beetles. Dill planted with cucumbers helps by attracting beneficial predators. Nasturtium improves growth and flavour. Keep sage, potatoes and rue away from cucumbers.

Dahlias: These beautiful, tuberous annuals that can have up to dinner plate size flowers repels nematodes!

Dill: Improves growth and health of cabbage. Do not plant near carrots, caraway or tomatoes. Best friend for lettuce. Attracts hoverflies and predatory wasps. Repels aphids and spider mites to some degree. Also may repel the dreaded squash bug! Dill goes well with lettuce, onions, cabbage, sweet corn and cucumbers. Dill does attract the tomato horn worm so it would be useful to plant it somewhere away from your tomato plants to keep the destructive horn worm away from them. Do plant dill in an appropriate spot for the swallowtail butterfly caterpillars to feed on. Even their caterpillars are beautiful.

Eggplant: Plant with amaranth, beans, peas, spinach, tarragon, thyme and marigold. Eggplant is a member of the nightshade family and does well with peppers. Avoid planting fennel near eggplant.

Elderberry: A spray made from the leaves can be used against aphids, carrot root fly, cucumber beetles and peach tree borers. Put branches and leaves in mole runs to banish them. Elderberry leaves added to the compost pile speeds up the decomposing process.

Flax: Plant with carrots, and potatoes. Flax contains tannin and linseed oils which may offend the Colourado potato bug. Flax is an annual from 1-4 feet tall with blue or white flowers that readily self sows.

Four-O'Clocks: Draws Japanese beetles like a magnet which then dine on the foliage. The foliage is pure poison to them and they won't live to have dessert! It is important to mention that Four O'clock are also poisonous to humans and animals. Be careful where you plant them if you have children and pets. They are a beautiful annual plant growing from 2-3 feet high with a bushy growth form.

Garlic: Plant near roses to repel aphids. It also benefits apple trees, pear trees, cucumbers, peas, lettuce and celery. Garlic accumulates sulfur: a naturally occurring fungicide which will help in the garden with disease prevention. Garlic is systemic in action as it is taken up the plants through their pores and when garlic tea is used as a soil drench it is also taken up by the plant roots. Has value in offending codling moths, Japanese beetles, root maggots, snails, and carrot root fly.

Researchers have observed that time-released garlic capsules planted at the bases of fruit trees actually kept deer away. It's certainly worth a try!

Concentrated garlic sprays have been observed to repel and kill whiteflies, aphids and fungus gnats among others with as little as a 6-8% concentration! It is safe for use on orchids too.

Geranium: Repels cabbage worms and Japanese beetles, plant around grapes, roses, corn, tomatoes, peppers and cabbage. Geraniums help to distract beet leafhoppers, carrier of the curly top virus.

Gopher Purge: Deters gophers, and moles.

Grapes: Hyssop is beneficial to grapes as are basil, beans, geraniums, oregano, clover, peas, or blackberries. Keep radishes and cabbage away from grapes. Planting clover increases the soil fertility for grapes. Chives with grapes help repel aphids. Plant your vines under Elm or Mulberry trees.

Hemp: Repels many types of beetles which attack brassicas.

Horseradish: Plant in containers in the potato patch to keep away Colourado potato bugs. Horseradish increases the disease resistance of potatoes. There are some very effective insect sprays that can be made with the root. Use the bottomless pot method to keep horseradish contained. Also repels Blister beetles. We have observed that the root can yield anti-fungal properties when a tea is made from it.

Horehound: like many varieties in the mint family, the many tiny flowers attract Braconid and Icheumonid wasps, and Tachnid and Syrid flies. The larval forms of these insects parasitize or otherwise consume many other insects pests. It grows where many others fail to thrive and can survive harsh winters. Blooms over a long season, attracting beneficial insects almost as long as you are likely to need them. For best results use horehound directly as a companion plant. Stimulates and aids fruiting in tomatoes and peppers.

Hyssop: Companion plant to cabbage and grapes, deters cabbage moths and flea beetles. Do not plant near radishes. Hyssop may be the number one preference among bees and some beekeepers rub the hive with it to encourage the bees to keep to their home. It is not as invasive as other members of the mint family making it safer for interplanting.

Kelp: When used in a powder mixture or tea as a spray, this versatile sea herb will not only repel insects but feed the vegetables. In particular we have observed that kelp foliar sprays keep aphids and Japanese beetles away when used as a spray every 8 days before and during infestation times. If you have access to seaweed, use it as a mulch to keep slugs away.

Kohlrabi: May be planted with cucumber, onion and chives. Kohlrabi and beets are perfect to grow with one another! Do not plant kohlrabi with pole beans, pepper, strawberry or tomatoes.

Lamium: This will repel potato bugs- a big problem for many gardeners!

Larkspur: An annual member of the Delphinium family, larkspur will attract Japanese beetles. They dine and die! Larkspur is poisonous to humans too.

Lavender: Repels fleas and moths. Prolific flowering lavender nourishes many nectar feeding and beneficial insects. Lavenders can protect nearby plants from insects such as whitefly, and lavender planted under and near fruit trees can deter codling moth. Use dried sprigs of lavender to repel moths. Start plants in winter from cuttings, setting out in spring.

Leeks: Use leeks near apple trees, carrots, celery and onions which will improve their growth. Leeks also repel carrot flies. Avoid planting near legumes.

Lemon Balm: Sprinkle throughout the garden in an herbal powder mixture to deter many bugs. Lemon balm has citronella compounds that make this work: crush and rub the leaves on your skin to keep mosquitoes away! Use to ward off squash bugs!

Lettuce: Does well with beets, bush beans, pole beans, cabbage, carrots, cucumbers, onion, radish and strawberries. It grows happily in the shade under young sunflowers.

Lovage: Improves flavour and health of most plants. Good habitat for ground beetles. A large plant, use one planted as a backdrop. Similar to celery in flavour.

Marigolds: Given a lot of credit as a pest deterrent. Keeps soil free of bad nematodes; supposed to discourage many insects. Plant freely throughout the garden. The marigolds you choose must be a scented variety for them to work.

One down side is that marigolds do attract spider mites and slugs:

- *French Marigold* Has roots that exude a substance which spreads in their immediate vicinity killing nematodes. For nematode control you want to plant dense areas of them. There have been some studies done that proved this nematode killing effect lasted for several years after the plants were These marigolds also help to deter whiteflies when planted around tomatoes and can be used in greenhouses for the same purpose. Whiteflies hate the smell of marigolds. Do not plant French marigolds next to bean plants.
- Mexican marigold is the most powerful of the insect repelling marigolds and may also overwhelm weed roots such as bind weed! It is said to repel the Mexican bean beetle and wild bunnies! Be careful it can have an herbicidal effect on some plants like beans and cabbage.

Marjoram: As a companion plant it improves the flavour of vegetables and herbs. Sweet marjoram is the most commonly grown type.

Melons: Companions: Corn, pumpkin, radish and squash. Other suggested helpers for melons are as follows: Marigold deters beetles, nasturtium deters bugs and beetles. Oregano provides general pest protection.

Mint: Deters white cabbage moths, ants, rodents, flea beetles, fleas, aphids and improves the health of cabbage and tomatoes. Use cuttings as a mulch around members of the brassica family. Mint flowers attract hoverflies and predatory wasps. Earthworms are quite attracted to mint plantings. Be careful where you plant it as mint is an incredibly invasive perennial. We have found that placing peppermint cuttings where mice are a problem is very effective in driving them off!

Mole Plants: Deter moles and mice if planted here and there throughout the garden. Drop a seed of this in mole runs to drive them away. This is a poisonous plant.

Morning Glories: They attract hoverflies. Plus if you want a fast growing annual vine to cover something up morning glory is an excellent choice.

Nasturtium: Nasturtium is an excellent companion for many plants. It is a companion to radishes, cabbage family plants deterring aphids, squash bugs, and striped pumpkin beetles, and improving growth and flavour. Plant as a barrier around tomatoes, cabbage, cucumbers, and under fruit trees. Deters wooly aphids, whiteflies, cucumber beetles and other pests of the cucurbit family. Great trap crop for aphids which it does attract, especially the yellow flowering varieties. It likes poor soil with low moisture and no fertilizer. Keeping that in mind there is no reason not to set potted nasturtiums among your garden beds. It has been the practice of some fruit growers that planting nasturtiums every year in the root zone of fruit trees allow the trees to take up the pungent odor of the plants and repel bugs. It is among the best at attracting predatory insects. It has no taste effect on the fruit. A nice variety to grow is Alaska which has attractive green and white variegated leaves. The leaves, flowers and seeds of nasturtiums are all edible and wonderful in salads! Try our recipe for: Nasturtium Salad

Nettles, Stinging: The flowers attract bees. Sprays made from these are rich in silica and calcium. Invigorating for plants and improves their disease resistance. Leaving the mixture to rot, it then makes an excellent liquid feed. Comfrey improves the liquid feed even more. Hairs on the nettles' leaves contain formic acid which "stings" you.

Okra: Plant lettuce around your okra plants and they will shade the lettuce in the summer giving you some more growing time. Okra also does well with peppers and eggplants as it helps protect these brittle stemmed plants from high winds. It also gets along with basil, cucumbers, melons, and black eyed peas. For planting with the peas plant your Okra first. When the okra is up and established plant the peas around the edges of the okra planting. You may find that the peas are far less bothered by aphids when near okra.

Onions: Planting chamomile and summer savory with onions improves their flavour. Other companions are carrot, leek, beets, kohlrabi, strawberries, brassicas, dill, lettuce and tomatoes. Intercropping onions and leeks with your carrots confuses the carrot and onion flies! Onions planted with strawberries help the berries fight disease. Keep onions away from peas and asparagus.

Opal Basil: An annual herb that is pretty, tasty and said to repel hornworms! Like the other basils it also does well with peppers, oregano, asparagus and petunias. Keep away from rue and sage.

Oregano: Can be used with most crops but especially good for cabbage. Plant near broccoli, cabbage and cauliflower to repel cabbage butterfly and near cucumbers to repel cucumber beetle. Also benefits grapes.

Parsley: *Allies*: Asparagus, carrot, chives, onions, roses and tomato. Sprinkle the leaves on tomatoes, and asparagus. Use as a tea to ward off asparagus beetles. Attracts hoverflies. Let some go to seed to attract the tiny parasitic wasps and hoverflies.

Peas: Peas fix nitrogen in the soil. Plant next to corn. Companions for peas are bush beans, Pole Beans, Carrots, Celery, Chicory, Corn Cucumber, Eggplant, Parsley, Early Potato, Radish, Spinach, Strawberry, Sweet pepper and Turnips. Do not plant peas with onions.

Peppermint: Repels white cabbage moths, aphids and flea beetles. It is the menthol content in mints that acts as an insect repellant. Bees and other good guys love it.

Peppers, Bell: Plant peppers near tomatoes, parsley, basil, geraniums, marjoram, lovage, petunia and carrots. Onions make an excellent companion plant for peppers. They do quite well with okra as it shelters them and protects the brittle stems from wind.

Don't plant them near fennel or kohlrabi. They should also not be grown near apricot trees because a fungus that the pepper is prone to can cause a lot of harm to the apricot tree. Peppers can double as ornamentals, so tuck some into flowerbeds and borders. Harvesting tip: The traditional bell pepper is harvested green, even though most varieties will mature red, orange, or yellow. Peppers can be harvested at any stage of growth, but their flavour doesn't fully develop until maturity.

Peppers, Hot: Chili peppers have root exudates that prevent root rot and other Fusarium diseases. Plant anywhere you have these problems. While you should always plant chili peppers close together, providing shelter from the sun with other plants will help keep them from drying out and provide more humidity.

Tomato plants, green peppers, and okra are good protection for them. Teas made from hot peppers can be useful as insect sprays. Hot peppers like to be grouped with cucumbers, eggplant, escarole, tomato, okra, Swiss chard and squash. Herbs to plant near them include: basils, oregano, parsley and rosemary. Never put them next to any beans, broccoli, cabbage, cauliflower, Brussels sprouts or fennel.

Pennyroyal: Repels fleas. The leaves when crushed and rubbed onto your skin will repel chiggers, flies, gnats, mosquitoes and ticks. Warning: Pennyroyal is highly toxic to cats. It should not be planted where cats might ingest it and never rubbed onto their skin.

Petunias: They repel the asparagus beetle, leafhoppers, certain aphids, tomato worms, Mexican bean beetles and general garden pests. A good companion to tomatoes, but plant everywhere. The leaves can be used in a tea to make a potent bug spray.

Poached Egg Plant: Grow poached egg plant with tomatoes, they will attract hover flies and hover flies eat aphids.

Potato: Companions for potatoes are bush bean, members of the cabbage family, carrot, celery, corn, dead nettle, flax, horseradish, marigold, peas, petunia, onion and Tagetes marigold. Protect them from scab by putting comfrey leaves in with your potato sets at planting time. Horseradish, planted at the corners of the potato patch, provides general protection. Don't plant these around potatoes: asparagus, cucumber, kohlrabi, parsnip, pumpkin, rutabaga, squash family, sunflower, turnip and fennel. Keep potatoes and tomatoes apart as they both can get early and late blight contaminating each other.

Pumpkins: Pumpkin pals are corn, melon and squash. Marigold deters beetles. Nasturtium deters bugs, beetles. Oregano provides general pest protection.

Purslane: This edible weed makes good ground cover in the corn patch. Use the stems, leaves and seeds in stir frys. Pickle the green seed pod for caper substitutes. If purslane is growing in your garden it means you have healthy, fertile soil!

Radish: One of the workhorses for the garden. Companions for radishes are: radish, beet, bush beans, pole beans, carrots, chervil, cucumber, lettuce, melons, nasturtium, parsnip, peas, spinach and members of the squash family. Why plant radishes with your squash plants? Radishes may protect them from squash borers. Anything that will help keep them away is worth a try. Radishes are a deterrent against cucumber beetles and rust flies. Chervil and nasturtium improve radish growth and flavour. Planting them around corn and letting them go to seed will also help fight corn borers. Chinese Daikon and Snow Belle radishes are favourites of flea beetles. Plant these at 6 to 12 inch intervals amongst broccoli. In one trial, this measurably reduced damage to broccoli. Radishes will lure leafminers away from spinach. The damage the leafminers do to radish leaves does not stop the radish roots from growing, a win-win situation. Keep radishes away from hyssop plants, cabbage, cauliflower, Brussels sprouts and turnips. For some good eating try our delicious Radish varieties.

Rhubarb: A good companion to all brassicas. Try planting cabbage and broccoli plants your rhubarb patch watch them thrive. Rhubarb protects beans against black fly. Some other interesting companions for rhubarb are the beautiful columbine flowers, garlic, onion and roses! It helps deter red spider mites from the columbines. A spray made from boiled rhubarb leaves, which contain the poison oxalic acid may be used to prevent blackspot on roses and as an aphicide.

Rosemary: Companion plant to cabbage, beans, carrots and sage. Deters cabbage moths, bean beetles, and carrot flies. Use cuttings to place by the crowns of carrots for carrot flies. Zones 6 and colder can overwinter rosemary as houseplants or take cuttings.

Rue: Deters aphids, fish moths, flea beetle, onion maggot, slugs, snails, flies and Japanese beetles in roses and raspberries. Companions for rue are roses, fruits, raspberries and lavender. To make it even more effective with Japanese beetles: crush a few leaves to release the smell. Has helped repel cats for us. You should not plant rue near cucumbers, cabbage, basil or sage. A pretty perennial with bluish-gray leaves. May be grown indoors in a sunny window. Rue may cause skin irritation in some individuals.

Rye: An excellent use of plant allelopathy is the use of mow-killed grain rye as a mulch. The allelochemicals that leach from the rye residue prevent weed germination but do not harm transplanted tomatoes, broccoli, or many other vegetables.

Sage: Use as a companion plant with broccoli, cauliflower, rosemary, cabbage, and carrots to deter cabbage moths, beetles, black flea beetles and carrot flies. Do not plant near cucumbers, onions or rue. Sage repels cabbage moths and black flea beetles. Allowing sage to flower will also attract many beneficial insects and the flowers are pretty. There are some very striking varieties of sage with variegated foliage that can be used for their ornamental as well as practical qualities. More on sage.

Spinach: Plant with peas and beans as they provide natural shade for the spinach. Gets along with cabbage, cauliflower, celery, eggplant, onion, peas, strawberries.

Southernwood: Plant with cabbage, and here and there in the garden. Wonderful lemony scent when crushed or brushed in passing. Roots easily from cuttings.

Does not like fertilizer! It is a perennial that can get quite bushy. We have started to cut it back every spring and it comes back in not time. A delightful plant that is virtually pest free.

Soybeans: They add nitrogen to the soil making them a good companion to corn. They repel chinch bugs and Japanese beetles. Why not try soybeans, they are good for you. They are many tasty ways to prepare them.

Squash: Companions: Corn, cucumbers, icicle radishes, melon and pumpkin. Helpers: Borage deters worms, improves growth and flavour. Marigolds deters beetle. Nasturtium deters squash bugs and beetles. Oregano provides general pest protection.

Strawberry: Friends are beans, borage, lettuce, onions, spinach and thyme. Foes: Cabbage, broccoli, Brussels sprouts, cauliflower and kohlrabi. Allies: Borage strengthens resistance to insects and disease. Thyme, as a border, deters worms.

Summer Savory: Plant with beans and onions to improve growth and flavour. Discourages cabbage moths, Mexican bean beetles and black aphids. Honey bees love it.

Sunflowers: Planting sunflowers with corn is said by some to increase the yield. Aphids a problem? Definitely plant a few sunflowers here and there in the garden. Step back and watch the ants herd the aphids onto them. We have been doing this for years and it is remarkable. The sunflowers are so tough that the aphids cause very little damage and you will have nice seed heads for the birds to enjoy. Sunflowers also attract hummingbirds which eat whiteflies. Talk about a symbiotic relationship!

Sweet Alyssum: Direct seed or set out starts of sweet alyssum near plants that have been attacked by aphids in the past. Alyssum flowers attract hoverflies whose larva devour aphids. Another plus is their blooms draw bees to pollinate early blooming fruit trees. They will reseed freely and make a beautiful groundcover every year.

Tansy: Plant with fruit trees, roses and raspberries keeping in mind that it can be invasive and is not the most attractive of plants. Tansy which is often recommended as an ant repellant may only work on sugar type ants. These are the ones that you see on peonies and marching into the kitchen. At least for us placing tansy clippings by the greenhouse door has kept them out. Deters flying insects, Japanese beetles, striped cucumber beetles, squash bugs, ants and mice! Tie up and hang a bunch of tansy leaves indoors as a fly repellent. Use clippings as a mulch as needed. Don't be afraid to cut the plant up as tansy will bounce back from any abuse heaped on it! It is also a helpful addition to the compost pile with its' high potassium content.

Tarragon: Plant throughout the garden, not many pests like this one. Recommended to enhance growth and flavour of vegetables.

Thyme: Deters cabbage worms. Wooly thyme makes a wonderful groundcover. You may want to use the upright form of thyme in the garden rather than the groundcover types. Thyme is easy to grow from seeds or cuttings. Older woody plants should be divided in spring.

Tomatoes: Tomato allies are many: asparagus, basil, bean, carrots, celery, chive, cucumber, garlic, head lettuce, marigold, mint, nasturtium, onion, parsley, pepper, marigold, pot marigold and sow thistle. One drawback with tomatoes and carrots: tomato plants can stunt the growth of your carrots but the carrots will still be of good flavour. Basil repels flies and mosquitoes, improves growth and flavour. Bee balm, chives and mint improve health and flavour. Borage deters tomato worm, improves growth and flavour. Dill, until mature, improves growth and health, mature dill retards tomato growth. Enemies: corn and tomato are attacked by the same worm. Kohlrabi stunts tomato growth. Keep potatoes and tomatoes apart as they both can get early and late blight contaminating each other. Keep cabbage and cauliflower away from them. Don't plant them under walnut trees as they will get walnut wilt: a disease of tomatoes growing underneath walnut trees.

White Geraniums: These members of the pelargonum family draw Japanese beetles to feast on the foliage which in turn kills them.

Wormwood: Keeps animals out of the garden when planted as a border. An excellent deterrent to most insects. Don't plant wormwood with peas or beans. A tea made from wormwood will repel cabbage moths, slugs, snails, black flea beetles and fleas effectively. The two best varieties for making insect spray are Silver King and Powis Castle. Adversely Powis castle attracts ladybugs which in turn breed directly on the plant. Silver Mound is great as a border plant and the most toxic wormwood. Note: As wormwood actually produces a botanical poison do not use it directly on food crops.

Yarrow: Yarrow has insect repelling qualities and is an excellent natural fertilizer. A handful of yarrow leaves added to the compost pile really speeds things up. Try it! It also attracts predatory wasps and ladybugs to name just two. It may increase the essential oil content of herbs when planted among them. Yarrow has so many wonderful properties to it and is an ingredient in our own Golden Harvest Fertilizer.

Zinnia: Pretty zinnias attract hummingbirds which eat whiteflies. Alternately the pastel varieties of zinnias can be used as a trap crop for Japanese beetles. All zinnias attract bees and other insect pollinators.

INTERCROPPING

Intercropping offers farmers the opportunity to engage nature's principle of diversity on their farms. Spatial arrangements of plants, planting rates, and maturity dates must be considered when planning intercrops. Intercrops can be more productive than growing pure stands. Many different intercrop systems are discussed, including mixed intercropping, strip cropping, and traditional intercropping arrangements. Pest management benefits can also be realised from intercropping due to increased diversity. Harvesting options for intercrops include hand harvest, machine harvest for on-farm feed, and animal harvest of the standing crop.

PRINCIPLES

Sustainable agriculture seeks, at least in principle, to use nature as the model for designing agricultural systems. Since nature consistently integrates her plants and animals into a diverse landscape, a major tenet of sustainable agriculture is to create and maintain diversity. Nature is also efficient. There are no waste products in nature. Outputs from one organism become inputs for another. One organism dies and becomes food for other organisms. Since we are modeling nature, let us first look at some of the principles by which nature functions. By understanding these principles we can use them to reduce costs and increase profitability, while at the same time sustaining our land resource base.

Diversity is Nature's Design

When early humans replaced hunting and gathering of food with domestication of crops and animals, the landscape changed accordingly. By producing a limited selection of crop plants and animals, humankind has greatly reduced the level of biological diversity over much of the earth. Annual crop monocultures represent a classic example. In response to this biological simplification, nature has struggled to restore diversity to these landscapes—that is her tendency. Our "war" with nature over the tendency to diversity is what we call "weed control" and "pest management." Of course we could hardly produce any crops if we simply allowed our fields to return to natural vegetation, but we can realise some of the benefits of diversity by planting mixtures of different crops.

Cooperation is More Apparent than Competition

There is far more cooperation in nature than competition. Cooperation is typified by mutually beneficial relationships that occur between species within communities. In *The Redesigned Forest*, ecologist Chris Maser offers a glimpse of the cooperation inherent in a northern temperate forest when he describes a relationship that exists among squirrels, fungi, and trees. The squirrels feed on the fungus, then assist in its reproduction by dropping fecal pellets containing viable fungal spores onto the forest floor. There new fungal colonies establish. Tree feeder roots search out the fungi and form a symbiotic association that enables the tree roots to increase their nutrient uptake. The fungi, in turn, derive food from the tree roots. Each benefits from the other's presence or actions.

If we view competition as the driving force in nature, we fail to see the complex relationships and feel compelled to take actions that may have unforeseen impacts. The rancher who views coyotes as competitors and kills them out may later find the predator helped keep rodent populations in check. With the predator gone, rodent numbers explode and cause more problems than ever before. The same is true with many insect pests of crops. When the only food for insects is crops, that is what they will eat. With no predator or parasite habitat present in a pure stand of crop, the pest insect could not possibly have it better. If we can shift our view of nature from a theme of competition to one of collaboration, we can act in ways that yield fewer negative consequences.

Stability Tends to Increase with Increasing Diversity

If left undisturbed and unplanted, an abandoned crop field will first be colonized by just a few species of plants, insects, bacteria, and fungi. After several years, a complex community made up of many wild species develops. Once a wild plant and animal community has reached a high level of diversity, it remains stable for many years.

When wild communities are in the early stages of development, or when they have lost diversity due to natural catastrophe or human actions, they are prone to major fluctuations, both in types of species present and in their numbers. Disease outbreaks in plants and animals occur more frequently—as do outbreaks of weed, insect, bird, or rodent pests. One good example is the grasshopper plagues that follow regional weather shifts. Another is the shift in weed species dominance following a soil disturbance.

The more complex and diverse communities become, the fewer the fluctuations in numbers of a given species, and the more stable the communities tend to be. As the number of species increases, so does the web of interdependencies. In both higher and lower rainfall years, there are fewer increases in any one species and fewer fluctuations in the community as a whole.

PURSUING DIVERSITY ON THE FARM

So, then, how can we begin to model our agricultural pursuits after some of these natural principles? Can we look for patterns in nature and imitate them? Some pioneering farmers have been able to utilize nature's principle of diversity to their advantage. Results of their efforts include lower cost of production and higher profits. Among the practices that promote diversity and stability are:

Enterprise diversification: Risk reduction through stability of income and yield are two of the reasons people diversify their crop and livestock systems. Increasing diversity on-farm also reduces costs of pest control and fertilizer, because these costs can be spread out over several crop or animal enterprises.

Crop Rotation: Moving from simple monoculture to a higher level of diversity begins with viable crop rotations, which break weed and pest life cycles and provide complementary fertilization to crops in sequence with each other.

Farmscaping: Diversity can be increased by providing more habitat for beneficial organisms, habitats such as borders, windbreaks, and special plantings for natural enemies of pests.

Intercropping: Intercropping is the growing of two or more crops in proximity to promote interaction between them. Much of this publication focuses on the principles and strategies of intercropping field crops. A related ATTRA publication, *Companion Planting*, provides more information on intercropping of vegetable crops.

Integration: On-farm diversity can be carried to an even higher level by integrating animals with intercropping. With each increase in the level of diversity comes an increase in stability. This publication focuses on intercropping and provides a section on integrating livestock with crops.

INTERCROPPING CONCEPTS

Most grain-crop mixtures with similar ripening times cannot be machine-harvested to produce a marketable commodity, since few buyers purchase mixed grains. Because of limited harvest options with that type of intercropping, farmers are left with the options of hand harvesting, grazing crops in the field with animals, or harvesting the mixture for on-farm animal feed. However, some intercropping plans allow for staggered harvest dates that keep crop species separated. One example would be harvesting wheat that has been interplanted with soybeans, which are harvested later in the season. Another example is planting harvestable strips, also known as strip cropping.

When two or more crops are growing together, each must have adequate space to maximize cooperation and minimize competition between them.

To accomplish this, four things need to be considered:

- Spatial arrangement,
- Plant density,
- Maturity dates of the crops being grown, and
- Plant architecture.

Spatial Arrangement

There are at least four basic spatial arrangements used in intercropping.

Most practical systems are variations of these:

- *Row intercropping*: Growing two or more crops at the same time with at least one crop planted in rows.
- *Strip intercropping*: Growing two or more crops together in strips wide enough to permit separate crop production using machines but close enough for the crops to interact.
- *Mixed intercropping*: Growing two or more crops together in no distinct row arrangement.
- *Relay intercropping*: Planting a second crop into a standing crop at a time when the standing crop is at its reproductive stage but before harvesting.

Plant Density

To optimize plant density, the seeding rate of each crop in the mixture is adjusted below its full rate. If full rates of each crop were planted, neither would yield well because of intense overcrowding. By reducing the seeding rates of each, the crops have a chance to yield well within the mixture. The challenge comes in knowing how much to reduce the seeding rates. If you are planning to grow corn and cowpeas, and you want mostly peas and only a little corn, it would be easy to achieve this. The corn-seeding rate would be drastically cut (by 80% or more), and the pea rate would be near normal. The field should produce near top yields of peas even from the lower planting rate and offer the advantage of corn plants for the pea vines to run on. If you wanted equal yields from both peas and corn, then the seeding rates would be adjusted to produce those equal yields.

Maturity Dates

Planting intercrops that feature staggered maturity dates or development periods takes advantage of variations in peak resource demands for nutrients, water, and sunlight. Having one crop mature before its companion crop lessens the competition between the two crops. An aggressive climbing bean may pull down corn or sorghum growing with it and lower the grain yield. Timing the planting of the aggressive bean may fix the problem if the corn can be harvested before the bean begins to climb. A common practice in the old southern U.S. cotton culture was to plant velvet beans or cowpeas into standing corn at last corn cultivation.

The corn was planted on wide 40-inch rows at a low plant population, allowing enough sunlight to reach the peas or beans. The corn was close enough to maturity that the young legumes did not compete. When the corn was mature, the beans or peas had corn stalks to climb on. The end result was corn and beans that would be hand harvested together in the fall. Following corn and pea harvest, cattle and hogs would be turned into the field to consume the crop fodder.

Selecting crops or varieties with different maturity dates can also assist staggered harvesting and separation of grain commodities. In the traditional sorghum/pigeonpea intercrop, common in India, the sorghum dominates the early stages of growth and matures in about four months. Following harvest of the sorghum, the pigeonpea flowers and ripens. The slow-growing pigeonpea has virtually no effect on the sorghum yield.

Plant Architecture

Plant architecture is a commonly used strategy to allow one member of the mix to capture sunlight that would not otherwise be available to the others. Widely spaced corn plants growing above an understory of beans and pumpkins is a classic example.

INTERCROP PRODUCTIVITY

One of the most important reasons to grow two or more crops together is the increase in productivity per unit of land. Researchers have designed a method for assessing intercrop performance as compared to pure stand yields. In research trials, they grow mixtures and pure stands in separate plots. Yields from the pure stands, and from each separate crop from within the mixture, are measured.

From these yields, an assessment of the land requirements per unit of yield can be determined. This information tells them the yield advantage the intercrop has over the pure stand, if any. They then know how much additional yield is required in the pure stand to equal the amount of yield achieved in the intercrop.

To calculate an LER, the intercrop yields are divided by the pure stand yields for each component crop in the intercrop. Here's the equation for a corn/pea intercrop where the yields from pure corn, pure peas, and the yields from both corn and peas growing together in an intercrop are measured.

(intercrop corn/pure corn) + (intercrop pea/pure pea) = LER

When an LER measures 1.0, it tells us that the amount of land required for peas and corn grown together is the same as that for peas and corn grown in pure stand. LERs above 1.0 show an advantage to intercropping, while numbers below 1.0 show a disadvantage to intercropping. An LER of 1.25 tells us that the yield produced in the total intercrop would have required 25% more land if planted in pure stands. If the LER was 0.75, then we know the intercrop yield was only 75% of that of the same amount of land that grew pure stands.

In a South Carolina study, researchers planted intercrops of southern peas and sweet corn at three different corn plant densities. The plantings were on raised beds with flat and wide crowns on six-foot centres. In the centre of each bed was a corn row, with two rows of peas planted 18 inches to either side of the corn row. The low corn-seeding rate was 6,700 plants per acre, medium corn was 9,500 per acre, and high was 11,900 plants per acre. Peas were established at a rate of 31,800 plants per acre in all intercrop plots. In the pure pea stand, each bed had two rows of peas spaced 24 inches apart. Yields of the intercrops and pure stands are shown in Table.

In this trial there was a yield advantage from intercropping over growing the two crops in pure stands. Pea yields suffered from the increased competition in the higher densities of corn. Some practical on-farm guidelines can be drawn to guide seeding-rate choices for a two-crop intercrop. To test seeding rates, experiment with three small plantings of two crops at the following percentages of their full seeding rates: 1/3 + 2/3, 1/2 + 1/2, and 2/3 + 1/3. From there, make adjustments for future plantings based on the results and your expectations.

Table. Yields of Sweet Corn and Southern Peas from Intercrops.

Seed Rates	Corn (pounds/acre)	Peas (pounds/acre)	LER
Full corn	5600	***	***
Full peas	***	1200	***
Low corn	4200	800	1.41
Medium corn	4600	800	1.48
High corn	5000	500	1.30

ESCALATING DIVERSITY AND STABILITY TO A HIGHER LEVEL

The diversity created by intercropping can be enhanced even further by integrating livestock (single or mixed species) into the cropping plan as harvesters. Allowing animals to harvest feed crops in the field puts gain on animals at the cost of crop production—considerably less than the purchase price of the grain. If you think about it, feed grains cost a lot less when they're not run through a $150,000 combine or hauled 1000 miles across the country.

Grazing animals and other livestock can be managed on croplands to reduce costs, increase income, and increase diversity. There are ways of incorporating animals into cropping without the farmer getting into animal husbandry or ownership directly. Collaboration with neighbours who own animals will benefit both croppers and livestock owners. Grazing or hogging-off of corn residue is one example where a cost can be turned into a profit. The animals replace the $6 per acre stalk mowing cost and produce income in animal gains.

Shasta College provides a unique demonstration of integrating livestock with intercrops. Shasta is a two-year community college located in Redding, California, that offers associate degrees in several branches of agriculture. Stan Gorden heads the college's holistic resource laboratory, where students get hands-on experience with ranching and farming. Stan and his students have taken intercropping to a high level of efficiency. They run hogs, sheep, cattle, and chickens together over 42 small paddocks of various forages and crops growing on 100 acres of college-owned land. One paddock is a pumpkin patch, another a garlic and carrot patch. Some are planted in alfalfa or mixes of grasses and clover. Not all the pastures have water sources for the animals, so water is moved on a trailer tank when necessary. The animals are moved daily in a planned grazing system during rapid plant growth and much more slowly, up to five days on a paddock, during slow plant growth.

Some of the paddocks are planted with mixtures of either winter or summer forage or grain crops. An intercrop of cereal grain, fava beans, and Canadian field peas is planted for winter grain, each crop at 1/3 normal seeding rate. The grain mixture is combine-harvested to make energy and protein supplement feed as needed. After harvest, the animals are turned into the paddock to glean what's left.

For summer feed, a mixture of milo planted on 18-inch rows is intercropped with a row of black-eyed peas planted six inches to either side of each sorghum row, using a drill with partitions in the seedbox. The milo provides a trellis for the pea vines to run on.

The milo/black-eyed mixture requires no herbicide. Before peas and milo were grown together, the milo pure stand would be plagued with whiteflies and green bugs. Mixing the two crops together ended the pest problem. Cowpeas have extrafloral nectaries that attract lots of beneficial insects. This could explain the absence of pest insects in the mixture. The milo/pea mixture is harvested by setting the combine to cut at the height of the milo heads. This yields a milo to bean ratio of 2:1—ideal for feed.

The college animal herd consists of 20 sows that farrow on pasture, 35 head of cattle, 50 sheep, and 30 laying hens that all range together. The hens are with the herd during the day and roost in a nearby eggmobile at night. Gorden selects breeds and genetics to fit this system, as opposed to selecting breeds for maximum production, and adapting a system to match the animal. The animals benefit one another. The sheep learn to stay close to the middle of the herd to avoid predators, which are fended off by the hogs. The cattle learn that the hogs know how to break the pumpkins open, so they stick close and get some too. The hogs eat the cow and sheep droppings and benefit from the predigestion. The hens scavenge wasted seeds from the various crops. There are three different kinds of hens, each of which lays eggs of a different colour. The eggs are marketed as rainbow eggs, with each dozen containing four white, four blue, and four brown eggs. The chickens also scratch apart cattle dung pats searching for insects, thus destroying cattle parasites.

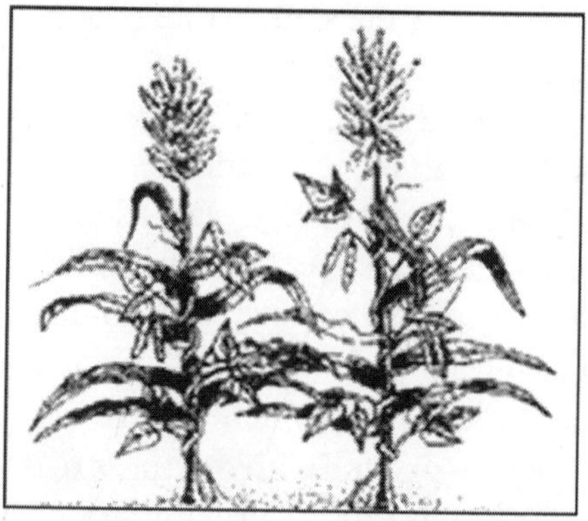

Fig. Cowpeas and Milo Growing Together.

Gorden, that developing and maintaining this high level of diversity has required creativity, selection criteria, constant monitoring, and re-examining traditional beliefs. By challenging long-held beliefs, he and his students discovered that hogs do not need standard farrowing crates and that sheep and cattle are compatible grazers. Animals and crops are selected and culled according to their ability to adapt to this complex system. Shasta College has one of the largest heritage hog herds in the country.

The hogs have been fitted with humane nose rings to prevent rooting. Also, hog breeds are selected that don't root up the ground nor eat the baby lambs when they are born. The sows farrow on pasture with only a single bale of hay for bedding. Hogs are not vaccinated, nor are needle teeth removed or other detailing done. Sows generally wean 12 pigs with no supplemental feed. The only purchased input is some nitrogen and phosphorus fertilizer applied to the pastures. The pigs are only touched twice; once to castrate and once to wean. As with the hogs, the cattle and sheep are selected to prosper on grass. Predators are not controlled in any way. Any animal that gets killed by wandering off is naturally selected out of the herd.

The sheep/hog/cow mix provides much better utilization of forage than single species grazing. Since the animals do most of the harvesting, less fossil fuel and labor-hours are expended. There are no pens to wash and no manure to deal with. The herd is controlled using an electric fence charged up to 8,000 volts to hold the sheep.

Before the 100-acre crop/animal integration project began in 1987, the College's agriculture resource laboratory was costing $8,000 per year. That was the first year the resource laboratory started managing holistically. By 1996, the resource lab's income was up $12,000, and expenses were down $10,000—rendering a $14,000 profit over the 1987 figure. During that same time the soil organic matter has increased from 1.7% to 3.2%.

INTERCROPPING FOR DISEASE CONTROL

Under direction of an international team of scientists, farmers in China's Yunnan province made some simple changes in their rice production methods. They changed from planting their typical pure stand of a single rice variety to planting a mixture of two different rice varieties. Their primary reason for trying this new technique was to reduce the incidence of rice blast, the main disease of rice. The technique was so successful at reducing blast disease that the farmers were able to abandon chemical fungicides they had been using.

The biodiversity effect is apparent here in that if one variety of a crop is susceptible to a disease, the denser the stand, the worse the disease can spread. If susceptible plants are separated by non-host plants that can act as a physical barrier to the disease, the susceptible variety will suffer less disease infection. Rice blast moves from plant to plant via airborne spores. These spores can be blocked by a row of a resistant variety. In this on-farm study, the rice was harvested by hand. Separating the varieties was easily done during harvest, since one variety towered above the other.

ADAPTING INTERCROPPING TO YOUR FARM

Intercropping has been important in the U.S. and other countries and continues to be an important practice in developing nations. In traditional systems, intercropping evolved through many centuries of trial and error. To have persisted, intercropping had to have merit biologically, environmentally, economically, and sociologically.

To gain acceptance, any agricultural practice must provide advantages over other available options in the eyes of the practitioner. Many of the impediments to adoption of new strategies or practices of diversification are sociological and financial rather than technological.

Farmers have generally regarded intercropping as a technique that reduces risks in crop production; if one member of an intercrop fails, the other survives and compensates in yield to some extent, allowing the farmer an acceptable harvest. Pest levels are often lowered in intercrops, as the diversity of plants hampers movement of certain pest insects and in some cases encourages beneficial insect populations.

MULTIPLE CROPPING

Planting two or more species in the same field in the same year. Preserved through history to maintain biological, economic, and nutritional diversity, multiple-species systems still are used by the majority of the world's farmers, especially in developing countries. Where farm size is small and the lack of capital has made it difficult to mechanize and expand, farm families that need a low-risk source of food and income often use multiple cropping. These systems maintain a green and growing crop canopy over the soil through much of the year, the total season depending on rainfall and temperature. Systems with more than one crop frequently make better use of total sunlight, water, and available nutrients than is possible with a single crop. The family has a more diverse supply of food and more than one source of income, with both spread over much of the year.

Multiple-cropping patterns are described by the number of crops per year and the intensity of crop overlap. Double cropping or triple cropping signifies systems with two or three crops planted sequentially with no overlap in growth cycle. Intercropping indicates that two or more crops are planted at the same time, or at least planted so that significant parts of their growth cycles overlap. Relay cropping describes the planting of a second crop after the first crop has flowered; in this system there still may be some competition for water or nutrients. When a crop is harvested and allowed to regrow from the crowns or root systems, the term ratoon cropping is used. Sugarcane, alfalfa, and sudangrass are commonly produced in this way, while the potential exists for such tropical cereals as sorghum and rice. Mixed cropping, strip cropping, associated cropping, and alternative cropping represent variations of these systems.

NO-DIG GARDENING

No-Dig Gardening is such a brilliant form of home-based agriculture. The TreeHugger archives would be rich with its merits. Was very surprised when one only found one mention, in a post chronicling Leonora's permaculture adventures in New Zealand. So one launched into the following first-person account of No-Dig, only to discover that in North America the same process might be better known as as Sheet Mulching. Nomenclature aside, it's worth covering the topic again. Especially if you want to grow your own veggies for a little food security.

BACKGROUND TO CULTIVATION FREE FARMING

No-Dig Gardening can probably trace its legacy back to visionary Japanese agricultural pioneer, Fukuoka Masanobu, who embarked on his Natural Farming experiment in 1938. His very productive organic farming methods did not require extensive soil tilling, weeding, or application of synthetic pesticide or fertilizer. Fukuoka Masanobu advocated returning grain and rice straw stalks to the fields as a way of enriching soil development.

Ruth, though maybe lacking some of the quiet humility and philosophy of her Japanese predecessor, also promoted covering gardens in a dense layer of straw and green mulch.

In the Antipodes we had Esther Dean, who released her own book *Growing Without Digging* in 1977, seeding a small cult following of No Dig gardeners. And, of course, Bill Mollison and David Holmgren who refined their concept of a nature-inspired agriculture with the publication of Permaculture One in 1978.

All would champion the idea that soil quality will dramatically improve if left undisturbed by cultivating, tilling, plowing, digging etc. They believed that soil was enriched with top layers of mulch decomposing to develop the appropriate communities of worms and micro-organisms that enhance food growth. Their ideas have since been embraced even in broad acre agriculture under the guise of no-till farming.

SO HOW DOES IT WORK IN PRACTICE?

There are many ways to implement a no-dig garden.

What follows is just one method:

- We selected a section of the yard that would get at least six hours of direct sunlight. Unfortunately we had to cut down a couple of trees to ensure this access when the sun dropped to lower plane in winter.
- We set up four main beds, so we can practice crop rotation, which rests the soil and reduces chances of plant pests making a comfortable home in the soil.

  Your first bed might get the root crops such as carrots, onions, beetroot and potatoes. The second is for Curcurbits, which are melons, pumpkins, squash, zucchini and cucumbers. Corn can also be planted here. For the third bed consider Acid Lovers: tomatoes, chillies, capsicums and eggplant. And in the last one go the Legumes, like peas and beans and the Brassicas. Each year plant the same vegetables per bed, but one bed further round the rotation.

  Separate non-rotating beds for herbs, and for perennials such as asparagus, strawberries and rhubarb, can also benefit from no dig methods.
- Because our soil is exceedingly clayey, we sprinkled gypsum through the grass to help loosen up the clay. Then we laid out salvaged railway sleepers to give the four main garden beds some definition. These beds were well watered down.

- Atop the wet grass we laid out big sheets of cardboard. This helps supress weeds. The cardboard was thoroughly wetted down too.
- A bale of chopped lucerne straw was spread over the soggy cardboard. And half a bale of long stem lucerne straw covered the lighter chop. This was watered in also.

- On this went a thick layer of what might be called soil 'matter.' It comprised material rescued from the floor of an old chicken coop that we'd shovelled out, and sieved through an old wire bed frame. It was a mixture of ancient chicken manure, soil, sawdust and compost scraps. Wetted down too.

- Over this soil matter we scattered a bale and half of plain straw and gave the whole shebang a deep soaking.
- We let it 'stew' a little while we waited for our organic seedling and seeds to arrive in the mail. And for the truck to drop off the the 2 tonnes of garden soil, mixed with cow manure.
- With these other ingredients in place we spread apart, with a trowel, strategic holes in the decomposing layered no-dig garden bed. Into these holes we dropped a couple of scoops of the soil/manure. Using a scoop home-made from a juice container. The beauty of this approach is that you only need use soil where you have plants. It's cheaper and saves on the volume of soil that needs to be humped about in a wheel barrow.

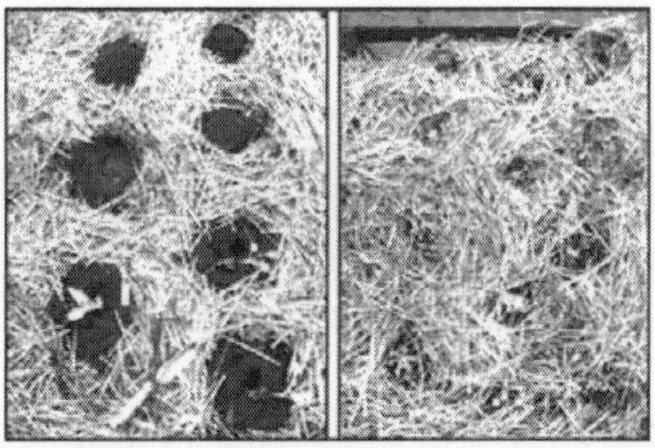

- Using a 'dibbler' stick we created a hole in the soil, and inserted the seedlings and seeds to their recommended depth and spacing. These were watered in with mixture of water and seaweed extract, to promote root growth. Then we pulled the straw loosely back over the mini-plots to reduce the soil from drying out.

- Of course it doesn't take long for snails and slugs to find these succulent new growths. So we cut up more containers to make ramps on the outside and shallow dished inside, which we filled with beer or wine. The slugs tempted by the sweet aroma slide up the ramp and succumb to alcohol poisoning. We also sprinkle some pine needles around the plants to create a spikey surface over which they need to crawl. Though this latter measure can make the soil a bit acidic, so we might experiment with wood ash from the slow combustion heater instead. We've also gone out at night with a head torch to pick off the sneaky slimy critters who don't fall for the beer traps.

- Water for the first couple of weeks to help the seeds and seedlings establish. Then let the straw mulch provide the soil with shade and to hold in any moisture from rain, dew or fog. But otherwise the garden should look after itself by-and-large. If weeds do poke through they can be pulled up, or simply smothered with another layer of straw.

The many steps indicated here might make it seem a drawn out process. But if you had everything together, it could all be set up one day on the weekend. Once set up, your No-Dig Garden shouldn't need more than a few hours tending each week. And besides it is far more satisfying to walk out into the backyard to harvest your own food, than to bump and grind around supermarket aisles and carparks. Cheaper, healthier and saves on the gym subscription too.

HOW TO SHEET MULCH

STEP 1: THE CONCENTRATED COMPOST LAYER

To prepare the site, knock down tall weeds and woody plants with a brush cutter, scythe, or simply by trampling the area. Then proceed to lay down the sheet mulch.

Whether you are mulching bare soil or weeds, the first step is to"jump start" microbial activity by adding enriched compost, poultry or stock manure, worm castings or the like at the rate of about 50 lbs/100 square feet. This high nitrogen matter stimulates soil life and gets things going. If the soil is acid, which it likely is if the area has been disturbed recently and treated with conventional fertilizers, add a layer of lime or crushed coral. A soil analysis will indicate the need for adjustment of pH or mineral amendments. This is the appropriate time to add the recommended doses of amendments such as rock phosphate and K mag. Soak the area well with water when the amendments are dispersed.

Step 2: The Weed Barrier

Most cultivated areas today harbor untold numbers of weed seeds. There are also weed seeds carried around by wind, animals and people. Soil borne seeds are lying dormant and waiting for the right conditions to sprout. Simply pulling or killing growing weeds will not erase the weed problem: more seeds will sprout almost as soon as the soil is exposed to moisture and light. Therefore the next step in mulching is to put down an organic weed barrier. This barrier prevents the germination and eventual emergence of weeds through your mulch.

Underneath this weed barrier grasses and weeds die and quickly become food for earthworms. From now on, the worms turn and aerate the soil, as they do naturally when in the right environment.

Of the four sheet mulch layers, the weed barrier has no natural counterpart on the forest floor. In the forest, weeds do not sprout because there is"no room for them," which simply means a lack of space above and below the ground, and a lack of light.

By planting an area properly, there will eventually be no room for weeds. The weed barrier is needed only for establishment of the mulch, and disappears with time. If your area is planted appropriately, weeds will not emerge after the decomposition of the weed barrier.

Materials for the weed barrier that work well are: 4-6 sheets of newspaper, cardboard, burlap bags, old rugs of natural fibre, worn-out jeans, gypsum board, or whatever you can find around. Banana, ape and ti leaves also work if laid down in several layers. Overlap the pieces of the material so as to completely cover the ground without any breaks, except where there are plants you want to save. Around these leave a generous opening for air circulation around the root crown. Care in laying down the weed barrier will save you the headache of emerging weeds later on.

Step 3: The Compost Layer

This layer is on top of the weed barrier - it must be weed seed free. Well conditioned compost, grass clippings, seaweed and leaves are ideal materials to spread over the weed barrier. Any weed-free material mixture at the right moisture level for a good compost will do. This should form a fairly dense layer about 3 inches thick.

Step 4: The Top Layer

The top dressing mimics the newly fallen organic matter of the forest. It also must be weed-free. Good materials for this include leaves, twigs and small branches, fern or palm fronds, straw, coffee chaff, macadamia nut shells, wood chips, sawdust, bark, etc.. The top layer will slowly decompose into lower layers, and therefore must be replaced periodically; it represents reserves of compost.

This layer should be about 3-5 inches deep. Many materials suitable for the top layer often have a pleasant cosmetic appearance. What luck! For this reason, there should be no hesitation in using sheet mulch in all cultivation from landscaping to gardening to permanent orchard crops. In fact, as you use mulch, bare soil will begin to seem ugly and undesirable.

When the soil is amended and sheet mulch applied properly, there will never be a need to turn the soil. Earthworms do the tilling. The only task left will be to keep the soil covered by replenishing the mulch. Warning: Feral pigs love good, moist soil, and will grub in sheet mulch if they have access to it. Do not use sheet mulch if pigs have access to the area; they will be attracted to it and will destroy both your work and your plantings.

Mulching Around Trees

- Plant tree.
- Amend soil around tree in a wide ring shape from a few centimetres from trunk out to 1 metre with a light layer of nitrogen fertilizer, such as chicken manure, and other amendments if necessary. Rake or water in.
- Spread a layer of permeable weed barrier around the tree in a ring shape, leaving about 15 cm diametre around the trunk of the tree for it to "breathe." Make certain there are no gaps in the ring shape through which weeds can emerge. Water the weed barrier layer thoroughly before the next step.
- Spread compost and/or mulch about 15 cm thick over the weed barrier, again making sure it is several centimetres away from the trunk of the plant.

The Ongoing Process

To make mulching as efficient and easy as possible, use mulch materials which are readily available. With good planning, mulching of gardens and orchards can become a regular part of maintenance-just mulch with handy materials such as grass clippings, plant prunings animal bedding, etc.. Eventually, other tasks such as watering, fertilization and weeding will be reduced. The overall maintenance burden in mulched conditions, when properly executed, is far less than in conventional systems.

Once a plant is properly mulched, its own leaf drop will constantly add to that mulch. But is natural leaf drop enough to maintain the mulch? The answer to this depends on the plant species and also how the plant is growing in relation to other plants. Certain trees produce tremendous amounts of leaf matter which decomposes rather slowly; examples are: avocado, macadamia, lychee, as well as many others.

These trees can be expected to generate sufficient mulch for themselves once vigourous growth is attained. Unfortunately, under most conditions many trees do not create enough long lasting mulch for maintenance of their needs. To explain this apparent deficiency, look once again at the forest. Here, plants are "stacked" in the vertical direction in ground-level, middle, and tall vegetation. This means that the ground under each plant receives organic matter from several plants.

There are many ways to produce sufficient mulch at your site. Grass clippings represent nutrient rich mulch material. Deep rooted, vigourous growing plants that readily come back from hard pruning or coppicing will also work. There are several nitrogen fixing trees which produce copious amounts of green matter. Each should be evaluated for the specific site before planting. Other plants that work well are kukui, hau, desmodium,, various bunch grasses, lemon grass, comfrey, etc.. Also, many water plants such as water hyacinth are good mulch materials. Since plants that produce heavy amounts of organic matter are by their nature nearly irrepressible, extreme caution should be taken not to let these plants escape your management and become weedy.

Sheet mulching should not be confused with composting, artificial weed barriers, or green manuring. Sheet mulching as described here is quite different from these in that it seeks to recreate the organic mulch layer of the forest with a minimum of effort from people. Properly planned, a backyard or orchard system will produce its own raw mulch in sufficient amounts and people are involved only in putting this material back onto the ground where it belongs.

POLLINATION MANAGEMENT

Pollination Management is the label for horticultural practices that accomplish or enhance pollination of a crop, to improve yield or quality, by understanding of the particular crop's pollination needs, and by knowledgeable management of pollenizers, pollinators, and pollination conditions.

POLLINATOR DECLINE

With the decline of both wild and domestic pollinator populations, pollination management is becoming an increasingly important part of horticulture. Factors that cause the loss of pollinators include pesticide misuse, unprofitability of beekeeping for honey, rapid transfer of pests and diseases to new areas of the globe, urban/suburban development, changing crop patterns, clearcut logging (particularly when mixed forests are replaced by monoculture pine), clearing of hedgerows and other wild areas, loss of nectar corridors for migratory pollinators, and human paranoia of stinging insects.

In 1989, following Hurricane Hugo, massive aerial applications for mosquitoes were done in South Carolina. The following year, watermelon growers who did not place beehives in the fields, observed the fruit begin to develop, then abort, or develop into small deformed fruit. There were entire fields that never yielded a single usable melon. Some growers went out of business; others began to seriously manage pollination. Since beekeepers were also heavily damaged by the mosquito spraying, the supply of bees for pollination was critically short for several years.

IMPORTANCE OF POLLINATION MANAGEMENT

The increasing size of fields and orchards increase the importance of pollination management. Monoculture can cause a brief period when pollinators have more food resources than they can use, while other periods of the year can bring starvation or pesticide contamination of food sources.

Table. Number of Hives Needed Per unit area of Crop Pollination

Common name	Number of hives per acre	Number of hives per hectare	Number of bee visits per square meter/minute
Alfalfa	1, (3–5)	2.5, (4.9–12)	
Almonds	2–3	4.9–7.4	
Apples (normal size)	1	2.5	
Apples (semi dwarf)	2	4.9	
Apples (dwarf)	3	7.4	
Apricots	1	2.5	
Blueberries	3–4	7.4–9.9	2.5
Borage	0.6–1.0	1.5–2.5	
Buckwheat	0.5–1	1.2–2.5	
Canola	1	2.5	
Canola (hybrid)	2.0–2.5	4.9–6.2	
Cantaloupes	2–4, (average 2.4)	4.9–9.9, (average 5.9)	
Clovers	1–2	2.5–4.9	
Cranberries	3	7.4	
Cucumbers	1–2, (average 2.1)	2.5–4.9, (average 5.2)	
Ginseng	1	2.5	
Muskmelon	1–3	2.5–7.4	
Nectarines	1	2.5	
Peaches	1	2.5	
Pears	1	2.5	
Plums	1	2.5	
Pumpkins	1	2.5	
Raspberries	0.7–1.3	1.7–3.2	
Squash	1–3	2.5–7.4	
Strawberries	1–3.5	2.5–8.6	
Sunflower	1	2.5	
Trefoil	0.6–1.5	1.5–3.7	
Watermelon	1–3, (average 1.3)	2.5–4.9, (average 3.2)	
Zucchini	1	2.5	

Most pollinator species rely on a steady nectar source and pollen source throughout the growing season to build up their numbers. Crops that traditionally have had managed pollination include apple, almonds, pears, some plum and cherry varieties, blueberries, cranberries, cucumbers, cantaloupe, watermelon, alfalfa seeds, onion seeds, and many others. Some crops that have traditionally depended entirely on chance pollination by wild pollinators need pollination management nowadays to make a profitable crop.

Some crops, especially when planted in a monoculture situation, require a very high level of pollinators to produce economically viable crops. This may be because of lack of attractiveness of the blossoms, or from trying to pollinate with an alternative when the native pollinator is extinct or rare. These include crops such as alfalfa, cranberries, and kiwifruit. This technique is known as saturation pollination. In many such cases, various native bees are vastly more efficient at pollination but the inefficiency of the honey bees is compensated for by using large numbers of hives, the total number of foragers thereby far exceeding the local abundance of native pollinators. In a very few cases, it has been possible to develop commercially viable pollination techniques that use the more efficient pollinators, rather than continued reliance on honey bees, as in the management of the alfalfa leafcutter bee.

It is estimated that about one hive per acre will sufficiently pollinate watermelons. In the 1950s when the woods were full of wild bee trees, and beehives were normally kept on most South Carolina farms, a farmer who grew ten acres (4 ha) of watermelons would be a large grower and probably had all the pollination needed. But today's grower may grow 200 acres and, if lucky, there might be one bee tree left within range. The only option in the current economy is to bring beehives to the field during blossom time.

TYPES OF POLLINATORS

Organisms that are currently being used as pollinators in managed pollination are honey bees, bumblebees, alfalfa leafcutter bees, and orchard mason bees. Other species are expected to be added to this list as this field develops. Humans also can be pollinators, as the gardener who hand pollinates her squash blossoms, or the Middle Eastern farmer, who climbs his date palms to pollinate them.

The Cooperative extension service recommends one honey bee hive per acre for standard watermelon varieties to meet this crop's pollination needs. In the past, when fields were small, pollination was accomplished by a mix of bees kept on farms, bumblebees, carpenter bees, feral honey bees in hollow trees and other insects. Today, with melons planted in large tracts, the grower may no longer have hives on the farm; he may have poisoned many of the pollinators by spraying blooming cotton; he may have logged off the woods, removing hollow trees that provided homes for bees, and pushed out the hedgerows that were home for solitary native bees and other pollinating insects.

PLANNING FOR IMPROVED POLLINATION

Before pollination needs were understood, orchardists often planted entire blocks of apples of a single variety. Because apples are self sterile, and different members of a single variety are genetic clones, this is not a good idea. Growers now supply pollenizers, by planting crab apples interspersed in the rows, or by grafting crab apple limbs on some trees. Pollenizers can also be supplied by putting drum bouquets of crab apples or a compatible apple variety in the orchard blocks.

The field of pollination management cannot be placed wholly within any other field, because it bridges several fields. It draws from horticulture, apiculture, zoology, ecology, and botany.

SHEET MULCHING

Agriculture with mulch in the tropics promotes plant health and vigour. Mulching improves nutrient and water retention in the soil, encourages favourable soil microbial activity and worms, and suppresses weed growth. When properly executed, mulching can significantly improve the well-being of plants and reduce maintenance as compared to bare soil culture. Mulched plants have better vigour and, consequently have improved resistance to pests and diseases.

"Mulch" is a layer of decaying organic matter on the ground. Mulch occurs naturally in all forests; it is a nutrient rich, moisture absorbent bed of decaying forest leaves, twigs and branches, teeming with fungal, microbial and insect life. Natural mulch serves as a "nutrient bank," storing the nutrients contained in organic matter and slowly making these nutrients available to plants. All forms of plant life from the ground layer to shrubs and trees thrive, grow, shed organic matter, die and decay, in a complicated cycle of nutrients.

Mulch forms a necessary link in nutrient cycling vital for our soils. When mulch is absent for whatever reason, the living soil is robbed of its natural nutrient stores, becomes leached and often desiccates. Natural environments without a litter layer are usually deserts. Non-desert plants grown in bare soil require constant fertilization, nutrient amendment and water, not to mention the work required to keep the soil bare.

Sheet mulching as described here is a suggested method for controlling weeds and improving soil and plant health with mulch. The process mimics the litter layer of a forest floor.

BASIC TECHNIQUES OF SHEET MULCHING

Once you get the hang of it, sheet mulching can be used anywhere plants are grown in the ground. Sheet mulching may be used either in establishing a new garden or tree planting, or to enrich existing plantings. In both cases, mulch is applied to bare soil or on top of weeds. New plantings are planted through the mulch, and a small area is left open to accommodate established plants and trees. The benefits of mulching justify putting the energy into doing the job right, using ample materials. Collect all of the materials and complete the mulching process in a day. A reduction in maintenance and increase in plant vigour will reward the initial effort. Sheet mulch is put down in layers to mimic natural forest mulch: well decayed compost, weed barrier, partly decayed compost and raw organic matter.

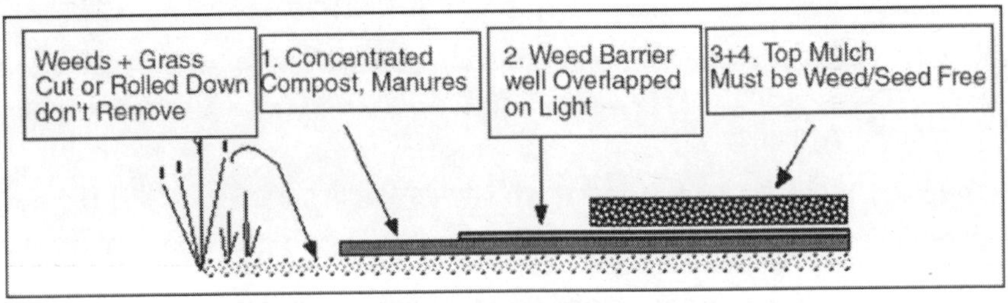

Bibliography

A.K. Tiwari: *Fundamentals of Ornamental Horticulture and Landscape Gardening*, New India Publishing Agency, 2012.

Arun K. Zingare: *A Manual of Gardening*, Satyam Publishers, Delhi, 2013.

Aruna Ludra: *Four Seasons Gardening in India*, Originals, Publication, Delhi, 2000.

B. L. Jana:*Hydroponics: Soilless Gardening*, Aavishkar Publishers, Delhi, 2015.

Buckland, Toby: *Gardeners' World Practical Gardening Handbook*, Random House India, 2004.

G Marshall Woodrow: *Gardening in India*, Daya, Publication, Delhi, 2001.

J. Coutts, A. Osborn and A. Edwards: *The Complete Book of Gardening*, Srishti Book, Delhi, 2004.

Kaushal Kumar Misra: *Ornamental Gardening in India*, Biotech Books, Delhi, 2011.

L.C. De: *Handbook of Gardening*, Aavishkar, Publication, Delhi, 2012.

L.H. Bailey and Ethel Zoe Bailey *Dictionary of Gardening and General Horticulture:* , Biotech, 2003.

L.L. Somani: *Dictionary of Gardening*, Agrotech, Publication, Delhi, 2009.

Laeeq Futehally: *A Sahib's Manual for the Mali : Everyday Gardening in India*, Permanent Black, 2004.

Leendertz, Lia: *Gardening SOS*, Random House India, 2008.

R.K. Chauhan: *Encyclopaedia of General Gardening for Common People*, Dominant, Publication, 2011.

R.L. Misra and Sanyat Misra: *Landscape Gardening : Design Elements Garden Planning and Pollution Monitoring*, Westville Publishing House, 2012.

Roy Edwin Biles: *The Complete Book of Gardening*, Biotech, 2003.

S.C. Dey: *Complete Home Gardening*, Agrobios, Publication, Delhi, 2012.

S.C. Dey: *Indoor Gardening*, Agrobios, Publication, Delhi, 2003.

Sudeep Guha: *Organic Methods for Ornamental Gardening and Floriculture*, Dominant, Publication, Delhi, 2011.

Supriya Kumar Bhattacharjee: *Landscape Gardening and Design With Plants*, Aavishkar, Publication, Delhi, 2012.

Syed Mahboob Ashraf: *A Handbook of Landscape Gardening and Environment*, Agrobios, Publication, Delhi, 2010.

Titchmarsh, Alan: *Alan Titchmarsh How To Garden: Greenhouse Gardening*, Random House India, 2004.

Titchmarsh, Alan: *lan Titchmarsh How To Garden: Greenhouse Gardening*, Random House India, 2004.

V.L. Chopra and Markandey Singh: *Ornamental Plants for Gardening*, Scientific, Publication, Delhi, 2013.

W.E. Shewell-Cooper: *Vegetable Gardening*, Biotech Books, 2005.

W.F. Gericke: *Soilless Gardening : A Complete Guide*, Biotech Books, Delhi, 2007.

Walter P Wright: *Encyclopaedia of Horticulture and Gardening*, Biotech, Publication, Delhi, 2002.

Index